AF323227

BARBARIANS OF THE NORTH:

Modern Chihuahua and The Mexican Political System

Manuel A. Machado, Jr.

EAKIN PRESS ★ Austin, Texas

Francisco Barrio Terrazas, PAN gubernatorial candidate in 1986 and successful candidate in 1992, at New Mexico State University 1986.
— Photo courtesy of María Telles-McGeagh.

Afectuosamente dedico este libro a mi amigo Dr. Armando Terrazas Borunda, su muy graciosa señora, Susana Ochoa de Terrazas y sus hijos Diego Armando y Federico. También extiendo mis gracias a todos mis amigos chihuahuenses que — aunque a veces no se dieron cuenta — participaron en las investigaciones que llevaron esta obra a cabo.

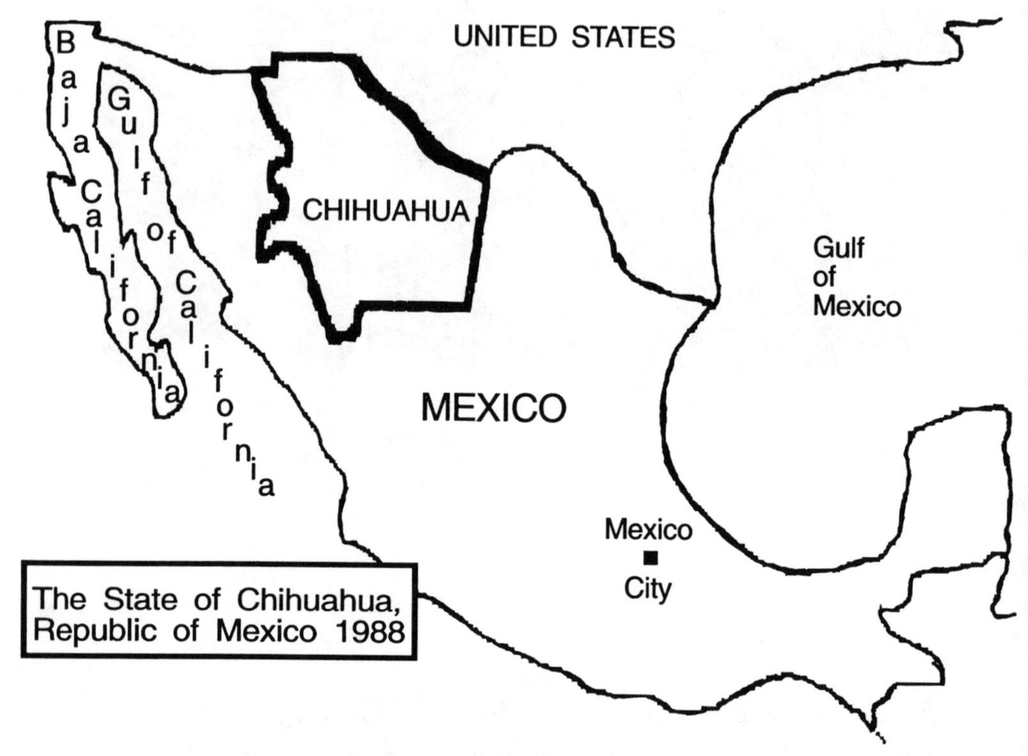

Map by Ronald Craig

Contents

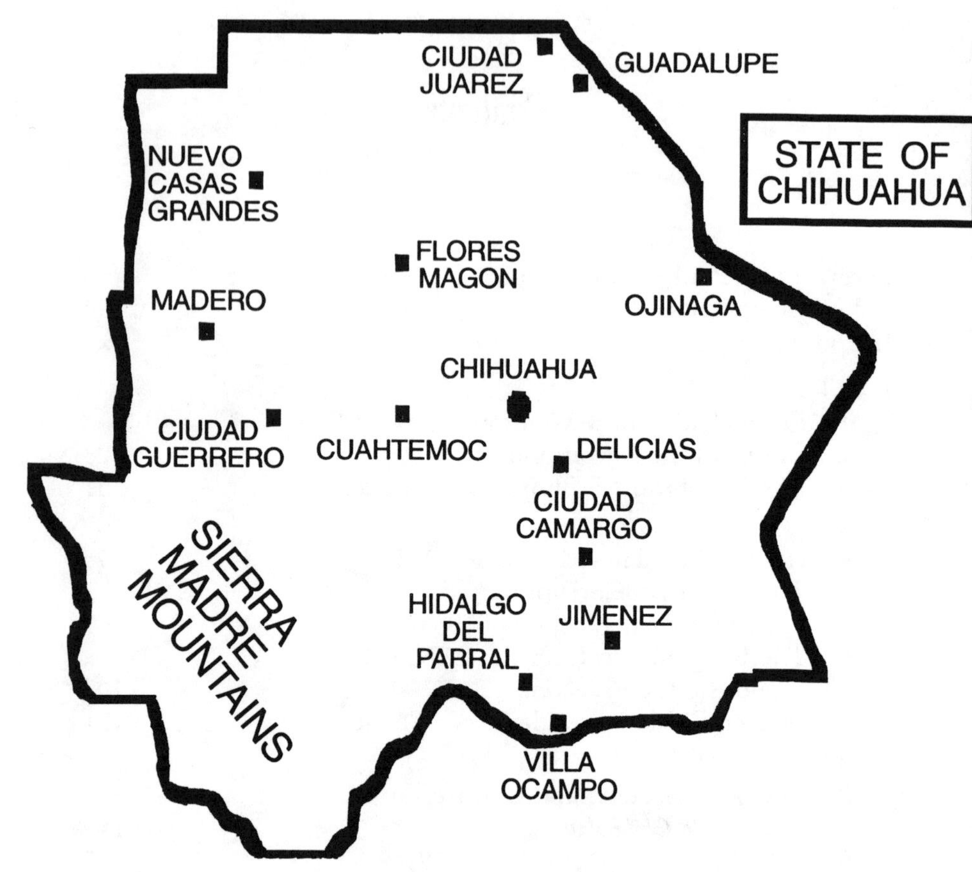

Map by Ronald Craig

Foreword:

The Dirt Under His Nails:
Manny Machado's Chihuahua

When I bumped into Manny Machado that simmering summer evening of 1984 in downtown Chihuahua City, he was seated at one of those enamel-topped card tables with the colorful beer advertisements that frequent the city's *cantinas*. Using *norteño* body language for punctuation, he chatted with a couple of locals, while taking an occasional draught of the local beer from an oversized water glass. That brew would be Cruz Azul, of course, maybe not the best of all those fine Mexican beers, but *puro chihuahuense*. Manny would not have had it any other way. Friends later explained that Manny Machado was more *chihuahuense* than most Chihuahuans themselves. That's why he could write such a personal book like this one about the place and its politics.

"Hey, Manny! Whatcha doin' here?"

"Just learnin' about Chihuahua the only way it can be learned," came the raspy reply.

It's not that Manny Machado had given up on the history books and the documents lying in any number of personal and official archives. In fact, he mastered a good many of them for this book. After all, he is a professional historian and has the written track record to prove it. But for this book he aimed to tap the soul of the site and that meant dealing with those Chihuahuan *rancheros* face-to-face. No doubt, if you mean to search for the spirit of Chihuahua, a *cantina* is a good place to look.

Chihuahua is not a Mexican tourist mecca in the sense of Aca-

pulco or Puerto Vallarta. It has neither the indigenous touch of
Oaxaca, nor the colonial style of Guanajuato. About the only thing
touristy about it at all is the famous (many would say infamous)
rail trip which traverses the magnificent heights of the Sierra
Madre and permits a peep into the Copper (colored) Canyon,
which reflects a rugged beauty rivaling that of the Grand. Some
50,000 Tarahumaras inhabit pockets in those mountains, but in the
main they steer clear of tourists and keep their crafts to themselves.

Nestled up against the southern boundary of New Mexico and
much of Texas, Chihuahua is Mexico's largest state and perhaps its
richest, especially in natural minerals like zinc, silver, and a bit of
gold. Agriculture, such as apples, and cattle contribute to the
bounty. Most impressive is the astounding growth of the *maquiladora* industry, not only along the border itself but encompassing
much of the periphery of the state capital. No doubt this phenomenal
growth is contributing to the political unrest that Manny Machado
has noticed and writes about here.

The entire state of Chihuahua tilts downward from west to
east, from the majestic Sierra Madre, which spills over the western
line into the neighboring state of Sonora, down into the broad expanses of the grassy Papigóchic Valley, and on past the state capital to the deserts that spill into the Rio Grande River. The mountains remain hostile to man and machine, for all but the
Tarahumaras whom, as far as we know, originated in the region
and continue to inhabit their *rancherías* scattered throughout the
area. Down in the fertile Papigóchic, cattle still graze the lands to
which they were introduced by the colonizing Spaniards, although
the great cattle estates of the nineteenth century have been pretty
well divided up amongst a growing population. Now apples are the
valley's major crop. On the eastern fringe of the Papigóchic lies the
relatively new town of Cuauhtémoc, energized by Mennonites who
nearly a century ago received title to expanses of surrounding territory and with disciplined hard work made it flourish, much to the
amazement of nearby Mexicans.

Ninety miles east lies the capital, which preserves but a hint of
its colonial past — the lovely *zócalo* at midcity dominated by a
handsome cathedral with its remarkably ornate facade. Otherwise,
Chihuahua City is quite modern, at least in a material sense. In
other ways, it retains the flavor of the Old West. In fact, inhabitants call it "our rancho grande." Pick-up trucks, tight blue jeans,

bandannas, and straw cowboy hats are *de rigueur*. Maybe that's what makes Chihuahua so attractive. For a romantic *gringo* it reminds him of unfettered, wide open spaces, sort of what the West must have been like a century ago. There is nothing quite like hitching a ride in a bucking pick-up and forging those rushing streams out in the countryside; nothing like shuffling a partner across those plank floors at a Saturday night *baile* where booze abounds and an occasional gun shot zings around; nothing as savory as *carne asada* burnt on a mesquite fire. Manny Machado fits right into this ambiance.

That time I met Manny Machado in the *cantina* was by no means his first visit to Chihuahua. He has been traveling back and forth from the area for most of his life. Just about everything Americans in the Southwest know about horse breeding and cattle raising is inherited from the Spaniards who first inhabited the place, and Manny learned his horse and cattle business the same way. So it was only natural that when Machado decided to hone his mind in college that he should get his academic license, a Ph.D., by studying the cattle exchange between the U.S. and Mexico around the great historic port of entry at El Paso/Ciudad Juárez. That research turned into a fine book. Furthermore, there's a saying that once the dirt of Chihuahua gets under the fingernails, there's no leaving the place. Manny dirtied his nails doing that book.

No one can wander around Chihuahua the way Manny Machado has done and not become infected with the state's number-one citizen: Pancho Villa. Outside of Chihuahua, one is tempted to call Villa a hero, but inside the state he is reviled as much as he is loved. Much of the revolutionary spirit that swirls around the state stems from the heritage of Pancho Villa. That's what attracted Machado to the man: his amorous affairs and unquestioned *machismo* on the battlefield, along with his hair-trigger temper and frequently wanton urge to murder and pillage.

Manny Machado has written a flavorful biography of Villa, and it is often said that biographers run the risk of falling in love with their subjects. Readers of the book can decide for themselves how closely the author identified with his subject.

When adventuresome Spaniards in search of a fast fortune in silver first arrived in the seventeenth century, they encountered fierce, nomadic Indian resistance that took more than two centuries to contain. Through most of this period, even into this century,

Chihuahua remained frontier country, far from the pull of the national capital at Mexico City and unfettered by formal demands of an organized Catholic church. If life under these circumstances was occasionally rewarding, it was always tough. Mother Nature saw to that. At the same time, these conditions molded a character which in many ways seems to be unique. Sure, these people are *norteños* — northern Mexicans — with a characteristic temperament and outlook on the world around them. But more than that, they are *chihuahuenses*, special in ways that Manny Machado has come to appreciate and wants to write about. Chihuahuans think themselves special. Super Mexicans. Super patriots. Free thinkers, ahead of the pack. And Manny agrees.

Driven by their ideal of independence, *chihuahuenses* have always proved to be a difficult bronco for the central government to corral. Backed by a strong economy, the state can afford to speak its political mind. There has always been a tension between the *políticos* in Mexico City and the people of the north. Quite frankly, they disdain one another. It's part of the country-versus-city/rural-versus-urban tension that exists most places, but in this case, differences between the *chilangos* and *provinciales* are profound and explosive. Manny Machado was in Chihuahua in the mid-1980s, when the ferment began to bubble and then explode into political action. In the book that follows he details these events and tells us why they happened.

Because of its economic strength and fractious temperament, Chihuahua is a key piece in the nation's political puzzle. It is in the forefront of the momentous political change that has begun to sweep the entire republic of Mexico. Sixty years of one party rule is ebbing away; the long dormant varieties of political persuasion are demanding a voice. It will be heard.

Unlike many other states in Mexico, the capital city of Chihuahua is not the only locus of political and economic power in the state. Juárez to the north is a burgeoning giant beset with all the turmoil of border cities along the U.S.–Mexico line. From Juárez issues the most persistent popular demand for both state and national political reform. In fact, this voice for change, which is captured by the author of this book, runs right down the state's major highway from Juárez through Chihuahua to Delicias and on to Jiménez and Parral. From these urban centers it is sweeping into the countryside, which has traditionally triggered profound social movements, including the great Mexican Revolution of 1910.

So this book is one of moment. Better yet, it is written from the inside out. It tells us about emotions, feelings, spirit, yearnings, ambitions, and all those other things that make us human rather than suffocating us in cold, statistical configurations. Manny Machado has celebrated these human sentiments for a long time, so it was only natural for him to write the kind of book that he did — one with passion and verve, plus understanding. Certainly, the political scientists, historians, and sociologists will have their say-so later on; we need their disciplined research and analysis freighted with the required footnotes and bibliography. But we also yearn to capture the vitality and humor of the occasion, and here Manny Machado points the way, as the reader learns to appreciate that dirt under his fingernails.

PAUL J. VANDERWOOD
San Diego, California

Acknowledgments

This is a very personal book. While all efforts were made to be as objective as possible, inevitably the contemporaneous nature of the work and the immediate involvement of the author either as a participant or as a close observer made the analysis a very personal one. The nature of the research proved highly subjective. Conversations in bars, with barbers, bank tellers, cab drivers, friends in Chihuahua, and any variety of folk helped to create a work not traditionally done by historians. Rather, it falls into the realm of retrospective journalism. But that is all right, for the function of writers is to convey information and analysis.

A lot of people deserve some thanks for their assistance in the project. Principal among them is Marianne Farr of the inter-library loan system of the Mike and Maureen Mansfield Library at the University of Montana. Always friendly and courteous, Mrs. Farr obtained materials for me to use before leaving for Chihuahua to finish the final research.

Financial support is an integral part of research. The Office of the Associate Vice President for Research at the University of Montana provided funding for me to go to Chihuahua to complete the study. For this, Dr. Raymond Murray and his staff deserve thanks.

In Chihuahua, the Centro de Información del Estado de Chihuahua (CIDECH) proved invaluable. Its director, Lic. Gáspar Gumaro Orozco Moreno, a friend and colleague from teaching days in Chihuahua, provided work space for both research and writing. He and his staff deserve generous thanks for the efforts they are making to bring pertinent information to the people of Chihuahua and to provide a research facility of which the state can be inordinately proud.

Once again, Ron Craig used his computer to my advantage. His computer wizardry produced some of the maps that appear in this book. Robert Ringstaff, a current student of mine, also provided maps for the work. To both of them goes my appreciation.

The rapid production of a final copy of manuscript can only be done by experienced, patient, and dedicated typists. Sue Koehn of the Word Processing Center at the University of Montana worked diligently at the completion of the final draft. Despite one of the most ghastly winters in Montana's history and the closure of the university because of that miserable Arctic blast, Ms. Koehn still beat the deadline. My thanks goes to her for her unstinting efforts.

Finally, there is my research assistant. Terry Hearst proved to be an invaluable asset in the preparation of this work. While I wrote, he checked information or brought me new data with which to work. His keen, critical eye and an ability to synthesize complicated information provided a shortcut that often is not available. In fact, he was more than a research assistant. Terry served more as a junior collaborator. He is, however, absolved of any error of interpretation, for that was solely my function. His editorial eye and perceptive ear for language did much to clarify the presentation. To him, I am eternally grateful.

Introduction

The smell of stale booze, the pall of cigarette smoke, and the sound of raucous voices — some acrimonious, some laughing, some somber — permeates the ambience of one of my favorite bars in Chihuahua City. It's a friendly bar. The booze is cheap and generous; the bartenders remember you and what you drink; you can always get some great tacos at a little stand just outside; and the patrons love to talk. My God, they love to talk. Many a morning I've stayed there discussing any variety of topics until the cops pointedly reminded the bartenders that it was afterhours. Inevitably the conversation turns to politics.

Politics runs as a constant theme through *chihuahuense* conversation. The political tensions that have characterized Mexico since the late 1970s clearly manifest themselves in Chihuahua. Growing dissatisfaction with a political system that only looks to Chihuahua for support without returning a lot of revenue to what is probably Mexico's richest state fails to make Chihuahua's quirky populace friendly toward the central government and the official party, the Partido Revolucionario de Instituciones (Revolutionary Party of Institutions, or PRI). Since the 1980s, what has always been felt *sub rosa* in Chihuahua — a sense of uniqueness, a feeling that *chihuahuenses* occupy a special place in Mexican history, an idea that they more than other Mexicans are deserving of special consideration — contributes to a sense of malaise, a perception that all is not right in Mexico.

My companions in the various bars that I frequent every time I go to Chihuahua (which is as often as possible) have gone so far as to declare that Chihuahua would be better off without Mexico City. Secession always is a conversational alternative; whether or not an organized secession movement could ever take flight would come into direct conflict with the strong sense of Mexicanness that *chihuahuenses* feel.

As I sat in my favorite bar one night, listening and drinking brandy and soda, one patron, already well in his cups, patently declared: *"¿Para qué chingados necesitamos a México?"* (What the f--- do we need Mexico [City] for?). Anytime someone in Chihuahua refers to "Mexico," he means México, D.F., the capital of the country (Federal District), not the whole country.

Chihuahuenses deprecate the denizens of Mexico City with a contempt that absolutely chills the atmosphere. *Chilangos* (the pejorative term that denotes someone from Mexico City) as a label is like a slap in the face. It implies that the individual is an insufferable snob who denigrates the northern provinces and thinks that the only good the north does is provide tax revenues and resources to keep the Mexico City monster fed, supplied, and generally living well. *Chihuahuenses* feel that all of their tax revenues — most of the taxes are federal — go to the support of a bloated bureaucracy that gives little, if any, benefit to the north in general and Chihuahua in particular. As one *cuate de cantina* (barroom buddy) of mine once put it: *"¡No me importaría pagar el pinche IVA se no fuera para el sostén del pinche metro de México!"* (I wouldn't mind paying the IVA [Impuesto de Valor Adicional, a value added tax, federal in nature] if it didn't support the f------ subway system in Mexico City!).

In 1983–84, I spent a year teaching at the Universidad Autónoma de Chihuahua. Of all things, I suddenly found myself teaching English, a truly frightening experience for an historian. One of my students in English was a *chilango*. The poor devil didn't stand a chance. His accent gave him away. The class took an instant dislike to the poor blighter. Some students constantly asked me to get rid of him. Out of a sense of fairness I told them that, like themselves, he had paid his money for the class and unfortunately had every right to be in there. Tragically, he was also a bit loony, operating out of an ozone layer that exacerbated the fact that he was a *chilango*. Somehow we made it through the term, but his constant presence in the class underscored for me why the *chihuahuenses* really dislike people from Mexico City. He was insufferable — rude, critical of the area, a generic pain that not even a leading hemorrhoid preparation could alleviate.

I've met other *chilangos* in Chihuahua as well. They complain about how backward Chihuahua is and decry the cultural backwater, the desert, the mountains, the capital city of Chihuahua, the booming industries — practically everything. Of one thing I am inordinately glad — the *chilangos* don't frequent the same bars that I do.

All of this is an attempt to explain, through personal experience, why the *chihuahuenses* really dislike their Mexican brethren from the south. Much of this animosity comes from Chihuahua's historically independent relationship to the rest of Mexico. Chihuahua was founded early in the eighteenth century, and its people have always felt that they had to do things for themselves rather than rely on Mexico City. As a consequence, the nearly 1,000 miles that separate Mexico City from Chihuahua provided the *chihuahuenses* with an isolation that forced them to be self-reliant, whether it involved dealing with nomadic Indians who pillaged and threatened settlements in the major parts of the state or working toward their hard-won economic development. Such a condition of independence fostered a sense of imposition once the central authority began to force its will on the entire country. Resented mightily by the *chihuahuenses*, central authority was something that one merely tolerated and did everything possible to circumvent.

What would those clowns from Mexico City know? They haven't even been to Chihuahua. Yet, reason the *chihuahuenses*, the *chilangos* are constantly trying to tell Chihuahua how to run its own affairs. Better that those arrogant bastards stay out of Chihuahua and let *chihuahuenses* attend to their own business without the ignorant interference of effete bureaucrats and picky snobs, they say.

One who stays around Chihuahua long enough gets trapped into the anti-*chilango* mentality. I can understand and even sympathize with it, for it reflects many of my own views about central government and overweening federal bureaucrats. Yet, Chihuahua is still a part of Mexico, an important part, and certainly glories in its Mexicanness. I still have cousins and one aunt in Mexico City. Though they all came originally from Sonora, a part of the northern phenomenon in Mexico, they have lived in Mexico City since the 1930s. Of course, I consider them as somewhat traitorous, and they consider me a northern barbarian who not only left his roots but resides in the cold northern climes of the United States.

In the most recent presidential election, the Partido de Acción Nacional candidate, Manuel Jesús Clouthier, was a prominent farmer and businessman from Sinaloa, part of Mexico's northwest. The *chilangos* made a reference to the northerners as "barbarians."

Proudly, bumper stickers began to appear all over northern Mexico, and especially in Chihuahua, proclaiming: *"¡Bárbaro del norte!"* (Northern barbarian!). There was a sense of pride here, something with which other regions of Mexico had a hard time coping and understanding.

Chihuahua occupies a unique geographical position in Mexico. It borders on the United States, for one thing. Americans have been initimately involved with Chihuahua for nearly 200 years, and have always maintained a stormy relationship with the central authority. It is a hard land, a land in which only the strong survive. As a consequence, a stubborn pragmatism rather than ideological niceties drives the *chihuahuenses,* be they soldiers, bandits, cattlemen, small farmers, miners, industrialists, bankers, or doctors. Write the Listers: "A race of strong men was needed to survive here, with enough love of the land to fight back."

Survival, in short, dictates the *chihuahuenses* ethos and self-perception. He still views himself as the fierce Indian fighter of the nineteenth century, holding off hordes of marauding Apaches while the incompetents in Mexico City argue over who might pay for the Indian campaigns. He thinks of himself as one of Pancho Villa's soldiers, fighting for the defense of a principle but also for the right to live his life as he sees fit. This is a land that has a series of geographic blessings and curses that ultimately determine the way in which the state develops.

Deserts, mountains, agricultural valleys — all of these comprise Chihuahua. A hot sun bakes you in the summer, and you can freeze in the winter. When John J. Pershing led his punitive expedition against Pancho Villa in 1916, some clown in the U.S. Army Quartermaster Corps issued tropical uniforms to the soldiers going to Mexico. He thought: *"Aha!* Mexico! Tropics!" They froze, for the temperature in the foothills of Chihuahua's western mountains is below freezing in late winter and early spring.

Sandstorms blow from Samalayuca just south of Ciudad Juárez to Villa Ahumada sixty miles south. Cars can get sandblasted in a really good blow. The relentless sun makes it difficult to achieve a degree of comfort in the summer, and the clay in the soil makes it almost impossible for the ground to absorb much-needed moisture when it rains.

Yet, for all of its geographic extremes, Chihuahua is a rich land. It produces an abundance of agricultural wealth. Rivers feed its crop lands, alfalfa fields abound, and cattle raising constitutes the principal activity of those who cling to the traditional enterprises. The land is so rich, in fact, that the average number of times an alfalfa crop can be harvested is around eight, usually beginning in March and ending in late October or early November.

A mere look at a map of Chihuahua clearly demonstrates the geographic extremes of the area. The mountains produce timber and minerals; the valleys and plains, agricultural produce and cattle. Industries surround the major cities of the state. And everywhere there is a sense of pride in the fact that *chihuahuenses* did this with little, if any, support from Mexico City.

Thus, the *chihuahuense* has learned to survive in a land that ruggedly fought against human occupation. He developed a symbiotic relationship with this land. And through blood and sweat he extracted a livelihood, often becoming wealthy, but usually just surviving. This factor alone gives Chihuahua a unique place in Mexican history. First and foremost, she is a survivor.

NEW MEXICO, U.S.
Palomas
Grandes
Ciudad
Juárez
Casas
Laguna de
Guzmán
Samalayuca
Río
Ascensión
Guadalupe
Laguna de
Santa María
Sierra
Janos
Laguna de Patos
Villa Ahumada
Corralitos
Carrizal
Nueva
Casas
Grandes
Santa María
Colonia
Juárez
Río
SONORA
Río del Carmen
Moctezuma
Colonia
Pacheco
Galeana
Buenaventura
Flores
Magón
El Sueco
Chuichupa
Laguna
Babícora
Madre
Madera
Namiquipa
Babícora
Laguna
Encinillas
Coyame
Conchas
Ojinaga
Cuchillo
Parado
TEXAS, U.S.
Grande
Yepómera
Encinillas
Río
El Sauz
Tutuaca
Sacramento
Aldama
Chuviscar
Río
Bachiniva
Chihuahua
Parigochi
Lago
de
Bustillos
Riva
Palacio
Aquiles
Serdán
Julimes
Río
Tomochi
Ciudad
Guerrero
Cuauhtémoc
Meoqui
Río Mayo
La
Junta
Cusihuiriáchi
General
Trías
Río San Pedro
Ciudad
Delicias
Saucillo
Río Chinipas
Creel
Camargo
Chinipas
Río Urique
Presa
Boquilla
San Francisco
de Conchos
Bolson
de
Mapimí
Urique
Río Conchos
Río Batopila
Batopilas
Huexotitlán
San Francisco
del Oro
Hidalgo
del
Parral
Río Florido
Jiménez
Occidental
Río Verde
Santa Bárbara
Allende
SINALOA
DURANGO
COAHUILA
Guadalupe
y Calvo
Chihuahua, Mexico
Continental Divide

PART I

Statue of Don Antonio Deza y Ulloa, founder of Chihuahua City. The statue faces the Cathedral.
— Photo by Travis Machado

The Cathedral in Chihuahua City.
— Photo by Travis Machado.

Statue of Pancho Villa on Avenida Universidad and División del Norte, Chihuahua City.
— Photo by Travis Machado.

CHAPTER 1

From Colony

to Revolution

The physical remnants of Chihuahua's historical past stand starkly in the desert sun. Wind, rain, heat, and the vicissitudes of man's inability to resolve his differences peaceably have failed to destroy the monuments to the tenacity of the Spaniards who settled Chihuahua in the early eighteenth century or of the subsequent Mexicans who remained there after Mexico achieved her independence in the 1820s. Churches, *cascos* (main houses) of *haciendas* (large landholdings also called *latifundia*), and small adobes provide testimony to the endurance and to the struggle for survival extracted by a hard and unyielding land.

As early as the mid-sixteenth century, the first generation of conquerors and settlers who had come to Mexico in 1519 and after felt a restlessness and a desire to expand the hegemony of their Crown, their Church, and their own desire for personal fulfillment. Closer they inched to the borderlands. Incursions had already been made in Sinaloa and parts of the Mexican West. By the mid-1540s, the discovery of silver at Zacatecas pushed the Spaniards further into unknown territory.

Yet the company of Spaniards who conquered Mexico never

grew excessively. The bulk of the force came to be composed of *mestizos* (mixed bloods) who shared sufficient cultural similarities with Indian and Spanish parents to make them the ideal colonizers of the northern frontiers. Both the Indian and Spaniard possessed an unquestioned faith in a theological system, in a political infrastructure represented by a God-chosen monarch, and in a social arrangement that carefully delineated the place of all members of a society.

But by the end of the sixteenth century, the social system imposed upon New Spain, or Mexico, by Spain found itself at a loss as to how to deal with the *mestizo*. The dominant racial group was now the mixed blood. The decline of the Indian population because of disease, labor exactions, as well as the subsequent production of hybrid children no longer left the first Mexicans in any kind of majority. Rather, they remained at the bottom of the social heap, patronized, coddled, punished, and generally exploited by the conquerors. It should be added, however, that the system that sought to protect and at the same time exploit the Indians became the subject of constant debate among policy-makers in Madrid. This debate regularly brought about modifications that sought to ameliorate the lot of the Indian without destroying the system that provided labor for the Spaniards and protection for the Indian.

By the 1560s, Spain sought to expand into the northern Mexican plateau. Spanish expeditions into the area in search of the fabled lands of Cíbola encountered Indians both friendly and unfriendly who perpetuated the Cíbola myth. Always further north, they said, lay the Golden Cities. The Spaniards, reared in a cultural tradition of chivalry and honorable adventure, proved gullible and continued to push to the north. Why not? Was there not a northwest passage to the Indies? Had not reliable reporters like Fray Marcos de Niza and even Coronado himself reported some of the wonders of those lands? Surely Spanish failure to reach those areas grew from inaccurate or incomplete information. By the late 1560s, Francisco de Ibarra, later to become governor of Nueva Vizcaya (which would include Chihuahua), established a capital at Durango. From there he sent further expeditions, one of which would penetrate southern Chihuahua and establish the first town and the twin industries that would make the area rich: mining and cattle.

Arrival of thirty families from Spain to work the mines at

Santa Bárbara failed to make Santa Bárbara productive. More labor was needed. Entreaties to bring Indians from central Mexico at first met with resistance by the viceroy in Mexico City; however, central Mexican Indians did arrive. A large problem that faced the settlement of Santa Bárbara, Chihuahua, was that the native population of the area was nonsedentary or inaccessible. Unlike the Indians of the center, those in the mountains of Chihuahua proved singularly resistant to Spanish incursions and sought refuge in the rugged *sierra*. As a consequence, the introduction of Indians from the center contributed appreciably to the cultural mixture that would comprise the modern *chihuahuense*.

The lure of the north, however, continued to nag at Spanish desire for the salvation of souls and for personal enrichment. By the 1590s, Spanish authorities decided to leapfrog over the vast Chihuahua territory and penetrate into what is now New Mexico. Juan de Oñate became the leader of the expedition that braved the deserts of Chihuahua to arrive at Paso del Norte (modern El Paso and Ciudad Juárez) in late April 1598. Like so many other conquerors, Oñate risked his private fortune as well as his reputation on the venture. When Santa Fe, New Mexico, was founded in 1609, Oñate had fallen out of favor and would no longer be the cherished servant of the Crown.

For the better part of a century the route followed by Oñate to Santa Fe became the principal highway that linked New Spain with its far-flung northern appendage. The seventeenth century saw the decline of Spanish power in the western world but not the lack of desire by Spain to continue in her mission of carrying the word and way of life to the outposts of the empire. Thus, Spanish settlers nibbled around the edges of Chihuahua. Missionaries in Sinaloa and southern Sonora crossed the Sierra Madre Occidental and attempted to bring salvation to the heathen. To be sure, there proved to be Indian resistance. The slaughter of missionaries by Tepehuanes and Tarahumaras plunged northern Mexico into a kind of hysteria accompanied by vicious reprisals. As yet, no major discoveries of precious metals had justified Spanish efforts in Chihuahua. Soon, however, nearly one hundred years after the first early nibblings around the edges of Chihuahua had occurred, bonanza would strike.

Silver! The cry went out over all of Mexico. Around 1629 (no one is quite sure of the date) a silver strike suddenly catapulted

Chihuahua and, more specifically, the area around Santa Bárbara into a boomtown. The new settlement, San José de Parral (later to be called Hidalgo del Parral in honor of Mexico's first leader of independence), attracted hundreds of miners. Bureaucratic prohibitions out of Zacatecas were imposed by the local magistrate because of wholesale abandonment of the declining Zacatecas mines. Mining claims were being filed at a rapid pace. Cattle ranches multiplied as the demand for meat and leather escalated almost geometrically. Spanish and Mexican faith in the possibility of treasure had finally borne fruit.

The twin enterprises of mining and cattle became and ultimately continued to be the principal business of Chihuahua. In the nineteenth century foreigners came to dominate the mining business, but Mexicans predominated in the production of cattle. There exists a close relationship between the cattle ranches and the mines. As the Mexican frontier expanded northward in the sixteenth century, it became increasingly difficult and dangerous to bring supplies from Mexico City. Consequently, the opening of the mines at Zacatecas in the 1540s saw the growth of cattle *haciendas*. While mining played out, cattle remained and expanded in terms of holdings and production. The same pattern that unfolded for Zacatecas held true for Chihuahua almost one hundred years later.

Throughout the seventeenth century, pressures from miners brought greater parts of Chihuahua, especially the Indian areas in the Sierra, under Spanish dominion. Coupled to this was the activity of missionaries who sought the salvation of souls — if not that, then martyrdom. Franciscans and Jesuits proselytized with zeal, hoping to bring more souls to Christ. Sometimes they met bloody ends, and the heathen remained unsaved. At other times the missionaries counted successes. In large measure, the missionaries helped subdue and pacify Indians who became the source of labor for the great mining enterprises. In addition, other racial stocks came in: blacks soon went to the mines in Parral, as did Indians from central Mexico. Thus, a hybridized race of Spanish, Indian, and black created the first autochthonous *chihuahuense*.

Indians of Chihuahua did not accept passively the blandishments of Christ or of the Spanish civil authorities. As the Indians resisted, many missionaries found their martyrdom. But the inexorable push of the Spaniards, utilizing tamed Indians, ultimately pacified the resistors. The pacification took nearly one hundred years, though, and some tribes, like the Apache, would not be defeated until the late nineteenth century.

Continual expansion of mining and ranching accompanied the pacification of the different Indian tribes. San Francisco del Oro and Cusihuiriachi yielded important mining discoveries and continued to enrich the Spanish Crown and the mining concessionaires. Spain constantly pushed northward. In the far north, however, trouble brewed. New Mexico would soon erupt.

By 1680, an Indian rebellion in Santa Fe forced the Spanish inhabitants who could escape with their lives to take refuge at Paso del Norte. A defeated and despirited group of settlers arrived at El Paso, and fifteen years would pass before Spain could recoup her losses in the far north. She had too much invested in the area to allow the heathen to drive the Crown and the True Faith out of New Mexico. By the dawn of the eighteenth century, Chihuahua began to fill up around the edges. Only the center, along which stretched desert country and river valleys, required settlement.

By 1709, the town of San Francisco de Cuellar was established. This would ultimately become modern Chihuahua City In large measure its founding was a response to the incursions of the Apaches who capitalized upon the Spanish debacle in Santa Fe to carry the war to the intruders in their southern settlements. Far removed from Mexico City, Chihuahua lay almost helpless to attack by very mean and very ugly-tempered Apaches. Defense of the city rested in the hands of the citizenry since the powers-that-be in Mexico City could not or would not dispatch sufficient soldiers to defend the northern frontier. Thus began almost two centuries of concerted warfare against the Apache, a factor that contributes to the fierce independence of the *chihuahuense*.

With threats from the north, as well as a constant and almost unbridled ambition pushing upward from the south, Chihuahua became a scene of debauchery and wild living. Eat, drink, whore, and be merry, became the philosophy, for tomorrow some bureaucrat might annihilate your precarious fortune or some crazed Indian might dismember you. Fortunately, the Franciscans established themselves and acted as a moderating influence on the area. But they, too, proved ambitious, for they wanted to construct a proper edifice to the glory of God, and by the 1730s began construction on what would become the Cathedral of Chihuahua City.

By the late 1700s, Chihuahua had grown. Its Cathedral dominated the Plaza de Armas and became the center of civic life. Yet, the town was, like most towns of that century, a collection of low, squat buildings that lined streets filled with the wastes of the population, animal and human. Sanitation was not a primary consideration. Garbage and excrement notwithstanding, a segment of the population became rich. They held *haciendas* and shares in the mining enterprises. And they learned to do for themselves, for they lived in a splendid isolation from the whirling currents of discontent and political tensions that began to beset Mexico City by the end of the century.

The latter part of the eighteenth century brought profound changes to the Spanish Empire. The expulsion of the Jesuits in 1767, the creation of a new administrative infrastructure in New Spain, and the sanctioning of a colonial militia in 1765 with all of the perquisites of the regular army provided a training ground for the future leaders of Mexican independence. In Chihuahua, the tensions that afflicted the center were also felt.

In 1776, the English colonies engaged in an exercise of ridding themselves of a monarch. By 1783, they had accomplished this feat. But the newly formed United States was, if nothing else, ambitious. Despite internal problems, the writing of a constitution, and conflict with some European powers, the United States aimed at expanding its hegemony to the west. But Spanish territory occupied all of that land west of the Mississippi. In 1803, President Thomas Jefferson acquired the Louisiana Territory from a Napoleon who desperately needed the money for his own ambitious campaigns. Three years later, the first Americans would travel from St. Louis, Missouri, to Santa Fe, New Mexico.

The capture and subsequent imprisonment of Zebulon Pike and the transporting of Pike and his followers to Chihuahua only acted as a temporary glitch in the desire of Americans to get into Spanish territory. By opening this first trade route with Mexico in the last days of Spain's occupation of that land, Pike and others initiated a constant and at times mutually beneficial relationship between Americans and northern Mexicans. Trade began to grow on a regular basis, and not even the onslaught of the Mexican War for Independence (1810–1822) failed to disrupt the newly established commercial relationship.

Two months before Miguel Hidalgo y Costilla, the renegade

priest from Guanajuato, issued his *grito de Dolores, chihuahuenses* armed themselves to withstand the rumored onslaught of Napoleon's soldiers. The *chihuahuenses* proved loyal to Ferdinand VII, even after his ouster by Napoleon, and prepared to withstand any attempt by Napoleonic forces to take over Mexico. Thus, they were armed and ready, eager to take on a foreign invader. Instead of French forces, they faced a more difficult choice: support of an incipient independence movement or loyalty to Napoleon's brother, crowned Joseph I of Spain. The guiding principle in their decision was the same one that had dictated most local action in Chihuahua: survival. Chihuahua sided lukewarmly with independence.

But the Hidalgo Revolt died aborning. The slightly mad priest from Dolores, Guanajuato, failed as a military commander. Desertions, internal disputes among the rebel leaders, and the superiority of Spanish arms drove the rebel army north, hopeful of finding aid among the denizens of the northern provinces. Unfortunately, the northerners proved more loyal to Spain at this point. Hidalgo and some of his followers were captured and marched in chains to Chihuahua City. Executions of rebel leaders began; Hidalgo was the last one. His death was delayed because the Crown and the Church wanted a recantation from him. Finally, he recanted, made his peace with God, the Inquisition, and the Crown, and faced a firing squad. The bishop defrocked him, circulated his recantation, and relaxed him to the secular arm for execution of sentence. All of the major leaders of the initial phases of independence had been shot, their heads removed and packed in salt and then sent south for exhibition as a warning to those who would oppose royal authority.

Yet the *chihuahuenses*, though at first supportive of the Crown, remained uncomfortable about the death of Hidalgo. A niggling feeling that something terrible had occurred nagged at the collective conscience. Even the bishop who defrocked him had appealed for a commutation of sentence for Hidalgo. Also, it became apparent even in the isolated north that the Crown was in deep trouble, its power waning. If Chihuahua was to survive — the guiding principle of its existence — then a reevaluation of its position *vis-à-vis* the Crown was necessary.

Another eleven years (1822) would go by before Mexico achieved her independence. Unfortunately, that independence did not result from the leadership of statesmen like Father José María Morelos y Pavón, the successor to Hidalgo, but rather from an opportunistic popinjay who had the effrontery to crown himself as Mexico's first emperor. Agustín de Iturbide (Agustín I) in many respects set the pattern for the chaos that would afflict Mexico for most of the nineteenth century. Unstable government punctuated by barracks' revolts became the *sine qua non* of political life.

In Chihuahua the citizens remained staunch royalists. They even dispatched an army to support Mexico City against Iturbide. But the infection of nationalist independence had even struck the local soldiers. In southern Chihuahua they declared for independence, turned north, and marched on Chihuahua City to support Iturbide and his Plan de Iguala. Chihuahua, the Spanish province of Nueva Vizcaya, was incorporated into the Mexican nation. By 1823, Chihuahua appeared on Mexico's first national map as a state of the Mexican Empire. The imperial status, however, was short-lived. Iturbide, overthrown by Antonio López de Santa Anna, fell from power in much the same way he had achieved it: through violence and a *coup d'etat*.

Mexico's independence brought with it a flurry of patriotic symbols. A national flag commemorating Mexico's Indian heritage came into being, as well as the declaration of a national holiday on September 16, the day Hidalgo called for a class war against the hated Spaniards. The bodies of Ignacio Allende, Father Hidalgo, and others were sent to Mexico City for burial in a place of honor. *Chihuahuenses*, lukewarm about the whole independence notion, still disinterred the bodies and dispatched them to the new capital. But provincial animosity toward the impositions of the center continued to lurk in the psyche of the *chihuahuenses*.

In addition, the relaxed relationship between Creoles and Spaniards suddenly deteriorated. In 1829, a time in Mexican history when there was a renascent Hispanophobia because of Spanish attempts to retake Mexico, Chihuahua felt its first jolt. Screams of death to the *gachupines* (Spaniards born in Spain) resulted in the expulsion of thirty Spaniards from Chihuahua City. No concrete evidence existed, but it was believed that the Spaniards resident in Mexico generally and Chihuahua specifically served as a sort of fifth column for an ultimate retakeover of Mexico by Spain. In a fit of xenophobia the *chihuahuenses* came close to destroying their economy, for much of the wealth of the state was concentrated in the hands of Spaniards. Those who were expelled took their money with them and thus deprived Chihuahua of substantial revenues. Various exceptions were made for some Spaniards to stay in Chihuahua, but the xenophobic indulgence cost the state dearly.

In its first quarter-century of independence, Mexico struggled to attain respectable nationhood. But the venality of public officials even made this attempt a joke within the nation. The long tenure of Antonio López de Santa Anna as kingmaker in Mexico's political processes (1823–1855) assured that bullets rather than orderly transitions would dominate the political scene. Against that backdrop the *chihuahuenses* attempted once again to look out for themselves.

Chihuahua envisioned ambitious programs of public health, education, and industrial development. Smelting, one of the city's largest industries, produced huge revenues because of its volume. Of course, the pollution created by the smelters necessitated that the city fathers of the capital mandate the painting and restoration of buildings affected by the smoke. The tax revenues produced by the smelting industry essentially supported state government.

Taxes have constantly been a plague to the *chihuahuenses*. These ranged in the nineteenth century from five to fifty percent. Tobacco, for example, needed to be imported into Chihuahua for the local cigar industry. Then, as now, the locals attempted to circumvent these taxes by using substitutes. Chihuahua smokers, a tough lot traditionally, carried bags of tobacco substitute and cornhusks, and rolled their own cigarettes rather than purchase cigars made from tobacco imported from other parts of Mexico. The *serredas* are one example of Chihuahuan attempts to deal with what they considered impositions from the center.

Another constant of existence of Mexico's northern frontier came in the form of Indians. Apaches and Comanches continually plagued Chihuahua. Deals were struck with the tribes, often to the discomfiture of neighboring states. But attempts to mollify the marauding bands of nomadic Indians proved to be only stopgap measures. A real fear gripped Chihuahua. There sat the state, powerless in the face of increasing Indian raids and with little, if any, support from the federal government. To make matters even more complicated, the growing number of Americans coming into Mexico through Chihuahua caused concern to Mexico's government.

Yankee traders brought increasing revenue into Mexico. The *chihuahuenses* welcomed and sympathized with the Americans. They had come from similar country and had endured the hardships of frontier life. Americans were pragmatic in the same way that the *chihuahuenses* were pragmatic. Adaptations for survival were necessary. Though the Americans brought Protestantism and Freemasonry to northern Mexico, the denizens of Chihuahua, conservative by nature, rejected these ideas without rejecting the advocates of these heresies. The relationship between Chihuahua and the American traders proved beneficial to both sides. An active trade in livestock, especially pack mules for the long trip back to the United States, endeared the Americans to stockraisers in Chihuahua. Also, the *chihuahuenses* could obtain goods at a cheaper price from the foreign traders than they could from Mexican traders coming north from Mexico City because of the elimination of internal customs duties.

By the 1840s, the intercourse between Chihuahua and America had increased in briskness. But increasing tensions between Mexico and the United States over Texas and United States expansionist ambitions vitiated the good relations, for a growing paranoia amongst the *chihuahuenses* led to bitter resentments. Principal among leading citizens of Chihuahua to oppose the Americans was a man who would serve as governor more than six times, Angel Trías, Sr.

Trías owned a large *hacienda* over which the traders had to cross, and he steadfastly made life miserable for them. His undying loathing of all things foreign would have their repercussions when war finally broke out between Mexico and the United States. Trías would be acting as governor of Chihuahua when the Doniphan expeditions would occupy Chihuahua City for fifty-nine days in the spring of 1847. He would have to swallow the bitter pill of foreign occupation.

The war with the United States led the *chihuahuenses* to an almost irrational support of a war that was led by Santa Anna, a war that in many respects Mexico was destined to lose. Mexican internal stability still remained shaky at best. The constant comings and goings of Santa Anna after his defeat at the Battle of San Jacinto and the loss of Texas in 1836 left Mexico reeling from the shock. The country's treasury was a mess, political power shifted radically from one man to another, the provinces — Chihuahua included — proceeded to carry on their own affairs without much reference to Mexico City. But the Fatherland was now under attack. The dreaded *gringo,* whom *chihuahuenses* had fawned over before the 1840s, was coming. Rape, pillage, and destruction followed in his path. Should he enter Chihuahua City, all would be lost.

When Doniphan's bedraggled outfit reached Chihuahua City, they seized the state capital without much resistance and occupied it for fifty-nine days. The *gringos* did not prove to be the bloody barbarians depicted by xenophobes like Trías. Yet they did represent an occupying force, a foreign force that occupied Mexican territory. *Chihuahuense* nationalism has always risen to the defense of the Fatherland. Whatever arguments it might have with the creatures of Mexico City were subsumed in favor of a short-term unity with the suspect *políticos* of Mexico City.

In spite of the xenophobia, when Doniphan pulled out in April 1847 some American traders chose to stay in Chihuahua and carry on their trade. Chihuahua was too far north to be affected by the immediacies of the war, which had shifted to Veracruz and Mexico City. While they experienced some animosities, including the murder of one American trader, the bulk of those *gringos* who chose to stay continued to prosper.

The end of the war in early 1848 brought massive cessions of land to the United States. The United States paid Mexico $15 million for California, most of New Mexico, Arizona, Colorado, and parts of Utah. In the immediate postwar tension, the commander at Santa Fé, not believing that the war was over, dispatched forces to Chihuahua, where again the *chihuahuenses* headed by Angel Trías made a valiant stand against the American invaders. Trías would enhance his reputation among his fellow citizens, but that would be all. War in Chihuahua had, for the time being, ended. But development in far off California brought increased trade to the traders who remained in Chihuahua, and those who would come after 1848.

The cry for gold came from the Sacramento and American rivers in north-central California. Discovery of gold in what was formerly Mexican territory precipitated a massive gold rush that sent many of the seekers through El Paso del Norte, where they purchased goods from the increased number of traders in Chihuahua. Many gold seekers used Chihuahua City as an entryway to the Pacific, and traders there enjoyed a lucrative business. Mexicans also gained appreciably through the manufacture and sale of leather goods — pack saddles, water bags, rifle scabbards, and other items

— to the American caravans that passed that way. Less than a year after the war between Mexico and the United States had ended, American commercial activity again picked up in Chihuahua.

But United States commercial ventures in Chihuahua failed to overshadow the Indian threat, especially from Apaches. Moving from redoubts in southern New Mexico (still Mexican territory), the Apaches raided with impunity into Chihuahua and again threw the citizenry into nervous and justifiable fits. Recriminations flew on both sides. Technically, the United States could not pursue the Apaches into southern New Mexico. Mexican defenses remained incredibly weak and despirited after the war. In Chihuahua there even existed talk of restoring a brutal bounty system to keep the Apache at bay. The state was becoming devoid of population.

The Indian problem in Chihuahua in one sense played into the hands of Antonio López de Santa Anna. Back again for another go at the presidency, Santa Anna established an outright dictatorship, complete with regal trappings and a designation of himself as "His Serene Highness" and "President for Life." To pay for much of this, Santa Anna further contributed to the dismemberment of Mexico by selling the Mesilla Valley to the United States. The United States gained a southern railroad route to the Pacific and, additionally, territory that encompassed modern-day Las Cruces, New Mexico, and Tucson, Arizona, and an increased Mexican population. The treaty negotiated between James Gadsden and Santa Anna's minions transferred more than 45,000 square miles of land to the United States for $5 million. Angel Trías, again governor of Chihuahua, loathed the sale of the land and refused to publish the treaty in Chihuahua for six months. Thoroughly disillusioned with Santa Anna, Trías dragged his feet but in the end accepted the deal.

Santa Anna's days wound down. In rather short order, he spent the money gained from the sale of the Mesilla Valley. Suddenly, he found that the support he had bought no longer looked so favorably upon his continued tenure. In 1854 opposition crystallized around Juan Alvarez, one of the last war horses in the fight for independence. Alvarez was joined by such notables as Benito Juárez of Oaxaca, Miguel Lerdo de Tejada, and Melchor Ocampo. Within a year they successfully ousted Santa Anna, a man who would return to Mexico only once more and then only to die of natural causes, old, broken, and despised.

The advent of the Reform regime ultimately headed by Juárez in the mid-1850s polarized the nation. The liberal Reform included provisions for the nationalization of Church lands, the elimination of special privileges for the Church, and an attempt to create a rural peasantry that had a concept of real property. In addition, the Reform aimed to make the civil authority supreme over the ecclesiastical. Marriages, registries of births and deaths, and other functions normally performed by the Church now fell within the civilian sphere. The upshot of the nearly monomaniacal attempts to transform Mexico appeared in evergrowing political tensions and polarization, a situation that eventually erupted into civil war and foreign intervention.

The polarization that afflicted the nation in general with the onset of the Reform also manifested itself in Chihuahua. There, too, the split between conservatives and liberals appeared, and the problem was complicated by the Indian threat. Apaches dominated Chihuahua and kept its citizenry at bay. Again, Mexico's northern tier felt abandoned by the center. Write the Listers: "A central government, secure for three hundred years from overthrow by Indians, frequently failed to appreciate the northern dilemma. Confederation of the northern states was the topic of discussion in cafes and *cantinas*."

The internecine warfare that erupted between liberals and conservatives in 1858 also manifested itself in Chihuahua. Conservatives from Durango seized Parral, and liberals among whom Luis Terrazas figured prominently moved to eliminate the conservatives in their midsts. These men opposed the clericalism that made the Church dominant as well as the overweening influence of the army in civilian affairs. Thus, they fought their way through Chihuahua City until they successfully ousted and executed the conservative fanatic, Domingo Cajén.

Luis Terrazas began his rise to power in Chihuahua during the Reform struggle. He personified the contradictions that underscore the *chihuahuense* existence. Loved and vilified, Terrazas became the man who would dominate the state for the next fifty years. His rise to power began when he inherited his father's butcher shop operation in the early 1850s and started to become prominent in local politics in Chihuahua City. Eventually his influence spread throughout the state. He began to acquire lands and with these lands, increasing wealth. A wise marriage to Carolina Cuilty brought him additional influence and land. Early on, Terrazas perceived that land ownership would ultimately dictate a man's ability to acquire wealth in other areas. Land would become the basis of his eventual fortune.

Elevated to the rank of colonel because of his daring leadership in the ouster of the conservatives, Terrazas took to the hills to rout out pockets of resistance. A grateful state legislature elevated him to the governorship in 1860 at the age of thirty, technically not yet the legal age for that high office. Luis Terrazas was the most powerful figure in the politics of Mexico's largest state, so little constitutional proscriptions about age could be easily ignored.

Nevertheless, royalist sympathies that had made Chihuahua at best lukewarm to independence forced many *chihuahuenses* to favor the establishment of royal authority in Mexico. Certainly, the confusion engendered by Juárez and his coterie of followers did not inspire confidence in the north. In addition, the United States was also enmeshed in its own fratricidal struggle and could do little to control the Indian problem on the border. Again, the *chihuahuenses* had to look after themselves. Mexico generally was ripe for plucking.

In 1862, France, with conservative support, began an imperial adventure in the New World. Under the pretext of collecting debts suspended by Juárez, the French invaded Mexico. Juárez, embattled, put out the call for recruits to repel the French invaders. But the north, whose principal occupation was survival, did not respond with alacrity. When Juárez asked for 2,000 men, Terrazas had to make a choice. Sending men to central Mexico to help fight the French meant weakening defenses at home. The choice was clear. What aid had Chihuahua received in the constant and unrelenting struggle against the Indian menace? None! Local militiamen stayed home, for the threat of Indian depredations loomed more immediately than did invasion of a bunch of ambitious monarchists and Frenchmen in central Mexico.

In some quarters, criticism over Terrazas' refusal to send troops described him as a traitor. Yet his motives were purely localistic. Northern conditions needed attention first. It was Terrazas ultimately who gave refuge to Juárez and his liberal allies when French and conservative forces drove the reformers out of Mexico City. Juárez, however, remained the impassive, almost maniacal reformer who failed to appreciate the problems of the north. He violently criticized Terrazas for his administrative errors that revolved around the amortization of Church lands and their resale to the private sector, problems dealing with forests and grazing lands, and the handling of customs revenues from ports of entry to Chihuahua. In many respects, Terrazas became the victim not only of political enemies, but also of his own youth, as he was in power at a time that required greater experience.

Consequently, from his redoubt in Monterrey, Nuevo León, Juárez appointed a new governor for Chihuahua as well as a new military commander. Moreover, Terrazas suffered the confiscation of his properties. Angel Trías, the father, had to seize Terrazas' lands while Luis sought refuge in Paso del Norte. But Terrazas would not be out for long. Soon Juárez would have need of the appeal that Luis Terrazas had generated in Chihuahua.

Juárez governed on the wing. As royalists moved toward Monterrey, Juárez headed west and was met south of Chihuahua by Trías. For the first time a president, though one in flight, visited Chihuahua. However, this was not really a visit; it was a search for refuge. Festering under all of the visual unity, of course, lay the fact of central government refusal to aid the *chihuahuenses.* Rarely had Chihuahua's real enemy been the foreigner. Rather, the enemy was an insensitive central authority. Juárez did represent that legitimate authority, however, and for a while animosities stayed subsumed.

For the *chihuahuenses,* the presence of Benito Juárez presented a series of contradictions. He was an Indian, born of Zapotec stock from Oaxaca, who espoused essentially white liberal theories. Additionally, Juárez seemed humorless and insensitive to the needs of local areas. He placed nation above all else, yet for the *chihuahuenses* the nation had not done much for the benefit of the state. Still, Juárez was the president, and Chihuahua could take pride in the fact that he had sought aid and refuge there.

Juárez moved in and out of Chihuahua City between 1864 and 1866 on three different occasions. French and monarchist occupation of the town again forced him north to Paso del Norte. Terrazas and other Juárez supporters rallied liberal elements to help expel the French intruders. While many *chihuahuenses* had pronounced royalist sympathies, they still remained nationalistic Mexicans. French insensitivity to Mexican customs and traditions alienated the sympathizers, who then threw their support to the liberal or nationalist cause.

Finally, in early 1867, France pulled out of Mexico. The days of Maximilian of Hapsburg were then numbered. Pressures from the United States (whose civil war had ended in 1865) as well as conflict in Europe forced Louis Napoleon to withdraw. Maximilian, however, chose to stay on and attempt to rally his followers. Ignoring pleas to abdicate, the Austrian clung tenaciously to his precarious throne. But it was too late. The foreigner had alienated the Mexicans. Juárez succeeded in overcoming regional animosities to rally the nation long enough to oust the usurper. In June 1867, Juárez, having successfully swept down from the north, captured Maximilian and some of his generals and ordered their execution at the Cerro de las Campanas (Hill of the Bells) in Querétaro.

Juárez had left Chihuahua in December 1866. Like all good *políticos,* he soon forgot the supposed affront to him committed by Terrazas when Don Luis failed to send troops. Terrazas joined the party that escorted Juárez to the Chihuahua-Durango border as the dour little Zapotec began his march toward Mexico City.

The return of Juárez to power in Mexico City brought sweeping reprisals against the supporters of the French. Their lands were summarily confiscated. Luis Terrazas, again serving as governor of Chihuahua, began his program of personal land acquisition by obtaining title to the *hacienda* at Encinillas. This would lead, ultimately, to the creation of the largest *latifundium* in Mexico — six and a half million acres of land devoted mainly to cattle.

To this day, Luis Terrazas inspires strong emotions in Mexico and Chihuahua in general. Often he represents everything evil about the regime of Porfirio Díaz. At times he emerges as the true modernizer of that unique Mexican state. As such there are some odd contradictions, for Terrazas never supported Díaz while Díaz sought power. At the same time, Terrazas took advantage of the Díaz pacification of Mexico to expand his own fortunes.

In 1872 Juárez again stood for reelection, won, and rather quickly died of a heart attack. Porfirio Díaz, the leading general of the republican forces, also stood for election. When he lost, he went into revolt. Terrazas refused to support Díaz' Plan de La Noria, which denounced Juárez for attempting to perpetuate a dictatorship. Four years later, under the banner of the Plan de Tuxtepec, Díaz successfully ousted Sebastián Lerdo de Tejada and was installed as president. He would remain in office, with one four-year break from 1880 to 1884, until 1911. It was not until the turn of the century that Díaz and Luis Terrazas began to achieve at least a livable peace.

Porfirio Díaz found some support in Chihuahua. Angel Trías, Jr., supported Díaz and eventually became governor of Chihuahua. The time had come for Terrazas to take a backseat in politics. He did so with a certain amount of grace, for he had fortunes to make and could still indulge in the rough and tumble politics of Chihuahua without being wholly visible.

Land still formed the basis of the Terrazas fortune. The six and one-half million acres he had acquired encompassed twelve *haciendas* for the Terrazas family. Some of these lands were acquired through marriages arranged for the Terrazas offspring; others Don Luis obtained himself. He came to represent everything associated with the Porfirian era. After 1872, the history of Chihuahua in many respects remains the history of Luis Terrazas. There is yet to be a fair biography written about the man. He is either vilified or adored, held up as a hero or a monster who lived off of the labor of poor *peones* whom he held in inescapable thrall through a network of company stores, debt, and the peasant orientation to a little plot of land.

Large landholdings characterized Chihuahua from the time that mines near Parral began production. The *haciendas* provided food for the miners. With the decline of mining, the *haciendas* continued to grow and develop a life of their own. By the time Terrazas came to maturity during the turbulent 1850s and 1860s, large landholdings formed the pattern for the acquisition of power and influence. The confiscation of royalist lands gave Terrazas his impetus. In large measure, the northern tier of Mexican states had their modern start with the large cattle estates. This certainly was the case with Luis Terrazas, for he aimed his production and his energies at the traditional *chihuahuense* market — the United States.

Terrazas' cattle herds spread over vast expanses of land. But, like the rest of Chihuahua, it was a hard land, and only the hardiest of cattle could survive much less thrive. In Chihuahua, cattle require 75 to 125 acres per cow-calf unit for year-round pasturage. From about 1890 until 1910, the Terrazas *haciendas* branded an average of 35,000 head of calves per year. Changing tastes in beef in the United States forced Terrazas to adapt. The tough, hardy *criollo* cattle of northern Mexico needed upgrading. At about the same time that United States ranchers began the importation of blooded stock — Hereford, Angus, and Shorthorns — so, too, did Terrazas, since his market lay north and not in central Mexico.

After cattle formed the basis of Terrazas' incredible wealth, he expanded into urban real estate and began to buy and develop large urban tracts in Chihuahua City. His urban wealth soon brought him control of public utilities, and he must be credited with urban improvements such as street lighting and trolley cars. In order to capitalize upon the agricultural wealth of Chihuahua, Luis Terrazas and his associates constructed flour mills there. Textiles also attracted Terrazas as a money-making venture, and in the early 1870s he acquired a woolen mill, thus giving him some control over the prices paid for wool. While Terrazas himself did not become involved in mining, he served as an intermediary for the acquisition by United States firms of mining properties in the mountains of Chihuahua.

The logical outlet for all of this wealth ultimately became banking. Initially, he and some associates founded the Banco Mexicano with a capital of 77,000 *pesos*. In 1884, thirty years after he inherited the butcher shop from his father, Luis Terrazas and friends began the Banco Minero Chihuahuense. This beginning ultimately would lead Terrazas and his son-in-law, Enrique C. Creel, to consolidate all banking in the Banco Minero. The Banco Minero would become, ultimately, the bank for the deposit of all state government funds and the bank to be used for capitalization of government projects. In effect, a banking monopoly was born that effectively excluded any other would-be bankers. By 1900, Terrazas and Creel owned or controlled sixteen separate enterprises valued at over 27 million *pesos* (the *peso* was worth about 2:1 to the dollar).

There is no question that Terrazas proved as adept in business as he had in the rugged politics of the Juárez era. He skillfully acquired fallow lands, some of which resulted from nationalizations and some of which merely had lay there, unused, for over a century. Previous occupants had fled either Apaches or a vindictive government.

No doubt exists that Díaz helped Terrazas. Díaz' desire to modernize Mexico through industry and a rapidly improved transportation resulted in railroads. These railroads facilitated the shipment of cattle to market, and this in turn allowed Terrazas to turn some handsome profits. But much of the initial profit-taking came as a result of a system that bound peasants to land and seemed manorial and reminiscent of a medieval Europe rather than a modern nineteenth century.

Terrazas cannot be condemned for excessively harsh treatment of his *peones*. The system was already in place, and Terrazas did provide good lands for the *peones* to raise food for themselves. But the peasant was still bound to the land through a system of debt peonage. The *hacienda* communities were essentially self-sufficient entities that provided all of the bare necessities for existence.

There is no question: Luis Terrazas dominated the Chihuahua landscape. To him goes the credit for the ultimate pacification of the Apaches, though it was his cousin Joaquín who was the actual hero. The Apache ultimately began to infiltrate Mexico permanently as reservations in the United States threatened to reduce the proud warrior to a dirt grubber. By the early 1880s, Terrazas, still serving as governor, commissioned Joaquín to undertake the pacification. Finally, the Apaches were forced back to the United States, where they were captured and pacified coercively. Joaquín Terrazas, acting under orders from his cousin, the governor of Chihuahua, responded with a direct brutality that helped break the Apache spirit. Yet Joaquín is overshadowed by Luis' accomplishments.

The long reign of Porfirio Díaz brought peace to Mexico. Concessions to foreigners and a brutal pacification of lawless elements outside the government assured that Mexico would be acceptable in the eyes of foreigners. By the time Díaz had succeeded, critics of the regime declared that Mexico was "a mother to foreigners and a stepmother to Mexicans."

And it was an odd mixture that came to Chihuahua. Chinese worked on the railroads and stayed. In the 1890s, Mormons came from Utah after reaching some generous agreements with the government. As a result, Chihuahua became increasingly varied in its ethnic mixtures and in its values. In the 1920s, to jump ahead, Mennonites occupied what is now Cuahtémoc and turned it into the apple center of Mexico.

The nature of the state of Chihuahua lends itself to extensive exploitation of the land. In 1900, for example, seventeen persons owned forty percent of the land mass of the state. About ninety-five percent of the population owned no land whatsoever. This was not necessarily a wholly evil or inequitable situation. The large *haciendas* were productive, though they had their attendant drawbacks which ultimately led to revolutionary strife. But pressures threatened to disturb the tranquility of the Porfirian peace in Chihuahua.

In 1891, in Tomochi, an Indian rebellion inspired by charismatic religious leaders kept government forces at bay for a month. In large measure, the causes of the revolt were both religious and economic, for much of the land surrounding Tomochi belonged to José Yves Limanatour, Díaz' minister of finance, and he took great quantities of timber out of the area.

Labor problems also ruffled the tranquility of the state. In 1881 a miners' strike at Pinos Altos in the municipality of Ocampo led to severe repressions. These antagonisms would fester and make the miners ready recipients for the idea of revolution. By the time the copper workers struck in Cananea, Sonora, in 1906, laborers in Chihuahua were fully apprised of labor agitation and of possible action when necessary.

By 1900, Díaz and Terrazas had mended their political rift. In 1903, Luis Terrazas was again elected governor of Chihuahua. In the next year, he left the governorship to be succeeded by his son-in-law, Enrique C. Creel. Creel was elected governor in his own right in 1907, and this resulted in a further bonding between Terrazas and Díaz. Creel served as an interpreter for Díaz when William Howard Taft visited Cd. Juárez in 1909. Díaz went to Chihuahua, the second time in a century that a president had visited the state. This time the president was not a refugee but a victorious and enduring politician. He would later appoint Creel as minister of foreign relations.

The victories of Díaz and coincidentally Terrazas ultimately proved ephemeral. For all of the development and enterprise that occurred under their aegis, many social problems continued to fester in Chihuahua and in the nation in general. Political exclusivity, social discrimination, problems of literacy and inequitable distribution of income and means of production, and a host of other problems produced conditions that led to an explosion. When that explosion came in 1910, it began as a small boom that later took on nuclear proportions and engulfed the nation in more than a decade of fratricide. In its path were produced monumental leaders who would dominate state and nation. And the revolution would bring real and ideological effects that have affected Mexico ever since.

CHAPTER 2

Cradle of the Revolution

He rode out of the western Sierra, bandoliers crisscrossing his chest, sweat streaking his horse's body, vengeance clearly emblazoned on his face. Francisco "Pancho" Villa came to personify the Revolution in northern Mexico. Grievances — personal, social, and political — had pushed Villa into a life of banditry where he preyed upon the rich, especially the Terrazas family, performed acts of charity with the goods he stole, and also kept himself and his band of men alive and constantly in the minds of *chihuahuenses*. Reviled and deified, Pancho Villa *was* the Revolution.

Chihuahuenses excluded from a share of the economic and political action welcomed the Revolution. The exploitation of peon and mine labor, the influence of foreigners, especially in mining, and the closed system headed by Luis Terrazas clearly made Chihuahua a breeding ground for discontent. Even Díaz, with the rift between himself and Terrazas healed, could not stem the swelling opposition to the regime. To overthrow the national government would in effect topple the Terrazas clan, who were the unwitting personification of the system in Chihuahua. Inarticulated feelings of inequity in land and income distribution, political impotence,

A photo of Villa in uniform inscribed
``to my esteemed friend, Rudolfo
Fierro."
— Muséo de la Revolución
en Chihuahua,
photo by the author.

Villa leading the charge. Purportedly, this
was taken on the way to the first battle of
Torreón (October 1913).
— Muséo de la Revolución en Chihuahua

A postcard, issued in 1977 by what
would become a left-wing political group
in Chihuahua, calls up the spirit of
Pancho Villa to unite the north of
Mexico against the impositions of
Mexico City. The postcard denounces
aristocrats and political leaders who dis-
parage the north and refer to that area
merely as ``the provinces." A long message printed on the reverse calls for the
northerner to ``defend himself! ... Fight!
... Prepare for the long and hard battle
that awaits us!" The pictorial part of
the card states: ``Viva Villa, you bastards! The Revolution isn't over."

and a general rage against a system predicated on privilege rather than merit or talent impelled many *chihuahuenses* to join with a national movement headed by another northerner, Francisco Madero.

Mexico's Revolution began essentially as a political movement aimed at the removal of Porfirio Díaz. Francisco I. Madero, scion of a wealthy Coahuila family, issued the first warning when Díaz in 1908 had declared his support of opposition parties and had stated that Mexico was ready for democracy. But Madero, ascetic, a spiritist, a vegetarian who had been trained by Jesuits and the University of California at Berkeley, saw that Díaz' ploy was but a sham. In 1909, Madero published a small political tract entitled *La sucesión presidencial de 1910 (The Presidential Succession of 1910)*. In it he flatly stated that Díaz merely wanted to gull the Mexican public and had no intention of stepping down. By 1910, Madero had become the only active candidate against Díaz. In the splendor of Mexico's centennial year celebration, presidential elections were held: Díaz, of course, emerged the overwhelming winner. Madero found himself in prison, first in Mexico City and later at San Luis Potosí. In October, Madero escaped prison, made his way to the United States, and launched a revolution against a system that allowed one man to remain in power for more than thirty years.

Madero, in typical Mexican fashion, published a political manifesto, the Plan de San Luis Potosí, in which he denounced the election as a fraud, reluctantly called upon the Mexican army to turn against the government, and set the date for the revolt at November 20. Madero's first call to arms failed to garner nationwide support for Díaz, who, although perhaps getting a little fuzzy because of age, still had sufficient political savvy to crush *loci* of opposition. Díaz did not, however, succeed in Chihuahua.

Sufficient opposition to the regime existed in Chihuahua. But that animosity toward the system was directed more against Luis Terrazas, now a man in his early eighties, than against Díaz. It was reasoned that a destruction of the Terrazas hold on Chihuahua would force the whole Díaz machine to collapse. Active recruitment began for the formation of a rebel army.

A principal spokesman for the Madero cause in Chihuahua was Abraham González. In many respects González typified the middle-class opposition that began to coalesce around Madero's call to arms. At one time, González had hoped to establish a bank in Chihuahua. Yet he found his way effectively blocked by the consolidation of all banking in the state in the Banco Minero de Chihuahua, a major enterprise of the Terrazas-Creel union. Frustrated, González looked for another way to make a living. He ultimately became a cattle buyer, and one of his best sources of supply was Pancho Villa. González readily recognized that most of the cattle he purchased from Villa were rustled; however, since much of that stock came from Terrazas' ranches, he was not too careful about reading the brands. Consequently, he knew Pancho when Madero issued his call to arms.

Men joined the Revolution for different reasons. Chances for self-aggrandizement and social improvement certainly figured prominently as motives for joining the opposition. Pascual Orozco from Guerrero, Toribio Ortega from Cuchillo Parado, and others began to answer the call. So, too, did Francisco Villa.

As the *maderistas* attempted to gather themselves nationally in order to renew the struggle against Díaz, in Chihuahua Abraham González began his recruitment of troops. By January 1911, troops headed by Orozco, Calixto Contreras, and Villa scored some minor victories. Yet the center of the country remained essentially secure for Díaz, with the exception of Morelos, where in 1909 Emiliano Zapata had begun a localized revolt against the aging dictator. Some common factors exist between Zapata and the revolt in Chihuahua. Principally, they centered on land, though the approaches advocated by the *zapatistas* who were communitarian differed markedly from those of northern Mexico.

Madero himself in the Plan de San Luis Potosí made some fuzzy promises about land reform, and this proved sufficient to entice Zapata to join with the northern rebel. As a consequence, the *zapatistas* successfully prosecuted a guerrilla action just south of Mexico City and kept a substantial portion of Díaz' army occupied while northern Mexico pressed downward on Díaz. Madero reentered Mexico in early 1911 and attempted to make some military decisions but was derided in this by both Orozco and Villa because of his limited experience. Both Orozco the muleskinner and Villa the bandit knew the terrain intimately, and this intimacy provided the edge that they needed to befuddle the federal army.

By early May, Madero and his forces succeeded in capturing the Northwest Railroad, which gave them ready access to the border and rapid mobility for the revolutionary army. Rebel forces encircled Ciudad Juárez, just across the Río Grande from El Paso,

Texas. Madero hoped to settle the argument peaceably, and tried to negotiate with the federal commander. Ultimately, though, he failed. Villa and Orozco knew that they had the power to crush the federal forces, but Madero held them back. He feared that stray shells might cross the river and cause damage in the United States, thus giving the *gringos* cause to withhold support from Madero.

But Orozco and Villa proved impatient. They wanted to get the bloody fight over and done. Consequently, they provoked a federal attack on rebel emplacement and told Madero that their men had to "defend" themselves and were unable to retreat from the battle. It was tricky, for Madero was no military genius. Villa himself stated that Madero was not a military man and that he and his followers had to "put in motion the plans to reach a great victory or die in the trying."

For two days (May 8–10) the battle raged. The *federales*, thoroughly trounced and disillusioned, finally sued for peace and negotiations began. Additionally, the capture of the Juárez garrison provided great quantities of arms and ammunition for the rebel army.

But Madero's army no longer faced great military campaigns. Internal divisions began to appear in the revolutionary ranks as Orozco, with Villa's unwitting connivance, attempted to oust Madero. Villa, utterly desolated by this unknowing treachery, begged for Madero's forgiveness and left the army, returning to San Andrés to marry Luz Corral. Orozco, however, continued to nurture his growing animosity toward Madero.

At the same time Díaz began to feel the pressure from his advisors. The only major and significant victory achieved by the rebels had been Ciudad Juárez, but there they controlled the major port of entry into Mexico and the Mexican Central Railway. They now had revenue and greater mobility. Díaz' advisors encouraged the octogenarian dictator to resign. He resisted. They appealed to his patriotism: If he wanted to save the country from a bloodbath, he had best resign. Finally, Díaz relented and at the end of May boarded the German ship *Ypiranga* and headed for France. Suffering from an abscessed tooth, the old man left, declaring that "Madero has unleashed a tiger. Now let's see if he can ride it." Three years later, Díaz died in France.

By law, Mexico now required an interim government until new elections could be held. Madero selected Francisco Léon de la

Barra, the ambassador to Washington, as the interim president. Madero subsequently stood for election and defeated his conservative opponent. He then began to create problems with his innocent belief that all of Mexico's problems could be resolved politically. Other, deeper animosities festered and demanded resolution.

Chihuahua saw an improvement in its government when Madero took power. Abraham González, so instrumental to Madero's victory in Chihuahua, became governor. Like most *chihuahuenses* González proved a practical man. His efficient administration attempted to bring about needed changes without provoking massive economic and social dislocation. He felt no real passion against the big landholders nor against foreign entrepreneurs. He saw their value, especially for states like Chihuahua, but felt they needed to pay a fair tax valuation on their lands. This fact alone alienated González from the Terrazas family, the Creels, the Lujanes, and others who had enriched themselves in the latter nineteenth century.

Madero's inauguration at the end of 1911 failed to bring peace to Mexico. Already Zapata had broken with Madero because of the failure to restore village lands. In Chihuahua, strong feelings persisted because Madero selected a new running mate, José María Pino Suárez of Yucatán, instead of Vásquez Gómez. Moreover, Orozco, the principal commander of *maderista* forces during the struggle against Díaz, felt unrewarded. Madero had not appointed him secretary of war but had put him in command of irregular forces in Chihuahua. Madero prepared the basis for his own downfall by failing to place revolutionaries in high office. Instead, many of the Díaz crowd as well as Madero's family, some of whom reeked with venality, occupied cabinet posts and ambassadorships.

Revolutionaries felt unrewarded as well. They had bled for Madero but failed to garner any of the rewards that their participation in the overthrow of Díaz warranted. Former rebels were only asked to lay down their arms and go back to their pursuits. They wanted perquisites, reform, and recognition.

Villa proved in some ways an exception. While he wanted all of the things to which other rebels aspired, he worshiped both Madero and Abraham González. He continued to act as a conduit for Madero for events out of Chihuahua, even as he attempted once again to become legitimate through the operation of a string of butcher shops. Of course, most of the meat supplied for those shops came from the lands of Luis Terrazas, but such a nicety did not deter Villa from his search for respectability. Still Villa remained available, and soon the call would come.

By February 1912, rumors abounded that Orozco planned to rebel against Madero. Despite protestations by Orozco to the contrary, there was little doubt that he would soon be in open revolt. By March 1, Orozco declared against Madero and denounced the president for his failure to comply with the promises of the Plan de San Luis Potosí. Conservative elements including the Terrazas family supported Orozco, for they believed that he could be handled if given sufficient ego strokes. Old followers of the radical Flores Magón brothers also joined him. Though opposed to the conservative elements, the old *magonistas* saw in Orozco a chance to advance their cause. The Orozco rebellion in many respects provided a microcosm of the opposition in Chihuahua to the central government. In fact, Orozco, though ultimately breaking with Madero, still remains a revered historical figure in modern-day Chihuahua.

The *orozquista* rebellion began to make headway in Chihuahua. Governor González hoped to contain Orozco before the rebellion spread to the rest of the country. How could he offset Orozco? González turned to Villa. Villa left the connubial couch, put his "legitimate" business on hold, and began organizing irregulars to give battle to Orozco. Orozco recognized that Villa could be a threat and attempted to buy him. Villa, ever faithful to Madero, informed Pascual Orozco, Sr., who carried the bribe to Villa, that he had no truck with traitors and that the old man was lucky to leave with his life.

Villa was incensed. He responded by quickly organizing forces in Satevó and Zaragosa and placing them under the command of former revolutionaries. But it took a while for Villa to score some victories. In early March, Villa and González retreated from Chihuahua City as Orozco grabbed the town. Federal forces along the border asked that Madero send troops to Chihuahua to help quell the rebellion.

The United States soon took an active interest in the Orozco rebellion. In a move supposedly predicated upon judicious neutrality, President William Howard Taft imposed an arms embargo on all of Mexico. As a result, it became increasingly difficult for both Orozco and the Madero government to obtain arms from the

United States. Orozco, however, did have the advantage of rustling cattle and selling them across the border. In this way, he continued the pattern that Villa and other revolutionaries had established. But the lack of order brought other problems to the Chihuahua–United States border: refugees.

Floods of refugees headed for the border — Mormons, Mexicans, rich, and poor. Tough people, accustomed to survival in the unrelenting lands of Chihuahua, found themselves displaced by renewed civil war. Mexicans, Mormons, and others left Chihuahua as the war headed in their direction. But most of the refugees hoped or at least felt that the conflict would be short-lived and that they could return; many left their homes virtually intact. People who remained became more and more tense. Strife between Mormons and Mexicans intensified, and incidents around Colonia Juárez made the situation volatile. Gun smuggling increased into the Mormon colonies around Casas Grandes. Pillaging of Mormon areas by rebels unsettled conditions in northwestern Chihuahua even more.

Finally, the federal government did intervene. Regular forces under the command of Gen. Victoriano Huerta headed north. Villa and other irregulars were placed under Huerta's orders. This, unfortunately, caused some immediate tensions, for Huerta held the irregulars and especially their commander, Villa, in utter contempt. There is no question that Huerta succeeded. The rebels were crushed throughout most of the state, and by July González was back in the governorship.

But the incorporation of Villa and his men into the federal forces underscored the antagonism of the old regime toward the upwardly ambitious lower classes represented by Villa. Villa liked to do things in his own, sometimes bizarre, manner. More and more he conflicted with Huerta, following orders if they suited his way of looking at things. When Villa, a lover of fine horseflesh, acquired a lovely Arabian mare as booty of war, Huerta demanded that the mare be returned to her owner. Villa refused, and Huerta had him arrested for insubordination. Summarily, Huerta ordered that Villa be executed. Elements sympathetic to Villa obtained a stay of execution from Madero, a fact that infuriated Huerta. Villa was transported to Mexico City and housed in a federal penitentiary. There he became another victim of Madero's refusal to clean out the old *porfirista* army and bureaucracy.

By late December 1912, Villa's escape was arranged. He traveled from Mexico City *in mufti,* went to Sinaloa, and entered the United States through Arizona. From Arizona he made his way to El Paso, where he waited in exile, wondering if he could ever reenter Mexico. While in prison, Villa had learned of a plot to overthrow Madero hatched by former *porfiristas* who were also incarcerated. Villa communicated with González, attempting to get the word to Madero. González counseled patience, and there sat Villa, eating ice cream in El Paso, while evil forces threatened to bring down his idol.

Conservative elements with the unofficial connivance of the United States ambassador successfully staged a *coup d'etat* that toppled Madero. By February 18, Madero had resigned. Four days later he was dead, and Victoriano Huerta took over as interim president of Mexico. When news reached Villa about Madero's assassination, all other thoughts fled his mind except that of revenge. Village lands and other ideals could wait until Huerta, the man Villa described as "that drunken Aztec," was out and preferably very dead. The rage that often characterized Villa at this point became cold, and he systematically planned his return to Mexico and the vengeance he would seek against the murderers of Madero.

Borrowing money from his brother, Villa and eight men crossed the Río Grande in early March of 1913. Little did he know at that time that Abraham González, his other idol, was also dead. Slowly but surely he began to gather adherents, and soon the revolutionary-cum-*pistolero*-cum retail butcher began to make small guerrilla incursions against the federal forces loyal to Victoriano Huerta.

Villa, however, clearly recognized that his efforts in Chihuahua needed coordination with other groups throughout the nation which opposed the Huerta takeover. At the end of March, when Venustiano Carranza issued his Plan de Guadalupe denouncing Huerta and asking for adherence from all those opposed to the usurpation of power, Villa pledged his adherence. But Villa was no dummy. Carranza, though from Coahuila, still represented some of the centralized control that could hinder the movements of Villa and his ever-growing band of guerrilla fighters. Villa consequently pledged his alliance to the Plan de Guadalupe without making himself subservient to Carranza. Carranza would later regret this action.

No cavil exists about the impact of Villa's return. Huerta even tried to buy him off in order to weaken any resistance in northern

Mexico. Through an intermediary, Huerta, the man who drank nothing but the best imported brandies in large quantities, offered Villa 100,000 *pesos* and promotion to brigadier general in the federal army. Villa responded:

> Tell Huerta that with regard to the rank, I don't need it because I command as the Supreme Chief of all free men who conquer for liberty; with regard to the 100,000 pesos . . . let him drink it up in *aquardiente* [white lightning made from sugar cane or grapes].

Villa soon attracted some of the great and some of the infamous names of the Revolution — Tomás Urbina, a former bandit and Villa's *compadre;* Rodolfo Fierro, the former railroad engineer who loved to kill people; and Toribio Ortega, who was so honest he would only take his paltry soldier's salary, an anomaly rarely found in Mexico then or now. Others would join him later, but this was a start. Villa had a force that began to make a military impact on Chihuahua, capturing Casas Grandes, Guerrero, and Bustillos.

Meanwhile, Carranza, sitting in Coahuila, began to take on political trappings. He styled himself as *primer jefe encargado del poder ejecutivo del ejército constitucionalista* (first chief in charge of the executive power of the Constitutionalist Army). In short, Carranza had nothing. His military forces came from Villa and others throughout Mexico. He commanded no men of his own nor did he have military rank. But what he did possess was political skill, a factor that would ultimately cause trouble between himself and Villa and the first chieftaincy and the State of Chihuahua.

Throughout 1913, as Villa's *División del Norte* (Division of the North) grew and continued to achieve successes, other adherents to the Constitutionalist cause found themselves bogged down. Alvaro Obregón's troops in Sonora had become entangled in a siege of the port of Guaymas. Pablo González in Nuevo León proved that he lacked certain military skills. González' detractors purport that Don Pablo was the only general not to have won a battle. Zapata, who could rarely see beyond the confines of little Morelos just south of Mexico City, kept himself to his peasant army and to the very limited objectives found in his Plan de Ayala of 1911.

By October, Chihuahua was providing the supplies necessary for the *villista* juggernaut. No longer was this merely a guerrilla band; the Division of the North numbered in the thousands. Though it lacked some of the refinements of a modern army, such as trained artillerymen to operate captured cannon, Villa still put together a formidable force. By June, most of the *chihuahuense* leaders had selected Villa as their standard bearer. Chihuahua now could speak with one voice: that of Francisco Villa. Supply of that army proved relatively easy. The thousands of head of cattle that roamed Chihuahua allowed Villa to revert to his former profession. He simply stole cattle, especially Terrazas cattle, and sold it across the border. With the money thus acquired, he could purchase arms, ammunition, and military supplies for his forces.

Of course, the United States still maintained the arms embargo against all of Mexico that had been imposed by William Howard Taft in March 1912 when Orozco broke with Madero. But the United States had a new president, Woodrow Wilson, who sympathized with the Revolution. Wilson hoped to guide Mexico in her search for decent politics and unfortunately failed to understand some of the underlying tensions that impelled a variety of people to join the battle against Victoriano Huerta and the system that he represented.

In early October, Villa's *División del Norte* met its first major test: the seizure of Torreón. Torreón, Coahuila, capital of the Mexican cotton industry and a major rail junction, lured the *villistas* to seize it. The treasures held by Torreón certainly tempted Villa. So, too, did the opportunity to thump a bunch of Spaniards who controlled the cotton industry and who supported Huerta. The hispanophobic theme would come to represent a generalized xenophobia in the Revolution. In Villa, his anti-foreign tendencies proved quite selective.

Villa achieved a conclusive triumph at Torreón. The *federales* fled deep into Coahuila. From Torreón, Villa hoped to move north again to capture Chihuahua City. Strategically, this made eminent sense, for control of that capital city would give Villa and his men a firm base of operation from which they could gain control of the entire state. Unlettered he might be, but Villa still could discern effective strategy. Control of Chihuahua provided a secure springboard into the rest of the nation.

But immediate seizure of Chihuahua City failed. As yet, Villa proved insufficiently prepared to sustain a long siege. Instead, he looked further north. In a move that captivated the imagination, Villa seized a southbound train heading to Chihuahua City from Cd. Juárez. At various stops he kept sending telegrams over the name of the troop train commander announcing his return because of heavy concentrations of *villistas* as he got closer to Chihuahua City. On November 15, in a four-hour battle, the *villistas* captured Cd. Juárez. Their arrival had surprised the *federales,* and Villa now enjoyed a secure northern base plus control of Mexico's major railhead.

With Juárez now under his control, Villa quickly moved to establish governmental forms in that major border city. Villa appointed Col. Juan Medina as the civil administrator of Juárez. Medina, a former federal officer who had joined the Revolution, began a systematic process of civilian administration including the collection of taxes and some regulation of the more tawdry side of life in Juárez. Initially, Villa, the teetotaler, wanted to close the saloons, gambling houses, and bordellos because Mexicans could waste themselves there. Even then, Juárez provided a haven for Texans who wanted to shake the stultifying influence of a strict Protestant ethos. Instead of closing down the vice dens, Villa began a regular tax collection and, thus, increased the municipal revenues of Cd. Juárez. With an administration functioning along the border, Villa prepared to head south again.

Within a week he dispatched his forces. On November 24 they met *orozquistas* (who had joined with Huerta) in pitched battle at Tierra Blanca. The battle raged into the night. By noon of the next day, Villa's men emerged triumphant. The ferocity of the battle, the unparalleled bravery of his *dorados* (Villa's hand-picked cavalry unit), and the unrivaled individual valor of his men impressed Villa. Of Rodolfo Fierro, Villa declared:

> In rain of bullets [Fierro] leaped from his horse to the train and, climbing from one car to another, reached the brake cylinder, released the air, and stopped the train. A beautiful feat, *Señor!* Soldiers from the Corps of Scouts then fell on the train, and the slaughter was horrible.

Federal forces including Governor Salvador Mercado prepared to flee Chihuahua City. Panic permeated the atmosphere. *Villa would kill them all,* it was said. *Hide your wives and daughters, for the rapacious savages attacked anything in skirts. Bury your gold. When you come back you will have something on which to begin again.* The confusion and tension made retreat from the city disorderly and a rout. Old Luis Terrazas prepared to join the federal retreat to Ojinaga.

In many respects, Luis Terrazas precipitated his own ruin. During the initial phases of the Madero revolt, Terrazas ordered that his *peones* be issued weapons in order to control the increased cattle rustling that began to diminish the Terrazas herds. Unfortunately, the tactic backfired. The same peasants took Terrazas' weapons and rushed off to join Villa or other rebel leaders in Chihuahua. Still, Terrazas had done nothing to aid Díaz though he was constantly accused of being a stalwart of *porfirismo*. When Terrazas returned to Chihuahua following Madero's victory, he hoped at least to come to terms with the new government. But the monster was unleashed. Rebel leaders — some of them *orozquistas,* some original *maderistas,* some without any political affiliation whatever — began to rape systematically the Terrazas holdings. Cattle disappeared, buildings suffered destruction, and the labor force became increasingly rebellious.

As a result, by late November 1913, just when Villa and his forces were glaring down the throat of federal forces in Chihuahua City, Terrazas decided to join the long march into exile. As preparations were made by General Mercado for the orderly evacuation of Chihuahua, Terrazas made his own arrangements as well. He left a son, Luis, Jr., to look after family affairs there. Some of the women in the family also stayed. Don Luis, now an octogenarian, mounted his coach and headed for Ojinaga with Mercado.

Villa's occupation of the city came on December 7. Flushed with victories from Torreón, Cd. Juárez, and Tierra Blanca, Villa moved into Chihuahua as a conqueror, his head filled with a sense of social vengeance against the system that had vilified him and others like him and had kept them from achieving their full potential. Enemies of the Revolution had to pay, and on December 12, in a sweeping decree, Villa made a major thrust at his enemies. In that decree of confiscation, Villa grabbed the property of the Creels, the Terrazases, the Cuiltys, and other leading families in order to pay for the price of revolution. Their goods and properties would be used to provide pensions for the widows and orphans of soldiers who had fallen in the conflict. Additionally, the lands would be used to establish military colonies of former revolutionaries. These men would work the lands and still provide a military reserve in the event of renewed strife.

Villa understood perfectly well that he had no penchant for this sort of administrative detail. As a result, he selected Silvestre

Terrazas, a distant cousin of Don Luis but on the wrong side of the political fence from the old patriarch, as the administrator of confiscated properties. While much of the Reform program envisioned by Villa failed to reach fruition, the intention was there, interrupted by the exigencies of civil strife.

But Villa ran into trouble. How to capitalize a government? Use of federal currency merely lent credence to the validity of the Huerta regime. No economist, Villa ordered the printing of over four million *pesos* worth of unsupported currency drawn on the newly created Bank of Chihuahua. In part, Villa hoped to back the currency issue with confiscated lands. As a stopgap measure, the Terrazas family inadvertently and unwittingly provided the funds for Villa to continue to function.

Luis Terrazas proved the avenue for *villista* financing of the Revolution. Luis, Jr., sought refuge in the British vice-consulate. Villa kidnapped him and held him ransom, demanding initially almost $1 million. The currency problem needed resolution. As a result, in partial payment of the ransom, the younger Terrazas signed checks drawn on the Banco Minero ranging from a few *centavos* to five *pesos* to serve as a substitute currency until such time as the government could acquire a revolutionary scrip.

Throughout 1914 and part of 1915, the younger Terrazas remained Villa's prisoner. He was, as Villa apologized, "slightly tortured" but generally allowed freedom of the city of Chihuahua. Villa's reasoning for holding Terrazas proved impeccable. He declared that *cuando se amarra el becerro, la vaca no anda lejos* (when the calf is tied, the cow won't wander far). Villa readily recognized that the elder Terrazas could funnel funds to Huerta and Orozco and thus undercut the Constitutionalists. By holding the son, Villa successfully averted Terrazas' assistance to the enemies of the Revolution and also extorted much needed goods and monies for his own forces.

Villa felt the need for action. He knew he must rid the state of the *federales,* who had taken refuge in Ojinaga. In part, Villa had a strategic motive. When he moved the bulk of his forces north for the capture of Chihuahua City, he left an undermanned contingent in Torreón. As a result, Huerta's army recaptured that major city. Villa needed to take the town again. But first, he had to assure the protection of his rear from attack by *federales* holed up in Ojinaga.

Villa dispatched Pánfilo Natera and Toribio Ortega to Ojinaga in early January. The siege carried on. Villa became impatient and took the field himself. He handed the government over to Manuel Chao and joined the battle. In a bloody and vengeful confrontation, Villa personally defeated the federal army at Ojinaga, driving the survivors into Presidio, Texas, for detention at U.S. military facilities in Texas.

Time had come to plan the retaking of Torreón, and Villa made his way to Cd. Juárez to give his troops rest and to reprovision his growing army. It was there that Villa began to fall out of favor with the United States, but not before Wilson lifted the arms embargo on February 4, 1914. Originally, President Wilson seemed more favorable to Villa than to Carranza, principally because Villa gave the impression that he would listen to the *gringo* president's homilies. But Villa's quick temper and the way in which the United States became embroiled in the affair tarnished Villa's Robin Hood image in the United States. Ironically, the explosion came not over a United States citizen but rather a British subject, one William Benton.

Benton had lived in Mexico for years. He had married a Mexican woman and owned a ranch north of Chihuahua City. Benton possessed a reputation of being quick-tempered and not prone to take offenses lightly. As a result, when *villista* troops seized some of his cattle, he went to Juárez to remonstrate with Villa. That proved to be a fatal mistake, for he drew a gun and was quickly subdued by Rodolfo Fierro. Summarily, Villa ordered Benton executed and handed the job over to Fierro. Fierro then took Benton to Samalayuca, ordered him to dig his own grave, and probably bashed the hapless Scotsman on the back of the head with a shovel. In all probability, Benton was buried alive.

A furor bubbled when Mrs. Benton asked the British consul in Juárez for help in finding her husband. Inquiries were made, and Villa readily admitted that Benton had been executed. Soon the British Parliament was demanding strong action against Mexico. The United States was asked to intercede, which it did. A commission was formed, demanding to examine the corpse as well as the military tribunal proceedings. Villa ordered his advisors to dummy up some court papers and to exhume the body and to shoot it in proper military fashion. However, Villa's knowledge of forensics was quite limited. He thought that one merely had to shoot a corpse to make it seem as if the cause of death had been a firing

Generals Obregón, Villa, and John J. Pershing at the customshouse in Ciudad Juárez in 1914. Over Pershing's shoulder is Lt. George S. Patton.

Trains provided the principal means of transportation for the growing revolutionary armies.

squad. The Benton matter horrified many United States supporters of Villa, including Woodrow Wilson.

But the time had come to turn toward Torreón once again. First Villa had to deal with Máximo Castillo, who operated in northwestern Chihuahua. Castillo ruled through sheer terror. He pillaged Mormon colonies, destroyed lumbering operations, and killed Americans indiscriminately. Both American and Mexican alike recoiled at the horror of the man. Castillo, however, received his comeuppance, for he was forced to face Villa. Defeated, Castillo died in exile in Cuba. Now Villa was free from distractions.

Torreón continued to glow like a jewel, beckoning Villa to come again. Villa by this time had accumulated sufficient artillery that he needed an expert for its operation. He turned to Felipe Angeles, former commandant of the military academy at Chapultepec and currently serving as undersecretary of war with Carranza. Angeles welcomed Villa's request, for the former federal officer felt uncomfortable with Carranza and his advisors, including Obregón.

Angeles' arrival in mid-March also brought Venustiano Carranza to Chihuahua for the first time. Carranza's advisors had consistently urged the first chief to make the trip in order to straighten out the mess Villa had created with the confiscated lands and the Benton affair. Carranza, however, proved reluctant, for he felt uneasy about having to deal with a barbarous peasant like Francisco Villa. The meeting proved disastrous. Villa, ever effusive, wanted to hug Carranza in the traditional Mexican *abrazo*. Carranza rebuffed the emotional greeting from his most able and visible commander. Villa declared that he felt that this bearded, bespectacled Coahuilan aristocrat's blood ran cold. Carranza's advisors were dubbed *chocolateros perfumados* (perfumed chocolate drinkers) by Villa's cronies. Tensions began to surface between Villa, the armed might of *constitucionalismo*, and the political directorate represented by Venustiano Carranza. Though both men seemed in harmony and Villa continued to profess his loyalty, the tensions already were apparent. Villa, however, did thank Carranza for bringing Angeles to the *División del Norte*.

By the end of March 1914, Villa moved against Torreón. For four days the battle raged, fought in bloody streets and alleys and with little respect for persons or property. But the *villistas* triumphed. Torreón again was secured for the Constitutionalist movement. In his initial test, Angeles proved his worth to Villa and to the Revolution that sought to oust Huerta. Torreón helped form the Division of the North into a disciplined army, and it was here that Villa began a dizzying series of victories that contributed significantly to the downfall of "that drunken Aztec."

Problems between Villa and Carranza surfaced again early in April. Villa supported the United States' invasion of Veracruz on April 21 because it would help to strangle Huerta. Carranza, however, roundly denounced the action, claiming that Mexico's internal sovereignty had been violated. Villa said that as long as the invasion did not constitute an invasion of Mexico *per se*, then the *gringos* were welcome in Veracruz.

Actually, Carranza saw in Villa a threat to his own hegemony over the Constitutionalist movement. As such he began to ring Villa with restrictions: He held up coal shipments, he issued orders to Villa's commanders, and let Villa know, in effect, that Carranza was the dominant personality of *constitucionalismo*. The real rending came over command of forces in the siege of Zacatecas in June.

Carranza wanted to keep Villa away from Mexico City. Obregón had taken Guaymas, finally, and began to sweep southward along the Pacific Coast and into western Mexico. If Carranza could stop Villa, Obregón could then move against Mexico City. At any cost, that barbarian from Chihuahua had to be stopped.

As a result, Carranza ordered Villa to send additional troops to buttress Natera and the Arrieta brothers at Zacatecas. Villa demurred, declaring that only he could command his men effectively. A telegraphic conference between Villa at Torreón and Carranza at Saltillo led to Villa's impulsive resignation from the Division of the North. Outwardly reluctant but inwardly joyful, Carranza accepted Villa's action and ordered the other generals to select a new commander. They, of course, selected Francisco Villa. Carranza declared the choice unsatisfactory. Heatedly, the telegrams flew back and forth. Finally, Maclovio Herrera seized his pistol, pointed it at the telegraph operator, and demanded that he take a message that began: "Sr. Venustiano Carranza, Saltillo, Coahuila. Sir: You are a son-of-a-bitch . . . ."

Angeles and cooler heads prevailed. The telegram was never sent. Villa resumed command again and ordered his troops to move on Zacatecas. Effective use of artillery and the overwhelming numerical superiority of the *villistas* brought Zacatecas into Constitutionalist hands at the end of June. But the breach between Villa and Carranza refused to heal, due in large measure to the monumental egos of the principals. Personal antagonism overrode principle. Within three months, Mexico would again be plunged into civil war.

Carranza succeeded in stymying Villa through the simple expedient of withholding coal with which the Centaur of the North could run his trains. In spite of agreements reached between representatives of the two factions, the split that many predicted and an equal number hoped would disappear came to the surface again.

Huerta was gone. On July 14 he resigned, left for Veracruz, and departed the port on July 18. Obregón and his forces marched into Mexico City while Villa sat fulminating in Chihuahua, impotent, desirous of venting his rage against Carranza and all of those who opposed his march to glory.

For most of the summer, different factions within the Constitutionalist movement attempted to bring about a reconciliation between Carranza and Villa. Obregón in late August undertook a personal and dangerous mission to Chihuahua, where an agreement was hammered out. When Carranza saw the deal, he rejected it out of hand. Again, Villa flew into a rage. Obregón again went to Chihuahua. This time Obregón's visit suffered from Villa's orders to execute the commander of the Army of the Northwest. In all probability Villa played with Obregón's mind, keeping him off balance. He would order an execution and then rescind the order. In fact, in one instance he embraced Obregón, effusively professed undying friendship, and escorted him to a banquet. When Obregón left, Villa ordered that the train be stopped and Obregón removed and shot. Two of Villa's men, sensing the injustice in the order, maneuvered to get Obregón to safety and to Mexico City. Villa's impulsiveness cost him a potential ally in Obregón. By the time Obregón returned to Mexico City, he was firmly committed to the proposition that Villa should not be allowed to gain power.

Also in August, Carranza called a convention of military leaders to determine Mexico's political fate. Villa steadfastly refused to attend. By early September, with Carranza controlling the convention, it seemed that Villa might have been brought to heel. But the wily *guerrillero* still had a few moves that he could use. His first and most expedient action was simply to break with Carranza. At the end of September, he made the split with Carranza definitive. He accused the first chief of offending the honor and dignity of the Division of the North and of a refusal to grant open and democratic processes to Mexico. Increasingly, Villa put pressure on Carranza, and Carranza retaliated by branding Villa a symbol of reaction and the "perhaps inconscious instrument of *porfirismo* and *cientificismo*." Charges flew back and forth. Fiscal mismanagement, authoritarianism, and social discrimination were among the allegations. But clearly, a large factor in the break grew from the inherent reaction of a northerner, Villa, against the encroaching centralism of a man with national ambitions, Carranza.

Different leaders tried to convince each of the principals to leave the stage. Each vowed to do so provided the other did it first. Villa even advocated a mutual suicide pact for the good of Mexico. Carranza pointedly refused. Still, the convention hoped to bring about, if not reconciliation, at least some sort of working peace. They did, however, listen to Villa on one point. Without the *zapatistas* from the south and without Villa from Chihuahua, the convention was nothing more than a rump congress of Carranza adherents. Villa finally agreed to go to Aguascalientes (where the convention had moved from Mexico City) if the *zapatistas* would come. In an attempt at peacemaking, the delegates asked that Felipe Angeles go to Morelos to talk to Zapata and his men. In mid-October Angeles left and successfully brought a delegation of *zapatistas* back with him. The arrival of Zapata's men and those of Villa soon outnumbered the *carrancistas*.

Carranza suddenly felt isolated. The convention moved swiftly, selecting Eulalio Gutiérrez as the convention president and asking that Carranza resign as first chief. Carranza refused and gathered his supporters to prepare for flight to Veracruz. With battle lines clearly delineated, the convention declared Carranza an outlaw. Villa became military commander of the convention forces and began to move toward Mexico City.

From October 1914 until the first part of February 1915, Villa controlled the convention and the president of the convention. In December he entered Mexico City and met with Zapata for the first time. Though there had been contact between the two armies, neither chieftain had ever met the other. Now the time had come to solidify their animosity toward Carranza, who was comfortably holed up in Veracruz, using customs revenues to finance his counterattack. The upshot of the meeting between Zapata and Villa was an agreement that pledged mutual military assistance and defined areas of military authority. Zapata agreed to pursue Carranza and drive him into the sea. Villa pledged to send military supplies to Zapata.

Tragically, neither one lived up to his end of the bargain. Zapata and his peasant forces pursued Carranza as far as Puebla and then stopped, feeling lost so far from Morelos. Villa found that sending the arms required going through territory taken over by the *carrancistas,* which would jeopardize men and equipment.

From early February through June of 1915, Villa steadily declined in power. In decisive battles at Celaya and León between April and June, Obregón, the cunning tactician, lured Villa into one trap after another. Villa simply refused to listen to Angeles. He wanted a devastating cavalry charge that would obliterate Obregón. Angeles wanted to reduce the enemy with artillery. Villa won the argument, but barbed wire entanglements and machine-gun emplacements stopped the once powerful *División del Norte*. Villa, his army tragically wounded and radically reduced in size, retreated to Chihuahua to continue the battle against Carranza and Obregón. According to the Listers:

> To Villa himself and to numbers of loyal peasants, he was and always would remain the *gran hombre,* the leading actor in the pageant of the north. Let them have their colorless wishy-washy Carranza or their smooth-spoken, smooth-operating Obregón. Strong men of Chihuahua liked their idols forceful, devilish, and devastating.

No longer did Villa, a wounded animal, react with any sort of political rationality. He turned savagely on those who for one reason or another offended him. With cause, he hanged his *compadre* Tomás Urbina. He brutally persecuted the Chinese. Yet he attempted to avoid a direct confrontation with the United States, for he still hoped to keep the seeming support of President Wilson.

Throughout the summer of 1915, Villa fortified himself in Chihuahua. He still had Juárez and access to United States markets and could continue to sell Terrazas cattle to buyers in the Southwest, though his source of supply began to dwindle. The Terrazas herds, as large as they were, could not supply Villa indefinitely without allowing for replenishment. Still, Villa needed to show that he remained the mighty warrior, that he could vanquish the forces of evil represented by Carranza.

Against the advice of Felipe Angeles, Villa headed from Casas Grandes through Pulpito Pass and began to lay siege to Agua Prieta, right across the border from Douglas, Arizona. In the weeks that it took to move men and equipment over the mountains about 175 miles, Woodrow Wilson extended formal *de facto* recognition to Carranza and even allowed Carranza to move forces from El Paso to Douglas on American trains in order to reinforce Gen. Plutarco Elías Calles. Calles, no military genius, did learn from Celaya. Villa did not. The scene had an oddly repetitious flavor. Villa again tried cavalry charges. And again, machine guns mowed down his men. This time the *carrancistas* repelled night attacks, aided by lights powered from Douglas, Arizona.

By this time, Villa discovered the treachery of Woodrow Wilson and flew into a rage. He moved his men, captured two American doctors and systematically threatened to kill them, and began to run amok in northern Mexico. No amount of reasoning could assuage Villa's anger, and he began to plot vengeance against the United States as well as against Carranza.

First, he needed to renew old alliances. He again made approaches to Zapata, informing the southern leader of plans for renewed hostilities against the first chief. These approaches now materialized, for Zapata had his own troubles and was hemmed in at Morelos. Villa, however, continued to plan, and in one communication with Zapata informed him of a daring plan to invade the United States. No longer did Villa even want to court the favor of the United States. Instead, he wanted to repay *gringo* ingratitude with devastation, and this frame of mind infected Villa's followers.

In January 1916, at the town of San Ysabel (now General Trías), *villista* commanders stopped a train, grabbed American engineers from the Cusi Mining Company, and killed them. Though Villa did not personally command the raid and promised swift punishment of the perpetrators, there is no doubt that his attitude had influenced his followers.

A month later, Villa's men began moving around Palomas, Chihuahua, just across from Columbus, New Mexico. They gathered cattle but did not attempt to sell it in the United States. Instead, they kept the cattle for the provisioning of troops. More *villistas* began to gather. By the first of March, warnings to Washington about a possible Villa invasion of the United States went ignored. And then Villa struck.

Frustration over his inability to bring Carranza to heel as well as a sense of betrayal by the United States forced Villa into a desperate posture. In his desperation, he conceived a plan to attack the United States, provoke American intervention in Mexico as proof of Carranza's inability to control the country, and, in some way, have himself emerge as a savior of the nation. Fuzzy, illogical, and thoroughly nihilistic, Villa nevertheless hit his target with a ferocity that was rarely equaled in all of his exploits. In the dark hours of the morning of March 9, 1916, about 500 *villistas* rode whooping into Columbus, New Mexico, from Palomas and began to devastate the town. They attacked carefully selected buildings, shot at army barracks, and inflicted general chaos upon the sleepy border town. It took a while, but army personnel rallied and began a counterattack against the *villistas*, pursuing them into Chihuahua. About fifty *villistas* were killed in the U.S. Army action.

The spinoff from the attack on Columbus proved devastating. Immediately, Anglo citizens along the U.S.–Mexican border intensified their fear of Mexicans that grew out of the San Ysabel massacre and began to rampage along the Mexican section of El Paso, a region called Little Chihuahua. Demands were made to Congress and to the president for action. Action they received. President Woodrow Wilson ordered out the army under the command of Gen. John J. "Blackjack" Pershing.

The order given to Pershing seemed simple: destroy and disperse Villa and his men. A two-pronged attack was readied along the border. Pershing moved troops and equipment to Columbus from Fort Bliss, outside of El Paso. Within nine days, American troops were again in Chihuahua in force for the second time in seventy years. Fifteen thousand American soldiers ultimately formed two columns that met, finally, at Parral, where Mexican troops and citizenry (not *villistas*) thumped them thoroughly. The Punitive Expedition touched a sensitive spot amongst the *chihuahuenses*. They might trade with *gringos*, they might help them set up economic enterprises, they might even marry them — but by God, they would not be invaded by them. The strength of *chihuahuense* nationalism proved more potent than all of the complaints that Carranza and his minions could offer. The refusal of the people of Chihuahua to

*Villa seated on presidential throne, flanked on the right by Zapata and Urbina
and on the left by Fierro.*

— O.T. Aultman Collection, El Paso Public Library

lend assistance to Pershing ultimately contributed to a long, miserable stay in Mexico and to the decision to withdraw the expedition.

But where was Villa? He had headed to the mountains. Wounded at Guerrero by *carrancista* troops, he hid in his beloved *sierra* while Pershing and his forces looked all over Chihuahua for the elusive Centaur.

Villa's plan succeeded in forcing United States action against Mexico and demonstrating to the Mexican people the ineptitude of Venustiano Carranza. Demands for withdrawal of the forces availed Carranza nothing. Negotiations at Atlantic City failed to result in an agreement between Mexico and the United States. The United States refused to withdraw the Punitive Expedition as a condition to a new hot pursuit treaty.

But Carranza had other plans afoot. He needed to consolidate his power base, and to do this he had to deliver promised reforms. In good Mexican tradition, he called for the election of delegates to a constitutional convention to be held in Querétaro between December 1, 1916, and February 1, 1917. Elections were held wherever the *carrancistas* held sway. However, virtually no delegates went to Querétaro from the state of Chihuahua. In all probability, the convention was a minority gathering of Carranza's adherents.

Massive reforms — far beyond Carranza's objectives — underscored the convention. Instead of an updated political document, the Constitution of 1917 sealed into the organic law of the nation sweeping changes that often had no practical application to the realities of the various regions of Mexico. Land reform proved a case in point. The Constitution of 1917 incorporated the *zapatista* conception of land tenure: *ejido* or communal lands; restricted parcels; massive breakup of the large *haciendas*. All of these proved anathema to the *chihuahuenses* and in large measure have contributed to the never-ending struggle to make the land of Chihuahua productive but in ways only a *chihuahuense* would understand.

Back in Chihuahua, Pershing and his troops finally withdrew. In one respect, they had succeeded. While they did not capture Villa, they did succeed in dispersing the *villistas*. Never again would Villa be able to rally as many men as he had before the Columbus attack. Also, United States troops received essential training for the upcoming entrance of the United States into World War I.

Villa, however, was down but not out. He continued to harass Chihuahua, inflicting punishment on foreigners and Mexicans alike whom he believed had betrayed him. Yet, the government's answer to Villa was to send Gen. Francisco Murguía after the *villistas*. Murguía proved to be as big a thief as any man of Villa's band. He stole cattle from already depleted herds in order to stock his ranches in Zacatecas. He refused to work with the civilian authorities and arbitrarily overrode civil decisions. In the end, Carranza had to rid Chihuahua of Francisco Murguía.

Between Villa and Murguía, the beleaguered and exhausted *chihuahuenses* felt threatened. They formed *defensas sociales* (armed citizens groups) who were at the ready in the event of depredation by either side. Obviously, the government again would not or could not come to the assistance of Chihuahua. *Chihuahuenses* again were forced to look out for themselves.

Yet the *chihuahuense* still looked at Villa with a certain amount of pride. He was one of their own, defending what he believed against tremendous odds and against the behemoth federal government. Even with Pershing in Chihuahua, he had taken Chihuahua City on September 16, Mexican Independence Day. Later that year, at Christmas time, he seized Torreón. Neither Pershing nor Carranza could do anything to stop the growth and perpetuation of the Villa image.

Throughout 1917 and 1918, Villa continued to harass government forces in Chihuahua. In 1919, he made his presence felt even more when he attacked Ciudad Juárez in mid-June. Again, he provoked an invasion of Mexico, though it only lasted for twenty-four hours. Villa was denounced by Carranza initially, but cooler heads prevailed on the first chief to tone down his rhetoric. Still, it was obvious to everyone that Villa had grown tired. He needed a way out of the mess in which ten years of civil strife had left him.

By the end of 1919, Villa began to look for ways to come to peace with the government. Felipe Angeles, his loyal artillery commander, had been captured and executed in November 1919. By spring of 1920, Carranza was so at odds with Obregón and other political leaders from Sonora and from other parts of the north that rebellion again filled the air. By late April, Adolfo de la Huerta, governor of Sonora, joined by Obregón and Calles, declared against Carranza in the Plan de Agua Prieta. Villa offered his services. De la Huerta instead asked Villa to make his peace with the new government. In late May, with Carranza dead, De la Huerta became provisional president. Negotiations began with

Villa. By late July, the interim government of De la Huerta, over the strenuous objections of Obregón (who would become president in December), reached agreement with Villa.

Villa received the Hacienda de Canutillo in Durango, sixty miles south of Parral. He also retained a body guard (at government expense) as well as his pay as a brigadier general. In short, he had reached his own respectability. Villa the bandit was now Villa the modern *hacendado,* much of this purchased with his own blood and sweat and with the blood and sweat of thousands of followers.

The Revolution in Chihuahua did have some positive results. Chihuahua shared in the sense of nationalism that gripped the nation. Yet, in the bizzarely *chihuahuense* way, that nationalism would undergo transformation in the postrevolutionary period. Old traditions that had sustained Chihuahua in the past came to the fore again. While a new age was dawning, the historic past still retained some of its vestiges. *Señora* Carolina Cuilty de Terrazas died in 1919; her husband, Don Luis, in 1923. They served to sever the past of colony, early republic, and *porfiriato* from the twentieth century. But many of their attitudes survived into the 1920s, and Chihuahua would enter the postrevolutionary period with a curious blend of old attitudes and new optimism.

The 1923 Dodge in which Villa was shot. Note the bullet holes that ventilated the vehicle.

— Muséo de la Revolución en Chihuahua,
Photo by the author.

CHAPTER 3

The Revolution Triumphant, Officially

His body hung grotesquely out the door of the car, bloody from the countless dum-dum shells it had absorbed. Cowardly political troglodytes had prepared an ambush that eliminated from any political activity the most feared, hated, and, at the same time, the most adored man to come out of the Mexican Revolution. Francisco Villa lay dead in his automobile on July 20, 1923, accompanied by the corpses of some of his closest associates. The Mexican government of Alvaro Obregón had taken another step toward the inexorable centralization that resulted directly from the revolutionary turmoil of the last decade.

Mexico and Chihuahua specifically had undergone some profound changes during the decade of the Revolution. Venustiano Carranza, once officially ensconced in power, continued the process of centralization that had in every way been a bane of Mexican existence and had made Chihuahua the political maverick that it was. Clearly, no opposition would be tolerated from retired rebels who had successfully beat the government at its own game. Villa served as one example. The entire political process that Mexico would undergo during the period between 1920 and 1980 impacted directly upon Chihuahua, encouraged its sense of frustration, and produced political results for the next decade that further frightened the political sharks who inhabited the capital, Mexico City.

Rather early in the process, it became clear that centralization of political power in the capital would be the rule. Alvaro Obregón came to power in December 1920, carrying with him a burden of political debt that necessitated payoffs to certain elements within the body politic. Agrarian elements, labor organizers, former military comrades — all screamed for their piece of the action for services rendered to the Revolution. Obregón, as wily a political animal as Mexico has ever produced, began programs of land redistribution far in excess of anything that Carranza ever conceived. Carranza had even attempted to restore lands to the previous owner. In Chihuahua, however, these did not fare well, for the lands that had once belonged to the mighty Terrazas clan and their allies remained firmly in the hands of the state or had passed to other owners through Villa's own program of land distribution in the previous decade.

A plethora of political parties, all claiming to be direct legatees of the Revolution, pressed for different objectives, usually the personal advancement of their leaders. Political debate swirled throughout Mexico, and at the same time, Obregón was prohibited from seeking office again and needed to designate a successor. All the while, Villa sat in his Durango *hacienda* at Canutillo and watched with what was seemingly detached interest as the political winds swirled around Mexico.

Two candidates clearly seemed to be the logical successors to Obregón: Plutarco Elías Calles, the secretary of *gobernación,* and Adolfo de la Huerta, secretary of the treasury. Both of these men had at one time served as governors of Sonora. Both had been in the forefront of the opposition to Carranza. But only one had the burning ambition to be president. De la Huerta had already done his stint as interim president after the death of Carranza. Calles, more ambitious, more ruthless, ached for the job. Early in 1923, when the succession was being discussed by Obregón and his two cronies, De la Huerta disclaimed any interest in the position. Calles, however, drooled at the idea. But there sat Villa in Canutillo, hating Calles for his defeat at Agua Prieta in 1915 and despising the idea of what he considered a military nincompoop ever ascending to the highest office in the land.

In the summer of 1922, Villa, always the publicity hound, granted an interview to a Mexico City reporter. A series of straw polls during the spring asking who should be the next president rarely even mentioned Calles or else placed him at the bottom. Villa, however, was always in the third or fourth slot. Rumors even circulated that Villa was considering a run for the governorship of Durango, where he was now legally a resident. In the interview, Villa boasted about the support that he continued to enjoy. In fact, he bragged:

> I have lots of partisans! I have friends in every social stratum
> .... Yes Sir, I believe that no one has today the following that
> Francisco Villa has! For that reason they [Obregón and Calles]
> fear me; they fear me because they know that the day in which I
> throw myself into the struggle, I will, Sir, overwhelm them.

Villa continued his vitriol against the men who had rendered him impotent. He claimed that he would abide by his agreement with De la Huerta at the time of his retirement, that he would engage in no political activity as long as Obregón was in power. Typically, he added a caveat: Should the United States invade Mexico, he would again take up arms against the aggressors; or, if Adolfo de la Huerta needed him, then he would organize his *muchachitos* (boys) in order to serve the man who had saved his dignity. Thus, Villa, in his desire to gain some public luster again, frightened the political manipulators in Mexico City. And in so doing, he set up his own death. Soft living and relative calm had made Villa feel invulnerable. He died believing that he was the principal power factor in northern Mexico.

In all probability, Obregón and Calles set up Villa's death. They played upon personal and political antagonism toward the Centaur of the North, made discreet arrangements, and in the streets of Parral, Chihuahua, Francisco Villa died in an ambush. The road was now clear for Obregón to impose Calles upon the nation. Just as Carranza tried to play kingmaker in 1920, now it was Obregón's turn.

De la Huerta bristled at the death of Villa. Political tomfoolery by Obregón, plus what De la Huerta considered unjust arrangements with the United States, forced him finally to launch his candidacy for the presidency, to break with his chief, and to go into open rebellion against the Mexican government in December 1923.

Villa, his strong support in the north, lay buried in Parral. By April 1924, De la Huerta's forces would be scattered, and he would be in exile in Los Angeles, California, not to return again to Mexico until the 1930s, when Lázaro Cárdenas would call back all Mexican exiles to serve the country.

Calles' ascension to the presidential throne signaled the continuing centralization of the Mexican government. Dealing viciously with his opponents, he was even implicated, though indirectly, in the death of Obregón in 1928. Obregón had manipulated the system to allow for one reelection after sitting out a term in office. Calles, however, liked power, and while he would not violate openly the Constitution, he saw to it that his three hand-picked men served as president between 1928 and 1934.

Calles created the Partido Nacional de la Revolución (National Party of the Revolution, or PNR). From his office as head of the party, Calles guided the destiny of Mexico for another six years. At the same time, he accelerated the process of centralization that ultimately would cause tensions between Chihuahua and the federal government in the subsequent decades.

Though Lázaro Cárdenas was Calles' chosen candidate, Cárdenas proved to be his own man. He quickly assured his preeminence by sending Calles off into exile and moving his own men into high political office. At the same time, he reorganized the PNR into the Partido Mexicano de la Revolución (Mexican Revolutionary Party, or PMR), which placed increasing control into the hands of the central government. Many of Cárdenas' reforms, which included some that impacted Chihuahua directly, resulted from the move toward political and economic centralization.

From Cárdenas to the 1980s, the official party (changed to the Partido Revolucionario de Instituciones or the Revolutionary Party of Institutions, PRI, in the late 1940s) controlled every single state house and national senate seat in Mexico and dictated policy along party lines. Government and party were inseparable. A continuum of power ran from the president as head of the party and government through the governor and even into the *municipios*. President Miguel Alemán Valdez, who governed from 1946 to 1952, even imposed his own governor on Chihuahua.

While *chihuahuenses* resented the increasing centralization, they tolerated it as long as the federal government did not become excessive in its demands. In the late 1970s, however, the growth of Mexico City placed greater demands on Chihuahua, and the official organs of government geared their directives more at the sustenance of the capital than the benefit of individual states. By the 1980s, conflict between the capital and the state of Chihuahua became inevitable.

Villa's death brought a sense of relief to politicians throughout Mexico. Even while he lived, programs began that ran counter to what he had believed in, but he kept his mouth shut, honoring the agreement that he had made with De la Huerta. Principal among these was the deal for the sale of the Terrazas estates to A. J. McQuatters, an American land developer.

The Carranza government restored the lands of Luis Terrazas, but the old patriarch, suffering from a stroke, could not enjoy the fruits of the restoration. His wife dead, his vast fortune in disarray, and himself an invalid, the putative sale was handled by his sons and family. McQuatters proposed to pay 20 million *pesos* to the Terrazas family for the vast lands that composed the *latifundia*. In turn, he planned to build agricultural colonies for sale to private farmers. Protests swamped both the state and federal government. About one-third of the state of Chihuahua would be sold into the hands of foreigners. Bad enough that other foreigners already controlled a great part of the state, but to have the largest *haciendas* go to an American seemed too much.

At first, the governor of Chihuahua enjoyed some support for the project from Obregón. But political pressures in early 1922 began to mount. Radical *agraristas* howled their opposition to the deal, and both state and federal government temporized. Finally, the governor of Chihuahua declared that the sale would be canceled until such time as the state legislature worked out the details of its agrarian code. McQuatters, however, received a refund of the earnest money he had paid, the government compensated the Terrazas family for the land to the tune of 13 million *pesos*, and the lands were split up among agrarian colonies and *ejidos*. Shortly thereafter, Luis Terrazas died in Chihuahua. He was buried at the small cemetery of the Santuario de Guadalupe in the western part of the city that he for so long realistically called his own.

Shortly after the McQuatters deal collapsed, the state legislature of Chihuahua came to grips with the problem of land ownership. Serious problems existed. Chihuahua was not a land that could function on small parcels. Extensive agriculture had always characterized the area, and this was no different. Yet commitment to Article 27 of the Constitution of 1917 made the division of lands imperative. In response to pressures from still existing *hacendados,* the legislature mandated that the maximum ownership of land in Chihuahua would be limited to 100,000 acres, or roughly 40,000 hectares. In typical Chihuahua fashion, the legislature made an accommodation that kept the central government at bay but at the same time responded to the realities of Mexico's largest state.

Meanwhile, many of the old and illustrious families who had been dispossessed by the Revolution worked their way back into the state. They did it through the simple expedient of marrying into the revolutionary families that controlled the state of Chihuahua. While they did not achieve the political power once enjoyed by Luis Terrazas and his coterie, the names of Terrazas, Luján, and Creel still sparkle in Chihuahua, on boards of banks, in industrial development and opposition politics, and in the professions. These were the same ones who rather early pressed for the salvaging of some of the lands through the state agrarian codes. Revolutionary power brokers — many of whom came from lower and middle-class sectors of the society — willingly made their deals with the older families. Thus they hoped to gain for themselves and their descendants a sense of respectability that could only occur through alliances with the names of what passed for nobility in Chihuahua.

The decrees about land ownership did not save foreign landholders from pressures. The Palomas Land and Cattle Company, one of the largest cattle operations in the state of Chihuahua, also succumbed to pressures. Located in one of the most uninviting parts of Chihuahua bordering New Mexico, Palomas represented a foreign presence that needed to be removed. During the presidential tenure of Miguel Alemán Valdez, the Palomas Land and Cattle Company underwent expropriation.

But the biggest of the foreign landholders carried a lot of clout through his newspaper chain in the United States. William Randolph Hearst, owner of the Babícora Ranch in southwestern Chihuahua, had been an on-again-off-again friend of the Mexican Revolution. He had both opposed the Revolution and supported United States recognition of Alvaro Obregón in the early 1920s. Pressures began to build in Chihuahua in the late 1920s to get Babícora out of the hands of foreigners. But the state government, as well as the federal government, did not really want to tangle with Hearst. His newspaper chain in the United States carried a lot of influence, especially during the Republican years of the 1920s, and Mexico needed all of the goodwill that it could muster if it was to make any of its revolutionary programs a reality. Consequently, an arrangement was made. Under the Chihuahua agrarian code, no individual could own more than 100,000 acres of land. Government officials suggested to Hearst and his managers that the land be divided up among the board of directors, thus satisfying the law while maintaining control within the Hearst corporation. This arrangement lasted until the mid-1950s. At that time (1954), shortly after Hearst's death, Babícora passed into Mexican hands.

In the 1920s, Chihuahua and its people attempted to accommodate to the exigencies of a centralizing revolution that seemed to rob them of their hegemony while at the same time homogenized the *chihuahuenses* into a carbon copy of the Mexicans from the south. For all of the government blather about Mexicans being one people, citizens of Chihuahua continued to see themselves as something unique in the Mexican firmament. In the face of radical land reform, labor agitation, and religious strife, the *chihuahuenses* attempted to rebuild. The vicious decade of revolution had decimated cattle herds, left many people hungry, if not dead, forced thousands out of the state, and compelled the remaining population to confront a new age.

One of the first changes, if not the greatest change, to occur in Chihuahua came in the arrival of the Mennonites to the west of the capital. These frugal, hard-working, German-speaking religious ascetics revolutionized agriculture in central Chihuahua. Settling in San Antonio de los Arenales in 1922, really nothing more than a water stop for the trains, the Mennonites founded what is now Ciudad Cuahtémoc and converted it into the bread basket of northern Mexico. They sought refuge from Canada, where Canadians also attempted to incorporate them fully into the Canadian society. This the Mennonites rejected. They hit upon a deal with the Obregón government. They would develop San Antonio de los Arenales, provided they could maintain their own schools and follow their own curriculum, be free of obligatory military service, which violated their pacifist beliefs, and be allowed to run their own affairs while paying only a token homage to Mexico City. In an age of rabid anticlericalism, Obregón took a large risk in allowing the Mennonites to come into Mexico under their own conditions. The risk paid off.

In agricultural production, especially that of cheeses and grains, the Mennonites have proven to be superb. Their way of life, while occasionally mocked, is still an object of envy among Mexicans. Even today the Mennonites maintain the best schools in the *municipio* of Cuahtémoc, and there is a waiting list among the non-Mennonite population of the area to have their children attend school there. In this the Mennonites have liberalized. While for over thirty years they wanted to maintain their own separate identities, they made concessions and allowed a quota of Mexicans to take advantage of the school system available. Freedom from government regulation allowed the Mennonites to develop a strong school base.

Additionally, the use of cheese by the Mennonites has in some respects revolutionized the Mexican diet. Active salesmanship by the Mennonite agents brings Chihuahua cheese into every part of the Republic, and it is a food product much prized by non-Chihuahua residents.

Oddly enough, while well in advance in terms of agriculture, the Mennonites continue backward socially. Women must stay at home, inter-marriage with non-Mennonites is discouraged, if not outright forbidden, and for local transportation they continue to use horse-drawn carts — now equipped with rubber tires instead of iron wheels — to get around their "camps." Modern farm machinery and pickup trucks dot the Mennonite camps.

San Antonio de los Arenales, now Cuahtémoc, has grown to cater to the Mennonites. The money rolls in to the local cash registers while at the same time Mexicans in the area augment Cuahtémoc's economy through their sense of competition with the odd-sounding, German-speaking members of the community.

In response to the Mennonite success, local Mexicans began to put their economic house in order. They discovered that the soil and climate around Cuahtémoc lent itself to the cultivation of apple orchards. As a consequence, the growth of huge apple farms has made Cuahtémoc the leading producer of apples in the country. The area produces all of the apples used in the manufacture of soft drinks throughout the nation. They also produce a sufficient apple crop for the general market, as well as for baking and canning. As a result, the *municipio* has steadily grown and today rightfully boasts as being one of the most prosperous areas in Mexico.

Mennonite prosperity since their arrival in Mexico in 1922 has been matched by that of those Mormons who returned to Colonia Juárez and Colonia Dublán outside of what is now Nuevo Casas Grandes. Mormon farms and ranches mingle with those of Mexicans in the Chihuahua northwest. Nuevo Casas Grandes also boasts about its inordinate economic success.

To describe the national mixtures that Chihuahua has experienced since 1920, the Spaniards need to be mentioned. Thrown out by Chihuahua in 1829, allowed to reintegrate, and then expelled by Villa in 1913, the Spaniards returned once again. Between 1936 and 1939 a bloody civil war left Spain in ruins and exhausted. Sympathizers of the defeated Republicans sought refuge throughout Latin America. Mexico, under the leadership of Lázaro Cárdenas, opened its doors to the Republican refugees. Many went to Chihuahua, where some of their relatives had once wielded large economic clout. Again they became grocers and shop owners, accountants, and generally those directly attached to trade. Spaniards with a more rural bent made for what land was available and found some near Namiquipa. Spaniards in Chihuahua today enjoy all of the privileges of citizenship and probably will incorporate more readily into the culture because of the strong similarities that exist between *chihuahuenses* and the once loathed *gachupín*.

The government cut deals with Mennonites, allowed Mormons to reestablish themselves, and even made arrangements for Spaniards to reside in Mexico and Chihuahua specifically. But it chose, selectively to be sure, to ignore the religious nature of its people. The new Constitution of 1917 bristled with anticlerical pronouncements. The Church definitively found itself out of the school business; clerics could no longer become active political participants; and churches became the property of the state. The government now dictated school curricula. In short, religious institutions lost all juridical personality and were rendered nonentities. This would presage conflict in the 1920s and would leave a feeling of bitterness among the 95 percent Catholic population of Mexico.

The bitterness erupted in Guanajuato and Jalisco in 1926 and later spread to a large part of the nation. After nearly a decade of frustration, the faithful launched their own battle against the central government. The trouble began when the archbishop of Mexico, Mora y del Río, allowed the republication of an article originally appearing in the United States just prior to the promulgation of the constitution. Mora y del Río roundly condemned the anticlerical provisions of the constitution and called upon the faithful to reject the document. To the government, this seemed like a direct challenge to its authority.

Plutarco Elías Calles, now president, responded viciously. He decided to form a Mexican Catholic church to challenge the authority of Rome and at the same time expelled the papal *nuncio*. Church authorities responded with equal fervor. They ordered the closing of the churches in midsummer of 1926. The faithful lined up for days in order to receive the sacraments, for while they could worship individually in the churches, they would be bereft of the sacraments. Children would go unbaptized, marriages would not be consecrated, confessions would be unheard, and the Eucharistic sacrifice would cease. It was a stalemate.

But conservative Catholics in Jalisco, Michoacán, and Guanajuato issued the call of *¡Viva Cristo Rey!* (Long live Christ the King!), and the battle was joined between tradition and the reformist and radical spirit of the Revolution. For three years the battle raged. The intervention of the United States through its ambassador brought the conflict to a close in 1929, only to have it reemerge again in the period 1933–1935.

For *chihuahuenses*, the loss of the holy sacraments did not mean that one had to go to war over the matter. Chihuahua had been an outpost of the diocese of Durango for so long, virtually ignored in the spiritual as well as the secular realm, that going without the benefit of clergy did not constitute a need to go to war. Chihuahua was of a different tradition than central Mexico, a child of the rationalist eighteenth century rather than the counter-Reformationist Hapsburg sixteenth and seventeenth centuries. While the bishop of Chihuahua dutifully ordered a closure of the churches, he continued to have good relations with the secular authorities and cooperated in the solution of local problems where his participation could not be construed as clerical interference. Chihuahua thus weathered the Cristero revolt and again proved its capacity for adaptability.

But the mainstream of *chihuahuenses* found themselves struggling to acquire some sort of economic prosperity after the Revolution. They faced a government in Mexico City that remained essentially insensitive to the needs of Mexico's largest state. When it was necessary to rebuild a cattle industry, the government wanted instead to expropriate lands. As a consequence, cattlemen, both of the pre-Revolutionary variety and those who chose to get into the cattle industry after the Revolution, proved wary about making large investments in land. They feared that if lands were developed from pastures to more productive tracts through irrigation, these lands would fall to hungry *colonos* and *agraristas* wanting to cash in on someone else's investment.

Thus, for cattlemen, the 1920s became a holding operation. They hoped to keep the government out of Chihuahua as much as possible while at the same time make quiet improvements that would allow the continued exportation of livestock to the United States. Throughout the 1920s, this was a tricky maneuver that could only be carried off through a judicious use of bribes *(la mordida)* and the favored position that Chihuahua enjoyed *vis á vis* the United States.

Rapid urban growth in the United States placed increasing demands on United States cattle raisers to produce red meat for the cities of the burgeoning country. Cattlemen, straining to adapt to radical changes in their own operations, could not keep up with the demand. As in the period before 1910, they looked again to Mexico. Chihuahua cattlemen found themselves hard-pressed to supply the needed feeder stock because of their fear of government expropriation of their lands. Something needed to be done, but the late 1920s and early 1930s hardly seemed the time to do anything radical.

Worldwide depression shook the very foundation of the economic order. Coupled with a devastating drought, cattlemen in both the southwestern United States and northern Mexico watched what remained of their herds die and be rendered useless for market. But all sides attempted to rebuild. By the mid-1930s, cattle production increased, exports to the United States seemed good for Chihuahua cattlemen, and these same cattlemen now sought some protection from the agrarian madness that seemed to grip the rest of the country.

Lázaro Cárdenas ruled in Mexico at this time (1934–1940). He carried with him the *zapatista* dream of land redistribution and engaged in some fairly radical land reforms that he hoped would make the *campesino* a self-sufficient entity in the Mexican economy. Cattlemen throughout northern Mexico and especially in Chihuahua again began to press for protection. This time the central government, in spite of Cárdenas' radicalism, took note of the demands. Principally, the ranchers insisted that their lands be exempted from expropriation by agricultural communities. Cattle culture, they rightfully pointed out, demanded extensive rather than intensive use of lands. When a rancher required 75 to 125 acres of land per cow/calf unit for year-round pasturage, the breakup of ranching holdings into even smaller units would prove fundamentally counterproductive. Cárdenas actually listened.

In 1938 Cárdenas issued what were called decrees of disaffectability. These in effect exempted pasture land from expropriation of *denuncia* by third parties. Those lands that had been improved by irrigation for the cultivation of alfalfa and other animal feeds made the production of livestock more profitable, for now they could sell nearly finished cattle. Yet those same improved lands remained subject to expropriation. As a consequence, cattlemen in northern Mexico and in Chihuahua specifically had to work again with influence and the judicious *mordida* to keep their lands from falling into the hands of the unproductive *ejidos*. Almost another thirty-four years would elapse before the central government in Mexico City recognized the true economic value of the cattle industry in Chihuahua.

But Cárdenas did not abandon his beloved *ejido*. In exchange for the decrees of disaffectability, Cárdenas demanded that cattlemen in Chihuahua and other northern states contribute two percent of their calf crops to *ejidos* in the respective states in order to encourage cattle production among the small farmers.

Additionally, Cárdenas sought to consolidate cattlemen throughout the country. The formation of the Confederación Nacional Ganadera (National Cattlemen's Confederation) was a step toward the homogenization of the cattle industry. Cattlemen's groups already formed, especially in northern Mexico, faced the dilemma of protection for the pastures but with increasing interference from the central authority. Since the mid-1930s, the conflict between the Unión Regional Ganadera de Chihuahua (Chihuahua Regional Cattlemen's Union, or URGCh) has heated the relations between Chihuahua and the central government.

Demand for Chihuahuan beef grew as the United States moved into World War II. By 1945, more than 900,000 head of Mexican cattle crossed into the United States to supply both the civilian population and the tremendous war machine created to fight against Germany and Japan. It seemed as if the prosperous enterprise would continue unabated — until disease-infected cattle herds in central and southern Mexico stopped the exportation of all cattle into the United States.

In 1945 Mexican cattlemen imported some Zebu bulls (a cousin to the Brahma) from Brazil. Brazil suffered at the time from endemic foot-and-mouth disease, while Mexico and the United States both had been free of the infection since the mid-1920s. Under the articles of a Sanitary Convention signed between Mexico and the United States in 1928 and ratified in 1930, the importation by either party of cattle from a country declared to have endemic foot-and-mouth disease *(fiebre aftosa)* was forbidden, and the United States should have stopped all importation of Mexican cattle and fresh beef. However, in some sort of cooperative frame of mind, the bulls had been allowed into Mexico. This prompted the Mexicans to attempt yet another major importation from Brazil in 1946.

The 1946 importation proved disastrous. Controversy swirled around the bulls who remained in quarantine on the Isla de Sacrificios just off of Veracruz. Finally, they were allowed to land and were placed on test pastures in Veracruz. Declared free of disease, the bulls made their way to ranches throughout Mexico and the southwestern United States. But it was not over. In December 1946, foot-and-mouth disease broke out in the Veracruz pastures where the bulls had been quarantined.

For cattlemen in Chihuahua, tragedy struck. Their lucrative market in the United States no longer wanted their very good feeder cattle. Ruin faced them. Both state and federal governments, in conjunction with the United States government, responded to the emergency. While governments fought foot-and-mouth disease in central and southern Mexico, cooperative efforts led to the building of canneries in northern Mexico, concentrated principally in Chihuahua, in order to buy cattle from besieged cattlemen. The canned meat in turn went to feed occupation forces in Europe. While this did not make Chihuahua cattlemen rich, it still kept them from losing the investments that for so long had been nurtured under conditions of governmental stress and the vicissitudes of weather and market.

The disease that stopped exportation of cattle to the United States finally succumbed to the relentless cooperation and scientific ingenuity of both governments. In 1952 Mexico was declared free of the disease. The next year, another small outbreak occurred in the Veracruz area but was eradicated in 1954. From that point forward, cattlemen in Chihuahua began an active program of expansion in order to better their circumstances.

Still the bothersome worry of expropriation continued to hang over the heads of cattlemen throughout northern Mexico. From the outbreak of foot-and-mouth disease until 1972, cattlemen constantly worried about the capriciousness of government interference in their enterprise. More and more, Mexico City loomed as the monster to be fed. Even in the late 1950s and the 1960s, production and sale of livestock was often dictated by the needs of Mexico City and not by the market for which cattle were destined. By 1972, political pressure from cattlemen's groups in Chihuahua and the rest of the north brought some relief.

In that year, the landholding laws underwent radical change. No longer did the government feel that it could dictate the amount of land necessary for the profitable production of 500 head of cattle or 500 cow/calf units. Instead, the new law mandated that cattlemen could hold as much land as necessary for year-round pasturage of a 500-cow herd. Additionally, and this was a major concession from the central government, lands improved for the production of foodstuffs for livestock were exempted from expropriation. Thus, wells could be dug, fields planted in oats, alfalfa, milo, and corn, and the Chihuahua cattlemen could actually become producers of finished as well as feeder stock.

But such concessions carried with them a heavy price. Cattlemen became subjected increasingly to export regulations that often seemed imposed at the whim of a capricious central government, thus exacerbating the feeling that the government in Mexico City cared little for its *chihuahuense* citizens. Moreover, if cattlemen exceeded their quotas, they had to ship a designated number of cattle to the public slaughterhouse in Mexico City at a fixed price that usually resulted in a loss to the cattlemen. Since 1972, in fact, the conflict between the Secretariat of Agriculture and Hydraulic Resources (SARH) becomes an annual and sometimes monthly event. Representatives from the Unión Regional Ganadera de Chihuahua make their treks to Mexico City several times a year in order to get the order changed and to allow the continuation of exports. The *quid pro quo* worked more in favor of Mexico City and less in favor of the *chihuahuense* and perpetuated the animosity extant between the distant state and the political center.

Cattle, however, did not comprise the only economic enterprise in Chihuahua. Throughout the period from 1920 until 1982, dormant industries — some shut down because of the Revolution, others newly founded or expanded — gave a more complex economic picture of the state. Agriculture, mining, banking, tourism, diversified agriculture and its ancillary industries — all of these blend into an economic whole that gives impetus to the political independence which grew from economic prosperity.

Take agriculture, for example. The singular successes of Mormons and Mennonites in western and northwestern Chihuahua stimulated the growth of competition in the area. Mexican nationalistic pride demanded that some response be made. As already noted, that response came in the growth of other agricultural pursuits that competed, though often not directly, with the Mennonites and the Mormons.

Major advancements have been made in Chihuahua with irrigated farming. Chihuahua, while possessing some rivers, is not endowed with flowing waters like the Yaqui in Sonora. Instead, it must depend upon dams, deep wells, and reasonably sophisticated hydraulic technology to make a veritable breadbasket of the state. Not surprisingly, where water could be taken to the flatlands of Chihuahua, gardens sprang forth and provided abundant agricultural harvests during long growing seasons. With heavy investments before 1982 in dams and irrigation, Chihuahua has become the principal supplier of basic foodstuffs for a large part of the nation.

In the mid-1960s, farming grew at a rapid pace. The Listers quite rightly claim that the growth of farming in Chihuahua resulted in large measure from the movement of farmers from central and southern Mexico who wanted a chance at successful farming. This, in turn, has increased production markedly. In response to this demographic movement, the federal government in the 1960s initiated a series of irrigation projects that provided more land for farming and for diversified market-oriented agriculture.

As early as the 1920s, federal activity in opening up Chihuahua to farming became evident. In the basin lying between the San Pedro and Conchos rivers, irrigation projects turned mesquite-covered land into agricultural nirvanas. Since that time, more dams

and irrigation systems have come into use. Towns like Delicias
sport windbreaks of cottonwood trees that protect delicate walnut
groves and other crops. Cotton, long a preserve of the Comarca La-
gunera around Torreón, Coahuila, spread into Chihuahua.
Grapes, cotton, wheat, peanuts, and nuts such as pecans and wal-
nuts constitute a large part of the crops grown in these areas. Milo
and sorghum for cattle feed also make up a part of the agricultural
activity. To add to it all, this is wholly mechanized agriculture, not
merely a *campesino* poking a hole in the ground and dropping in the
seed nor plowing the land with a brace of scrawny oxen and a
wooden plowshare. The agricultural areas reek of prosperity, some
of it stimulated by federal intervention and assistance, much of it
the result of the *chihuahuense* desire to survive on his own, to make
the best of the hand dealt to him by God and nature.

The agricultural downside, however, appeared in the *ejido*. Insufficient tracts of land (a maximum of sixty-five acres nationally)
made the communally-owned system of land singularly unproductive. Extensive provision of credits through the Banco de Crédito
Ejidal and the Banco Rural failed to be accompanied by the necessary technology that private farmers so successfully utilized. Instead, the *ejidatario* (*ejido* holder) had little stimulus to do more than
grub out an existence in unrelenting and brutal terrain. *Ejido* pastures can barely support goats, much less horses and cattle. A drive
through Flores Magón, for example, on the road from El Sueco to
Nuevo Casas Grandes, amply substantiates the observation. As one
enters Flores Magón, there is an *ejido* on the left. No more tragic
sight can be found. Scrawny horses, goats (equally anorexic looking), and cattle in the last throes of survival compete for precious
few blades of grass. On the right, however, is a large private farm
that bursts with verdure and prosperity.

In large measure the system that Emiliano Zapata of Morelos
loved so much and had incorporated into the Constitution of 1917
simply has not worked in Chihuahua. In spite of government efforts
to stimulate the *ejido* system, crashing failure has marked the enterprise. This derives in part from the nature of the system. Since it is
communitarian in principle, the *ejido* system simply runs against
the grain of the individualistic *chihuahuenses*. Ownership of an *ejido*
does not constitute real property, nor does it become a part of one's
estate. An individual's children must apply for *ejido* ownership, and
if land is available, then it can be held and worked for the lifetime

of the *ejidatario*. The lack of ownership in a real sense has made the *ejido* in Chihuahua an agricultural albatross that has probably hindered even greater agricultural advancement.

Even with some glitches appearing in agricultural activity, that enterprise gave Chihuahua the bases for its prosperity. Concomitantly, mining and industry made surprising comebacks since the Revolution. Mining, largely shut down between 1910 and 1920, again became active. Smelters began processing ore, and much of the ore went to the United States. Copper, silver, zinc, and lead in the 1960s provided Chihuahua with about fifty percent of the mining income for the entire country. Millions of *pesos* poured into national coffers, providing income for the nation and for the owners. Mining districts around Parral, east of Villa Ahumada, Santa Bárbara, and Aquiles Serdán, pump out lead, silver, zinc, and some gold. Some of the ore goes to the ASARCO smelter in El Paso, where it is processed and sent on in the United States.

Many of the mining areas are composed principally of company towns that regulate the lives of the workers, though not as in the days of Porfirio Díaz. Located in the mountains, often inaccessible by car, these mines continue to produce. After experiencing some slumps in the 1930s, when the United States went off the gold standard, production is again going at a profitable clip.

Related to mining because of its locale, the wood products industry in Chihuahua is finally starting to make some progress. Throughout most of the period under consideration, the prime forests of the Sierra Madre Occidental suffered vicious destruction. Reforestation suffered because cattle, sheep, and goats ate the young seedlings. Wood was cut and burned. Houses made of great slabs of Ponderosa pine sprang up in Creel and Madera. Only in the last twenty-five years have systematic efforts been made to bring some order to the forests of the Sierras.

The renovation of the wood products industry brought foreign firms into the picture. Pulp production by Kimberly Clark aimed at the supply of good pulp for its plant in Mexico City. Viscosa de Chihuahua, an Italian firm, makes rayon as well as pulp. Along with Celulosa de Chihuahua, the supplier for Kimberly Clark, Viscosa broadened the economic base of the capital city and provided jobs. So, too, did plywood manufacture. Thus the traditional cowtown that had once been Chihuahua City broadened into a multi-faceted economic entity.

During the 1950s and 1960s, the government realized the importance of wood products operations in Chihuahua and began programs to stimulate and encourage that industry. Federally sponsored reforestation projects and fire-fighting plans kept the Sierra from going up in a blaze. Lookout towers sponsored by the federal government have made the Sierra a more productive area.

Major advantages came to Chihuahua with the growth of tourism in Mexico. A quick trip across an international bridge allowed Americans to step into an exotic foreign land. This became especially true when the United States indulged in its noble experiment to rid the nation of demon rum. Americans would not be denied their booze and their fun; they looked instead toward Mexico. When Texas of its own volition went dry, the bawdy houses, distilleries, and casinos crossed the border to Cd. Juárez. There they remained, stimulating business in both El Paso and Cd. Juárez.

For El Pasoans, the 1920s provided an unprecedented growth in tourism. The El Paso Chamber of Commerce shamelessly advertised the delights to be found in Juárez if large groups such as the National Cattlemen's Association should hold their annual convention in that area. They could cross the river, load up on a bit of illicit booze, pinch a willing though often not a very pretty girl, and go back feeling that they had been in Mexico. The sheer tawdriness of the border gave many Americans a wrong impression of Mexico.

But the border between New Mexico–Texas and Chihuahua also provided a source of illicit liquor going into the United States. While much of the liquor to enter the United States during Prohibition came from Canada or from homegrown stills, Mexico became a principal source of intoxicants for the Southwest and California. Regular runs of liquor made their way across the unguarded border. Prohibition also provided a source of income for Mexicans who participated in the smuggling. In 1925, for example, one enterprising Mexican living south of Fabens, Texas, had an ingenious way of getting his liquor to the United States. He loaded his burro with booze, led the long-eared critter across the border, and left him with an accomplice. The Texas connection unloaded the burro, sold the liquor, and sent the little animal home. The homing burro became a ready source of income for this one Mexican. It took months before Treasury agents tumbled to the plot by which reasonable quantities of liquor came regularly into the Fabens area. Demon rum, then, became an issue that directly affected relations between the United States and Mexico while at the same time giving stimulus to the growth of Ciudad Juárez.

The repeal of Prohibition in 1933 caused a certain amount of consternation along the border. Most of the operators of clubs and distilleries had come from the United States. A cutback in their enterprises forced a reevaluation of the activity. The 1930s, beset by an economic collapse, brought a high degree of stress to the tourist industry in Chihuahua.

There were, however, some bright spots. The first successful airplane flight in the late 1920s from Juárez to Mexico City made that capital even more accessible. Railway completion also opened up parts of Chihuahua to tourism. Slowly but surely, Chihuahua began to open itself to foreign visitors.

Completion of highways after the 1930s connected Juárez to Mexico City and encouraged the growth of hostelries in Chihuahua. Motels catering to the mobile tourist appeared along the major highway. Tourists attracted to Mexico City used Chihuahua as a stopping point while en route to some other place.

Local authorities wanted to tap the potential of tourists in the area. They began to tout the natural and historic sites of Chihuahua. Copper Canyon, along the Continental Divide, was compared to the Grand Canyon. The impressive waterfall at Basesiáchic, the quaint Tarahumara Indians of the Sierra, and the grandeur of the mountain towns soon began to attract tourists. Much of this would not have been possible had it not been for the completion in 1952 of the railroad that ran from Ojinaga to Chihuahua City. Chihuahua now had a direct route to the Pacific. The line ended at Los Mochis, Sinaloa, and carried tourists either to hotels at the Continental Divide or onward to the coast.

The newly named Chihuahua al Pácifico Railroad also provided an avenue for the shipment of Chihuahuan products to western Mexico. In this way, Chihuahua, for so long isolated from the rest of the country, opened itself even more. While it may have succumbed to integration, Chihuahua instead chose to remain the maverick, preferring to view itself as something unique within the Mexican system. The state exploited the tourists and the commerce that went to all parts of the republic while remaining the fiercely independent member of the system.

As it approached the 1980s, Chihuahua felt prosperous and full of vigor. The economy of the state blossomed with diversity. Traditional industries — cattle, mining, agriculture — were booming. Tourism grew at a rapid clip, and so did new industries such as wood products. In the early 1960s, another element was added to the growth of Chihuahua. *Maquiladoras,* or assembly plants, began to appear along the border. These took components from United States companies, assembled them in Mexico because of the lower labor costs, and then shipped the finished product for distribution in American markets. The business became a part of the border industrialization project and came to constitute a major economic innovation for Chihuahua. *Maquiladoras* spread to Chihuahua City and by 1982 provided nearly 100,000 jobs in the state.

Chihuahua entered an era of booming prosperity. The state's economy gave it one of the best living standards in Mexico. Economic opportunities abounded for those who wished to avail themselves of the chance. A growing middle class began to see real gains. But lurking in the distance stood economic disaster, a massive national debt, and a runaway inflation. These produced disenchantment with the system, the development of new or revived political parties to challenge the institutional monstrosity that was the Partido Revolucionario de Instituciones, and a growing sense of isolation once again from the political center of Mexico.

PART
II

Overview of Chihuahua City taken from the roof of the now-closed Presidente Hotel.

— Photo by Travis Machado.

Calle Libertad, downtown Chihuahua City. Calle Libertad is blocked to motorized traffic between Avenida Independencia and Avenida Guerrero. It is, in effect, and outdoors shopping mall.

Photo by Travis Machado.

CHAPTER 4

It's Election Time:
1982 and 1983

President José López Portillo faced the assembled Congress. Mexico was in crisis. Debt now overrode whatever consideration might be given politically. López Portillo had ridden a wave of success and unprecedented prosperity in the years that he served as president. Suddenly, in 1982, Mexico's economy began to disintegrate. Debtors started to call in their markers. A gigantic crap game rapidly became one in which the dice were loaded against Mexico. She had bartered her future on the basis of high oil prices, prices that everyone — the Texas oil patch, the Arab sheiks, Venezuela's oil companies, Mexico's PEMEX (Petroléos Mexicanos) — believed would remain in the clouds ever since the Organization of Petroleum Exporting Countries (OPEC) doubled the price of crude oil so disastrously in 1973. As a consequence, Mexico plunged into debt. The country had used its oil resources as collateral with the World Bank, the International Monetary Fund, and private banks principally in the United States. Now it was in debt. On the world market, the *peso* started to fall. In February 1982, a devaluation was necessitated. Other measures would ultimately have to be taken.

So there stood López Portillo, facing Congress, preparing to

Top: Pancho Villa in lights next to the Cathedral in Mexico City, November 20, 1988.
Photo by the author.

A political poster found plastered on Calle Aldama in Chihuahua City in 1985. Porfirio Díaz is superimposed on the PRI logo. The words read that the ``vote is free and secret. Vote for the PMT [Mexican Workers' Party]."
Photo by the author.

deliver his *Informe Presidencial,* roughly equivalent to the State of the Union Address. He began a summary of his last year in office and described Mexico's advances. Then he dropped a bombshell: The banks would now be nationalized. Private banking ceased to exist in Mexico. López Portillo also pledged to defend the *peso* and to keep it from further decline. In fact, he swore to fight like a dog to defend Mexico's currency from further devaluation.

But it was the nationalization issue that upset world and national money wizards. What was Mexico up to? Did they intend to suspend payment of the debt? With the second highest debt level of any Latin American country, Mexico was in severe trouble if the country could not get its economic house in order. A joke current at the time went something like this:

> López Portillo dies and goes to heaven. He is greeted by St. Peter, who asks his name. López Portillo replies: "I am José López Portillo. I was the greatest president that Mexico has ever had. In fact, I saved the country from ruin when I nationalized the banking system." St. Peter consulted a computer printout and told Pepe López Portillo that his name, for some bizarre reason, was not on the list. He said: "Listen, *Señor* López, go on down and see my buddy Satan until we get this mess cleared up. These damned computers are always screwing things up." So, down goes López Portillo. A week goes by, two weeks, three weeks. St. Peter becomes curious and wonders what happened to that funny little Mexican with the big sideburns. He picks up the phone and calls Hell. The phone rings, and a voice answers: "Good day! InfernoMex. Pepe López speaking. How may I help you?"

In good Mexican fashion, the people of Mexico instantly began to deride López Portillo for his nationalization. After his comment about defending the *peso* like a dog, he was greeted with howls and barks of derision when he appeared in public.

Poor Pepe López! Not only did he preside over Mexico's economic collapse, he also headed an administration that was rocked with scandal. He was a man whose wife traveled with her own *mariachi* band when she would go to shop in Paris, London, or New York. He was a man who could not keep his fingers out of the till, at least so declared the conventional wisdom in Mexico, and who had socked away billions in Swiss accounts. So, too, did some of his closest friends: Roberto "El Negro" Durazo, head of the Federal District Police; and Jorge Díaz Serrano, the head of PEMEX. Díaz

Panel 1

In a meeting, the PAN speaker was heaping invective on the mayor. "He is inept, a demagogue, and corrupt."

Panel 2

The presidente municipal complained excitedly to his trigger man. "Didn't I tell you to kill him when he began to tell lies???" "That's what I'm waiting for...

Panel 3

...but up until now he's said nothing but the truth."

Panel 1

Licenciado [Fernando] Baeza confidentially told the newspaper reporter "the Noisy Threat" a bit of news. "What a breat item for the first page!"

Panel 2

"Let me publish it, Licenciado!" "OK, Threat, publish it...

Panel 3

...but don't tell anybody!"

Serrano took a fall and spent some time in jail for skimming off the top, but as of the early 1990s he lives well. López Portillo himself bought or built castles in France and Spain plus a summer playground in Zihuántanejo, Michoacán, courtesy of his buddy Durazo.

But how did Mexico reach such a pretty pass? Fundamentally, Mexico relied too heavily on the price of oil staying high. This proved fallacious. Money borrowed from all kinds of sources subsidized massive programs in and around Mexico City, for the population of that major metropolis needed to be fed, transported, clothed, and served in every conceivable way. Population growth began to spiral in the late 1960s and early 1970s as more and more Mexicans came from the countryside hoping to find some sort of relief from the miserable conditions in which they lived in the rural areas. More and more, the Mexican government threw money into programs that failed to generate additional income. As a result, government revenues began to rely increasingly on what could be borrowed, a condition not unlike that which occurred during the early years of Mexican independence.

The year 1982 also provided Mexico with its sexennial sideshow: a presidential election. No doubt existed about who would win the contest. The official candidate of the PRI, Miguel de la Madrid Hurtado, had been the *secretario de planeación y presupuesto* (secretary of planning and budget). He was Harvard-trained and held a graduate degree in economics. As the scandals that buffeted the López Portillo administration revealed themselves, De la Madrid tried to distance himself from the administration. He promised a "moral regeneration"; no longer would such scandalous behavior be tolerated in Mexico. Clean government would now characterize Mexico's political system. As a people, the Mexicans issued a collective yawn. They had heard it all before. More political blather that signified another six years of the same old thing.

The impact of the economic collapse on Mexico eroded principally the middle classes who finally had begun to see a chance for advancement and financial security. Nationalization of the banking system converted all dollar accounts into *pesos,* and with a declining currency, the accumulated assets of the middle class began to disappear. Anger and frustration gradually replaced sheer amazement at the brazenness of the move. The Mexican government, through a single stroke, began to annihilate the most productive sector of its population.

Political opposition began to grow, principally in northern Mexico. At the forefront of the opposition was the Partido de Acción Nacional (National Action Party, or PAN), which represented conservative, wealthy, Catholic, middle-sector, and some peasant elements. Founded in the wake of the Cristero Revolt of the late 1920s, the PAN began as a party of conservative opposition and of religious elements, principally made up of the pious and some peasantry. In northern Mexico, it gathered strength in Nuevo León, especially in Monterrey, and in the entire state of Chihuahua.

Chihuahuenses felt the pinch when dollar accounts were canceled. No longer could they trade neatly in dollars, almost the coin of the realm because of the proximity to the United States. As a result, they felt their gains being eroded by the capricious action of the central government, always considered the enemy anyway. No longer could they make buying trips to El Paso. No longer could they purchase those material items that they thought essential to their well being. No longer could they dream of being able to buy a house or a second car. In short, the whole prosperous bubble that Chihuahua had created in the period after World War II until 1982 began to burst. Moreover, the *chihuahuenses* resented the increased demands being made on them for additional revenue to feed the Mexico City monster. A new tax — *el impuesto de valor adicional (IVA),* or a value added tax — made its impact. The new tax ranged from six to twenty percent, depending on the item. Foodstuffs and medicines were taxed at a rate of six percent; everything else was taxed on an ascending scale.

Chihuahuenses received the IVA with a lot of grumbling and attempts to circumvent its payment. Local merchants advertised that their prices did not carry IVA, and, given the slowness of the Mexican bureaucracy, it would take forever before the tax collector ever caught up with them. *Chihuahuenses* also grumbled and complained that they were paying taxes for the subsidization of the massive transport system in Mexico City, especially the subway, and saw little of the benefits that came from the payment of such a horrendous tax.

Mexico's presidential election in 1982 seemed uneventful, though the rumblings of the PAN could be heard in the north. In the previous October (1981), López Portillo had unveiled his hand-picked choice called *el destapamiento,* or the uncovering. Miguel de la

Madrid then began to campaign for the job, though such a campaign was unnecessary since the government machinery controlled the electoral process. Chihuahua began to gear up for the election.

All of the electoral preparations were made before the election. Polling places were installed and ballots printed. By July 1, the PAN began to complain that the local elections had already been rigged, that the PRI had already prepared the way for a massive De la Madrid victory in Chihuahua to confirm his selection by Mexico's largest and most prosperous state. The PRI, in response, declared that it would win cleanly, without the political shenanigans and the corruption of which it had often been unjustly accused. *Chihuahuenses* scoffed.

Came election day. *Chihuahuenses* broke their traditional absenteeism and flocked to the polls. Almost eighty percent of eligible voters turned up to vote. This brought the federal electoral commission an extra amount of work, for they had to get 200 more ballot boxes ready for the polling places. As the results were announced, opposition leaders wondered how long it took to stuff the extra ballot boxes.

In typical fashion, the PRI trumpeted its victory even before all of the votes were counted. Senator Santiago Nicto Sandoval, member of the federal electoral commission, affirmed that PRI candidates had won "resoundingly" throughout the state of Chihuahua. A week after the election, the official results became known. In Ojinaga and Camargo, the PAN won. In Delicias, just forty miles south of Chihuahua City, the Partido de Acción Revolucionaria Mexicana (Party of Mexican Revolutionary Action) carried the area. But this was insufficient to give the state to the opposition. Everywhere else in Chihuahua, despite massive opposition to the government, the PRI emerged victorious. Miguel de la Madrid ostensibly received an imprimatur from Chihuahua.

By the first of August, the opposition prepared for the upcoming state elections in 1983. They issued statements that roundly condemned the official party. Both the PAN and the Partido Demócratico Mexicano (Mexican Democratic Party, or PDM) blasted the official entity. PAN declared that the PRI was seriously divided. The official party, claimed the opposition, had fallen into the hands of *chambistas*, jobseekers, who merely wanted a good, undemanding, government job. The PDM alleged that the PRI was made up of people who existed only "for a job and for those interested in a bone" upon which to gnaw.

Furthermore, a series of moves by the PAN prepared them for the gubernatorial election in 1986. Rumors circulated that Francisco Barrio Terrazas of Ciudad Juárez would be the gubernatorial candidate. Barrio Terrazas, an accountant, had been active in PAN affairs but had not held elective office. He would have a tremendous impact on the National Action Party when that party gathered strength in the following year.

Men were not the only ones to become politically active in the opposition and in the official party. On September 19, 1982, the Asociación Cívica Feminina (Women's Civic Association) was formed. Officially, the group endorsed no single political party but rather aimed at the involvement of women in the politics of the state and nation. Over 700 women met, and, according to Treviño de González, marked the "civic awakening of women in Chihuahua." Such civic consciousness on the part of women was absolutely necessary for the upcoming state elections.

As the day arrived for the inauguration of Miguel de la Madrid, the economic crisis deepened. A public deficit of sixteen percent of the gross national product afflicted the nation. Inflation surpassed 100 percent. Money fled Mexico into accounts in New York and Switzerland. The massive corruption of the López Portillo administration began to make itself evident. In such an atmosphere, Miguel de la Madrid prepared to take office on December 10, 1982.

In his inaugural address, De la Madrid promised to face the crisis — *la crisis* — squarely. To do so required a "moral rejuvenation." He promised increased "democratic participation" by the Mexican people. In order for that to happen, Article 115 of the constitution needed strengthening and enforcement. This article dealt with the autonomy of the *municipios* of local governments. De la Madrid promised to put Mexico back on a strong footing through a massive cleansing of the body politic. He further asked Mexicans not to question the system but to believe in its ability to bring about its own reform, to purge itself from within.

As usual, Mexico collectively scoffed. The people had heard it all before. In Chihuahua, the electorate began to awaken to the fact that the PRI merely wanted to keep itself in power. They began to switch their allegiances to the PAN and to other opposition parties. By March 1983, the promises so ringingly delivered in December by Miguel de la Madrid proved empty. No arrests had been made. López Portillo quickly got out of town as did his crony "El Negro" Durazo. Obviously, *chihuahuenses* rejected De la Madrid's contention that to question the system was by definition to be an "unpatriotic reactionary."

Massive electoral activity marked the campaigns of 1983 in Chihuahua. *Chihuahuenses,* men and women alike, joined political action groups. The Women's Civic Association did not get all of the political action of women; they joined other political parties as well. This swelled the ranks of the Partidos Socialistas Unidos Mexicanos (United Mexican Socialist Parties, or PSUM), the PAN, the PRI, the Partido Mexicano de Trabajadores (Mexican Workers' Party, or PMT), and the Partido Socialista de Trabajadores (Socialist Workers' Party, or PST). The time had come to mount effective political action. Even within the PRI, *chihuahuenses* realized that they needed to bring about change if they were to survive the horrors of the economic crisis and the political stagnation that beset them.

The demand for electoral honesty made itself felt. Governor Oscar Ornelas Kuchle, the head PRI official in the state of Chihuahua, soon began to offend the national powers-that-be because of his honesty in dealing with the opposition. Rather early in the campaign he angered the aging Fidel Velázquez, head of the powerful Confederación de Trabajadores Mexicanos (Mexican Workers' Confederation, or CTM), because of failure to support a CTM minion in Camargo. Since the 1930s, the CTM had been the official labor confederation allied with the ruling party. Apparently, the PAN leader, Guillermo Prieto Luján, became involved in some name calling that reached the point of slander. He also had allegedly prepared some forged documents that put the CTM representative in an unfavorable light. Ornelas, instead of allowing the case to go to trial, ordered that the whole affair be shelved in order to avoid an accusation of political manipulation. This enmity would erupt fully in 1985.

The picture became further complicated when Oscar Ornelas apparently turned against the PRI candidates in Camargo. In the latter parts of the campaign, PRI supporters in Camargo — already angry about the shelving of the case against Prieto Luján — turned against a group of *panistas*, beating a goodly number of them and leaving one dead. Ornelas, enraged by such action, ordered that the *priístas* be turned over to the police. It became clear that Ornelas might be headed for trouble, for he supported the detention of the PRI candidate and one other accomplice.

Velázquez and the CTM fumed. Accusations were hurled at Ornelas about being a closet *panista*. So much pressure was brought to bear that some members of Ornelas' cabinet were forced to resign. Among these were Luis Monroy de la Rosa, his chief of staff; Alfonso Rivera Soto, the attorney general for the state of Chihuahua; and, later on, Jesús José Silva, the head of the State Judicial Police, which handled the investigation. This conflict between Ornelas, the chief PRI representative in the state of Chihuahua, and the powerful CTM eventually demonstrated the deep schism that beset the PRI. The old guard, called the dinosaurs, demanded party loyalty while Ornelas, among others, wanted to see electoral reform and a liberalization of the party.

Violence did not remain limited to the smaller towns like Camargo. In Chihuahua City itself, conflict broke out. On June 24 a gang of *priístas* broke up a PAN demonstration and attempted to do anything possible to keep the *panistas* from pursuing an active campaign.

A major factor in the PRI campaign against PAN in 1983 came in the form of accusations that the blue and white (the PAN colors) tended to favor the United States. They further averred that the *panistas* leaned too much toward the policies of President Ronald Reagan and the conservative Republicans. PAN spokesmen did not deny that they had certain ideological affinities for what they called "democratic Christians," and PAN further declared a strong distaste for those groups that were "excessively liberal." But, they continued, the free enterprise nature of their program was no different from many other such groups in the western world and did not make them, *ipso facto*, the hand-picked servants of the White House. The PRI campaign obviously attempted to impugn PAN's Mexicanness.

But all of the PRI activity against the opposition groups availed them nothing. On the first Sunday in July (the 3rd), the PAN won sweeping victories from Ciudad Juárez to Parral, far in the south of the state, and controlled approximately seventy percent of the population of Chihuahua. Treviño de González wrote that these were "days of hope; it seemed that democracy in Mexico would begin to seem a reality."

PRI leaders recoiled in shock. For the first time since 1929, the official party took a thorough drubbing. Though not as spectacular as Chihuahua, the neighboring state of Durango also posted PAN victories and left the official party in a state of utter confusion. While no governorships were at stake, the PAN gained control of major municipalities, including four state capitals. For the PRI, it was a time of reconsideration, of plotting new electoral strategies. In previous elections, the PRI had won up to ninety-nine percent of all votes cast.

As the first votes in Chihuahua continued to roll in, PAN clearly had control. They had won, at first count, seven municipalities, and the PST took the *municipio* of Cuahtémoc. Additionally, PSUM controlled Ignacio Zaragoza and the PSP had Gómez Farías. To make matters worse for the PRI, the state electoral commission validated all seven PAN victories as well as those of the other opposition parties.

PAN ended up winning the municipalities of Chihuahua, Ciudad Juárez, Delicias, Meoqui, Parral, Camargo, and Casas Grandes. The electoral commission refused to recognize victories in General Trías (San Ysabel), Madera, and Nuevo Casas Grandes. In this last instance, the dispute became so heated that the election was nullified, and a new contest was held eight months later (March 1984). The nullification of the election demonstrated a strategy that had served the PRI in the past: If you don't like the results and if you control the electoral machinery, change the rules and start over again. That March, the PRI won the election in Nuevo Casas Grandes.

The PAN victories required the exercise of vigilance. Three days before the elections, rumors began to circulate around Chihuahua City that 300 PRI strong-arms were coming from Mexico City with the specific intent of stealing ballot boxes. *Panista* women began a telephone campaign aimed principally at housewives. They urged the women to vote and requested that they remain outside the polling places to make sure that the vote was not violated. Finally, those who could were urged to take a camera with them to photograph anything untoward at the polling places.

When election day arrived, peace reigned in the city. Oscar Ornelas maintained order, and the huge turnout of voters did not produce any incidents of violence. Election night also proved quiet when the first votes began to trickle in to the different party headquarters. PAN and PRI both claimed victory, though the PRI assertions sounded hollow. Luis H. Alvarez, the PAN leader who would become the *presidente municipal* of the capital city, began to stake out territory for himself rather early. He declared that he expected to have good relations with the state government, adding, somewhat sarcastically, as civilized folk should.

Soon the charges of electoral irregularities began to fill the air. PRI claimed that they had won in Juárez because PAN committed irregularities. They also charged the clergy with outwardly favoring the *panistas*, a clear violation of the Mexican constitution. The PRI firmly averred that they continued to be "the party of the majority. We did not lose all of Chihuahua nor all of Mexico."

The PAN responded to *priísta* charges by claiming that ballot boxes had been tampered with in General Trías. The attorney general retorted that if such was the case, then the guilty parties would go to jail. It was, however, up to PAN to prove its allegations.

By July 10, the future plans of victorious *panistas* became matters of interest. Alvarez declared that he only wanted to be a good *presidente municipal* for Chihuahua City. He claimed not to be thinking about the gubernatorial race in 1986. Many interpreted this as mere disingenuousness rather than a clear statement of political intention. In Juárez, the victorious Francisco Barrio Terrazas, though his victory was still in dispute, had not denied rumors as early as 1982 that he would run as the PAN candidate for governor.

Already the PRI began to cover its tracks and to downplay what surely were devastating losses. They admitted that the PAN received a great number of votes because the PRI had failed to mount an effective political propaganda campaign. As a consequence, *priísta* candidates did not receive the kind of exposure necessary to familiarize the voters with the party's objectives and plans. Such an admission came as close to a confession of error as one could expect from a party that had exercised political power for over fifty years without effective opposition.

By July 9, six days after the election, the president of the state electoral college gave PAN a victory in Ciudad Juárez. The *priístas* groused about the decision. They raised the bloody shirt of United States intervention when they alleged that the PAN received covert assistance in Juárez and throughout the state from Washington, DC.

The long, tedious process of electoral verification dragged on throughout July. By July 23, the PRI admitted that some of its municipal organizations had some serious faults and demanded that new votes be held in certain areas. It seemed that since the official party could not win against an organized opposition, they could try again through the nullification of the first results.

Stridently, the PRI further accused the *panistas* of buying votes. One PAN spokesman declared that such an accusation lacked any sort of basis in fact. He continued that the votes tallied with official scrutiny at each polling place had overwhelmingly given major triumphs to the National Action Party. He asked: "What more does the PRI want? It has already violated its public promise of recognizing its defeat, and now it weeps, without juridical support or moral authority, and wants to overthrow the public vote."

The hassle did not abate. By August 2, both the PRI and the PAN asked the state electoral college to be objective and fair in its deliberations when it decided the results of the various municipal elections. Two days later, *El Heraldo de Chihuahua* reported that four parties demanded victories in different *municipios* or the elections should be nullified. The PRI claimed Saucillo, Ciudad Juárez, Nuevo Casas Grandes, Madera, and Parral. The PAN wanted the electoral college to award it General Trías and Madera, while the Partido Popular Socialista (PPS) claimed victories in Villa López, Bocoyna, and Bachínava. The PST firmly supported its victories in Aquiles Serdán, Rosario, and Namiquipa.

The result of a nullified election allowed the state legislature to appoint an interim government until such time as new elections could be held. This was a move that demanded the greatest of political finesse. In 1974 municipal elections were nullified in Santa Bárbara and Villa de Matamoros. To take such an action only demonstrated the political distress in which the official party found itself, and as a consequence, the electoral college needed to tread warily.

During the political wrangling throughout the summer of 1983, the economic crisis continued to worsen. When Miguel de la Madrid took office the *peso* dropped from 125 to the dollar to an official rate of about 144:1. This figure would hold until October 1983, when the Banco Nacional de México would allow a controlled slide of the *peso*. By summer of 1984, the value of the national currency slid to about 185:1. In the face of increasing debt and a controlled devaluation, both the PRI and the PAN called for calm. Disorder and panic could presage internal collapse. The PRI claimed that the system would allow for adjustments and asked that the citizenry have faith in Mexico's political system for a resolution of the crisis.

Economic crisis or not, politics still dominated the scene in Chihuahua. The PAN demanded its legitimate victories and damned the consequences. PRI proved equally adamant about Ciudad Juárez, while the PST strongly suggested that if they were not awarded Namiquipa they would take it over through direct means.

By mid-August the PRI allowed rumors to circulate that it planned to make changes in its political practices. The accepted version in effect in Chihuahua stated that if the PRI became less the official party, all of Mexico would benefit. PRI spokesmen charged that PAN wanted to dictate the election outcome; this was a function of the electoral college, not a political party.

The electoral college, dominated by the state PRI organization, found itself impaled on the most uncomfortable part of a dilemma. Clamors for victory swirled about the state electoral college. Finally, on August 12, they gave the PRI part of its demands. *Priístas* were declared the winners in Saucillo, Huejotitán, and Aquiles Serdán. Guillermo Prieto Luján, the state PAN president, immediately jumped into the fray when he described the PRI victories as resulting from "ruffianesque" tactics. He further pledged that PAN would mount a campaign of nonviolent opposition to electoral fraud. In response, the PRI threatened to seize Nuevo Casas Grandes. One CTM spokesman openly stated that the PAN was blatantly criminal and that its candidate for the municipal presidency should be arrested. Moreover, he said, the PAN was an obvious tool of the reactionary clergy. PAN called the PRI victory in Saucillo a "tragicomedy."

With the election over, the political rhetoric became even more stridently heated. Both sides wanted to establish their terrain for the upcoming congressional elections in 1985 and the gubernatorial contest in 1986. At the same time, both sides hoped to pressure the electoral college.

But the electoral college refused to yield to one side or the other. In almost Solomonic fashion, it nullified the elections in

Nuevo Casas Grandes and Madera and appointed interim governments for those two areas. Parral and Bachínava were awarded to the PAN, while the PRI received General Trías. Howls of protest began to fill the air. Full-page ads appeared in the newspapers denouncing the electoral fraud. The PRI, through its satellite organizations such as teachers' and labor unions, claimed PAN was fraudulent, that the clergy continued to exercise undue influence, and that the United States — the great bug-a-boo — had given assistance to the reactionaries.

On August 16, the PAN's electoral victory in Juárez was confirmed. National Action spokesmen praised this advance of democracy in Mexico, and Francisco Barrio Terrazas became *alcalde* (mayor) of Juárez. But the PRI had not yet finished. They threatened to take to the streets in protest against the PAN victory. They darkly declared that protests would innundate Juárez if municipal services suffered any sort of decline.

By the end of August, the PRI realized that it had been trounced. *Priístas* began to lay the groundwork for their upcoming opposition to all of the *panista* governments that controlled a huge number of the *chihuahuenses* population. PRI declared that all who collaborated with the PAN were traitors to the PRI and should be cashiered from the party ranks. Such action by the official party defined the guidelines which would, in many cases, regulate the relations between victorious opposition parties and the state and federal PRI authorities and create a tense atmosphere.

With economic crisis dominating the Mexican ambience, the political tensions created in Chihuahua built upon the fiscal difficulties that beset the nation. *La crisis* clearly threatened the economic benefits that had come to Mexico's largest state in the last two decades, and reactions began to manifest themselves both in Chihuahua and the United States.

Despite PRI allegations of United States support of PAN, no evidence surfaced to substantiate the contention. PAN itself declared an affinity for a more free market system and claimed that PRI merely wanted to create a smokescreen for its own ineptitude.

Chihuahuenses felt the crisis. They could no longer go to El Paso to buy the finished products so coveted by upwardly mobile and affluent *chihuahuenses*. For many years it was believed that El Paso–Ciudad Juárez formed a dependency model predicated upon the notion that Juárez depended wholly on El Paso for its sustenance. The crisis quickly disproved the theory. One businessman in Juárez reported that by December 1982 nearly sixty percent of the independent businesses in El Paso faced financial problems or bankruptcy because of the sudden loss of income from purchases made directly from Mexico. Instead of dependence, interdependency has been the rule, something denied by those who wanted to make an economic bully of the United States.

Allegations by PRI of United States involvement notwithstanding, Mexican officialdom suffered incredible losses. Unfortunately, they did not take the losses well. For the next two years they would mount a campaign that ultimately would cause violence in the streets of Chihuahua City, a desecration of the Universidad Autónoma de Chihuahua, and the downfall of a governor — all in the name of *el PRI.*

CHAPTER 5

The Politics of Corruption: The Off-year Election of 1985

"Twenty-one!" went the cry. "Red deuces and one-eyed jacks wild!" "My flush beats your straight!" "Bullshit!!" "Raise you twenty!" "Your twenty and thirty more!" "You're called, asshole!" "Son-of-a-bitch, you did have it!!" "I'm busted *¡pinche puta madre!*" It sounded like a high-school poker game, but the stakes were a lot more serious than toothpicks, a furtive night with some bimbo, or an extra beer or two.

It was Chihuahua City, August 1985, and I had returned to Chihuahua to do some last minute research on Pancho Villa. Of course, I went to the Escuela de Filosofía y Letras of the Universidad Autónoma de Chihuahua to visit. I had taught there in 1983–84 on a Fulbright Fellowship, so I thought I'd go renew old acquaintances with colleagues and former students. At first there seemed to be little tension around the school. It was summertime, a lax period, and very little was going on. Yet, as the time that I was in Chihuahua passed, the tensions that appeared subsumed began to surface, and the state university of Chihuahua became embroiled in the political in-fighting that has characterized Mexican politics in general and that of Chihuahua specifically. For a place that should have been immune from the whirlwinds of politics, the university became a focal point of political discontent, a malaise that ultimately overthrew the rector of the institution and successfully unseated a governor.

Chihuahua's off-year elections in 1985 presented a distressing problem to the PRI. Acción Nacional remained firmly entrenched in major population centers throughout the state. Oscar Ornelas, as honest a governor as even the opposition could ask for, demanded electoral recognition of any opposition victories. This failed to sit well with the powers-that-be in Mexico City. Something needed to be done to offset the stunning defeats suffered by the ruling party in 1983. In effect, the electoral machinery needed sufficient tinkering to assure PRI victories in 1985 and in the important gubernatorial race of 1986.

But first PAN needed to be understood, analyzed, and, finally, defeated by whatever means were available. Different ideas swirled around dealing with the phenomenal success of the PAN. One school of thought held that *la crisis* had done substantial economic damage to a growing and influential middle class. Business had been hurt by bank nationalization in 1982. No longer was there enough capital fluidity. Shopping trips to El Paso became rare luxuries, and it proved increasingly difficult to send one's children to the better private schools.

The official PRI position held that the Party of National Action had made a dark and unholy alliance with the Church hierarchy, with the big industrialists, and with the Republican Party as represented by Ambassador John Gavin. PRI displayed all of its bloody shirts, hoping to rally the *chihuahuenses* population against Acción Nacional. Leftist parties and aglomerations held another view.

To the committed left-wing groups all that had occurred simply was an accommodation between the PAN middle sector and that of the official party. To the left, this was a family affair that paid little, if any, attention to the needs of the working poor and the indigent. Groups like PSUM and the PST merely figured that establishment elements represented by PRI and PAN would eventually disembowel themselves and leave the political field open.

Panistas had their own perception of the conflict. The PAN genuinely believed that it received its greatest support out of conviction, not desperation. The people of Mexico and Chihuahua specifically had tired of government fraud and corruption. "This version," wrote Aziz Nassif, "has as its center the notion of setting the north apart as an exception; it emphasizes the nonsubmissive and committed character of northerners, who contrast with the pliable people of the south."

Thus, in 1985, all of these ideas had to deal with the reality of PAN success in municipal administration. All of these needed consideration and action if PRI hoped to recapture its hegemony throughout the state. They needed to reacquire a sense of common objective, of consensus, and the PRI had to rid itself of unpopular leaders and at least visibly clean up the corruption that had come to characterize its political *modus operandi.* If removing a governor and allowing a university to become a focal point of political manipulation were required, then so be it. The PRI would regain its power throughout Chihuahua.

A principal factor with which PRI had to deal was the utterly aggressive nature of the opposition in municipal elections. PAN got out the vote. They overcame the high percentage of abstentionism and literally overwhelmed the official party. For years, abstentionism provided PRI with a mighty weapon. They relied on the *chihuahuense* attitude of *"no vale la pena votar; sabemos quien va a ganar."* (It's not worth voting. We know who is going to win.) As a consequence, the all-out campaign caught the PRI off-guard. Never had they had to contest so furiously for municipal elections. And, to make matters worse, they lost. The year 1985 became the time to redress the problem.

Throughout the north, PAN aggressiveness made itself felt in 1984 and early 1985. In Sonora, noises emanated from a popular *panista* who did not exclude the possibility of a run for the governorship. He made the run in the summer of 1985; unfortunately, the PRI rigged the election. In Coahuila, in both Monclova and Piedras Negras, rioting broke out after the PRI imposed its own man in municipal elections. The Coahuila problem became acute as violence continued. Three presumptive PRI office-holders were stripped, had their heads shaved, and sent into the desert. While PAN officially decried such activity, it did say that if the popular will continued to suffer ever-growing frustration, such violence would be almost inevitable. Northern volatility, long pent-up, would erupt should there be continued vote tampering.

In Ciudad Juárez, Francisco Barrio Terrazas, the charismatic *panista* mayor, continued his open and unorthodox style of governance. He refused to wear a tie; he seemed much more the carefree businessman than the politician. While some of the projects he wanted to initiate progressed slowly, much of the blame was laid at the feet of state and national authorities who seemed loath to cooperate with someone from the opposition. Yet Barrio maintained an open-door policy whenever he was in town. He saw on the average twenty to twenty-five people per day. They came with their problems to see if he could help resolve them. He also took long walks throughout the city, seeing at first glance what needed doing, and then tried to do something about the growing problems of Chihuahua's largest city. Inspired by this, the PRI began a program of citizen visitation. Barrio instilled hope in his constituents. He declared: "Our credibility remains high . . . It's not that we are doing so well, but the people have hope, and when you have hope you resist letting it die." PRI was learning this lesson too.

Thus, in 1985, PRI began to upgrade its political approach to the people of Chihuahua. Media usage, personal contacts by candidates with the voters, and a few judiciously placed *mordidas* came into play. In all probability, the official party began to question itself. Did it, in fact, need to modernize? Did it need to streamline its approach to the retention of political power in a country that it had dominated for so long?

And then came the bloody shirt of American intervention. In late March 1985, *El Día,* a Mexico City daily, claimed a strong link between the Central Intelligence Agency and PAN. PAN leaders had met with the ambassador in 1984 to take their orders from the National Security Council. Without doubt, claimed *El Día,* the Reagan administration wanted the PAN to win because of the amount of coverage that state and local elections received in the United States press. The paranoia of the left about U.S. intervention clearly made itself manifest and successfully played into the political hands of the PRI.

Three months later, the same cry went up. *Excelsior* (Mexico City) reported that major leftist parties — PSUM, PPS, and PMT — requested that John Gavin be expelled because he had dabbled in Mexico's internal affairs. Also, these same groups demanded that PAN lose its party designation because it had consorted with foreign elements. These parties averred that Gavin's fiddling with Mexican politics could lead to violence in the July 7 elections. Scare tactics now became the order of the day. Nationally, a climate was created that justified almost any move to retain PRI dominance.

Meanwhile, in the north, problems began to surface at the Universidad Autónoma de Ciudad Juárez that seemed to have a direct relationship to the growing political tensions in the state. Demands were made for the resignation of the rector of that institution. The rector, Carlos B. Silveyra Sayto, had asked for a leave of absence because of his political activities. His opponents argued that his openly PRI sympathies tended to push the university in one political direction rather than another, and a strong pitch was made for the nonpolitical nature of a university. In April, Silveyra Sayto quickly resigned as the rector of the Autonomous University of Ciudad Juárez. Already it was apparent that the universities of the state of Chihuahua would become political battlegrounds that would leave permanent scars on faculty, students, and on the state.

Clearly, the PRI was worried. In late June 1985, President Miguel de la Madrid visited Ciudad Juárez. He wanted to lend his personal support to PRI candidates in the state and congressional elections. The prestige of the Office of the President was needed if popular support could be swung to the PRI.

Then came election day, July 7, 1985. Tensions ran high and tempers short. By the evening of July 7, PRI officials claimed a massive sweep by margins of 3:1. Already they had trumpeted these claims, and the PRI intended to make good its prognostications through whatever means available. By the evening of July 7, also, the PAN began to note the existence of systematic voting irregularities. Voters with known *panista* proclivities found their names excluded from voting lists. Additionally, no one was around the election offices to resolve problems. The whole affair emitted a somewhat noxious air. PRI desperation to win led it to indulge in much the same sort of political games that had stood it in good stead at a time when people seemed rather bored by politics.

The *panista* campaign revolved around the national motif of "For a new majority." In Chihuahua, they took this quite seriously and campaigned actively. Municipal President Luis H. Alvarez of Chihuahua predicted, quite rightly, that the official party would not respect the outcome of the July 7 elections. PAN only had one election confirmed. "What occurred in the elections of 1985," wrote Treviño de González, "shook everyone like a rag."

Two key congressional seats fell to the PAN but were nullified:

Chihuahua City and Ciudad Juárez. In Chihuahua City, the problem became complicated by the attitude of Governor Oscar Ornelas, when he refused to support Doroteo Zapata, the CTM candidate for the VII Congressional District. Zapata should have won the election in a walk, but Ornelas' steadfast hands-off policy made the CTM candidate work and lose. Fidel Velázquez, the aging but still powerful labor czar in Mexico City, railed against Ornelas and set the stage for the subsequent removal of Ornelas from office.

In Juárez it was a repeat. PAN candidate Juan Saldaña won, but like his counterpart in Chihuahua City, Guillermo Prieto Luján, his election was nullified. It was estimated that nearly 100,000 votes were nullified through electoral manipulation. Luis Alvarez and his wife began a hunger strike that lasted until they had collected 100,000 votes on a petition to demonstrate that they had, in fact, the number of votes necessary to overturn the PRI. The official party genuinely feared that they might lose control of the state legislature. In addition, too many PAN congressmen at the national level might give that party too large a national exposure and negate the effective control exercised by the PRI.

The day after the election, Ornelas received a surprise visitor. Then Senator and today Governor José Ramírez Gamero of Durango brought Ornelas a direct word from Fidel Velázquez: Straighten out the electoral mess! Ornelas refused to see Ramírez Gamero, and instead the frustrated senator visited with Doroteo Zapata. In addition, he detailed some people to shadow Ornelas and report his movements. On July 9, one of the goons rushed in, interrupted Ramírez Gamero's lunch, and reported that Ornelas was heading for the airport, bound for Ciudad Juárez in a private plane. The senator from Durango jumped from his seat, ran to a car, and headed recklessly toward the airport, where he was able to intercept Ornelas and convince him to talk. Ramírez Gamero bluntly informed Ornelas that unless Doroteo Zapata won the VII Congressional District, all CTM support would be removed from Chihuahua. A deal was made. A few days later, the official position became public. Zapata won the VII District, but the PAN candidate for the I District in Juárez — Eduardo Turati (only three years a resident in the district) — emerged the winner there.

PRI officials in Mexico City remained unhappy with the deal negotiated by Ornelas. Powerful elements outside of Chihuahua reasoned that if Ornelas, obviously a scrupulously honest man, should remain in power, then PAN could capture the governorship in 1986. This would also confirm the PAN hold on the municipal governments it had captured in 1983 and would cause the spread of *panismo* throughout the country in the following year.

Thus, part of the national PRI strategy to undercut PAN influence in Chihuahua came in the elimination of Oscar Ornelas as governor of the state. It boiled down to the disgrace of an honest man in an essentially dishonest political job. To begin with, Fidel Velázquez despised Ornelas. PAN had lauded Ornelas' honesty in his respect for electoral results. Within Mexico's presidential cabinet and the official party, a division appeared. Manuel Bartlett Díaz, himself soon to be considered for president in 1988, as secretary of *gobernación* wanted to keep Ornelas. But party officials, spurred on by Velázquez, dictated that Ornelas had to go. The stage was readied, then, the actors were in place, and Ornelas was about to receive the *tiro de gracia (coup de grace)*.

Ideally, universities should be devoid of political involvement. They are places of contemplation and study and the transference and expansion of knowledge. While this may be the ideal, rarely is it seen, especially in public institutions. Public universities in the United States are constantly embroiled in budget fights with state legislatures and they covertly support candidates who will vote for bigger university budgets. In Mexico, political participation becomes much more direct and much more tied to the political vagaries that are current. Such was the case at the Universidad Autónoma de Chihuahua (UACH).

It all began with the reappointment of the rector of UACH, Reyes Humberto de las Casas Duarte, known as *El Pato* (the duck). In June of 1985, deans of the various schools all voiced their initial approval of the reappointment. They approved of the continued tenure of De las Casas, the University Council ratified the action, and the governor was pleased. However, some elements in the university community had not yet received their marching orders from the national PRI.

El Pato had twice served three-year terms as rector. A second reappointment, while unusual, did not seem necessarily out of line. The University Council gave its approval in June, but lurking in the wings stood the politics of the national PRI organization, ready to goad opposition to Governor Ornelas through the creation of chaos at the university.

In large measure, the reappointment came at an auspicious time. Students had been in final exams, faculty were ready to take off for a while before they began any summer assignments, and time seemed ripe for a questionable move. But elements surrounding State Treasurer Saúl González Herrera, with the support of anti-Ornelas elements in the national party, began to manipulate students, deans, and faculty into creating a chaotic situation. The orders were up: Get rid of *El Pato*. De las Casas and Ornelas were tied in together. The rector had been a law student of Ornelas and then went on to become dean of the Law School when Ornelas was rector. In typical Mexican fashion, personal friendships played a significant role in the appointment of academic and political office-holders.

As early as the 1970s, the split between Ornelas and González Herrera had manifested itself. Ornelas' faction triumphed, and González Herrera and his cronies found themselves without substantial political support. Yet, at a time when the political situation was critical, González Herrera came to the fore as the leader of a group who wanted to avoid, ostensibly, the creation of an autocracy at UACH.

In part a reflection of the economic crisis and of the perpetuation of *El Pato* in power at UACH, students in early August learned some alarming news. They were informed that their fees — initially nominal at most — would jump to between eight and ten thousand *pesos* for the year. Free education, a long tradition in twentieth-century Mexico, was coming to an end. This, coupled with the reelection of De las Casas to the rectorship of the university, engendered student discontent. This was ultimately the objective of those who wanted to use the university as a means to unseat Ornelas.

As a reflection of the economic crisis as well, the rector proved penurious. Every time a request came to his office for new programs, equipment, travel money, or any other expenses associated with the university, the purse strings closed. Always it was the same answer: more money was needed to justify any extra expenses. Discontent began to brew. High-handed administration plus the economic pinch made themselves felt.

By the second week of August 1985, the opposition to *El Pato* gathered strength and voiced its discontent. De las Casas moved quickly to avert any sort of conflict, knowing little that the whole affair was probably programmed. On August 7 he fired two deans who voiced their opposition to him. The deans of animal husbandry and chemical sciences fell. Also a move was afoot to expel "rebellious" students. Soon *El Pato* began moving deans around with a certain amount of impunity in an attempt to retain his position.

The political motivation behind the opposition to De las Casas became apparent. Saúl González Herrera, the state treasurer and leader of another PRI faction, and himself a former rector of UACH, declared that a "deadly precedent had been set that would be profoundly damaging to the life of the University." The opposition began to intimate some sort of physical reaction to the reimposition of *El Pato*. De las Casas categorically stated: "We are not cavemen who beat each other with clubs in order to obtain something."

By August 22, the purge had continued, and, as yet, no real opposition had coalesced. Ten teachers, some of them among the most respected in the different faculties of the university, received termination notices. In Delicias, the headquarters of the UACH School of Agronomy, the entire research department was wiped out. Six professors and a secretary found themselves in the streets. In the School of Philosophy and Letters, four faculty members — some of them leaders of the opposition — also found themselves jobless. Reputedly, there also existed a black list of twenty-five professors who, if they proved uncooperative, would get walking papers.

The opposition now began to make its demands known. They wanted a general university assembly to decide the issue. Also, they demanded the immediate resignation of De las Casas. One dean, now in opposition, said they could fire him if they wanted, but that he would continue his opposition to the imposition. More professors seemed destined to be fired. Tensions began to build.

In late August, students at the School of Agricultural Sciences seized the premises and demanded the resignation of the rector. Oscar Ornelas, preoccupied with the political whirlwind caused by his own honesty, viewed the university problems with little concern and genuinely believed that the university was undergoing some minor periodic social adjustments.

But the social problems proved more than little. Philosophy and Letters was the next school to fall to student protesters led by disgruntled faculty members. Students from Animal Husbandry, who had bodies to spare, sent delegations to help hold the School of Philosophy and Letters.

I was visiting the university at the time, not necessarily in support of the student strike but to see old colleagues and students. That my visit should occur during a disturbance did not bother me in the slightest. Suddenly, a student from Philosophy and Letters whom I had known from my earlier year as an instructor at UACH approached me. This student said that I should probably get out of the school because the word was out that *El Pato* and some of his henchmen were coming to try to disrupt the student takeover. She was absolutely right. A foreigner caught under those conditions would not be welcomed in Mexico. Given the Mexican sensitivity about foreign intervention, such an action could actually have had me declared an undesirable alien.

Apparently, De las Casas felt that he had the situation under control. He claimed support from the *secretariat* of education in Mexico City. The fired teachers, he averred, were stirring up discontent and spreading gossip in order to undercut his position. One of the fired teachers, Francisco Flores Aguirre of Philosophy and Letters, became the vortex of the fight to reinstate the dismissed professors.

Accusations began to fly back and forth. Opponents to De las Casas claimed that he was mysteriously involved in narcotics trafficking. They also accused him of flagrant nepotism, something that unfortunately was true. Both his father and his father-in-law worked for the university in different capacities. Additionally, many of his supporters drew more than one salary. Some even had as many as four paychecks every two weeks. For example, one highly placed administrator drew a professor's salary in addition to a handsome administrative wage plus other benefits that provided him with an impressive lifestyle that would have been the envy of faculty and administrators in the United States.

The opposition gathered increasing strength by early September. Students in an organized and militant fashion seized the rectory, located downtown across the plaza from the Governor's Palace. Their sense of frustration continued to grow. They had made other marches to the Governor's Office in an attempt to talk to Ornelas. At one such march, they even burned a large plush duck, chanting *"¡Muera el Pato!"* (Death to *El Pato*!).

Seizure of the rectory was accompanied by a grabbing of every available public bus that they could commandeer in order to block major thoroughfares. To prevent movement of the buses, the students let the air out of tires. They did this in an attempt to bring public pressure to bear on Ornelas to fire De las Casas. Five hundred thousand *chihuahuenses* found themselves without public transportation. The streets of Chihuahua City seemed strangely empty. Only people with cars or who could afford taxis moved about the city. One beneficial sidelight of the seizure of the buses came in the form of clean air. For a few days the stench of diesel fuel did not permeate the nostrils and aggravate hangovers.

Opposition to De las Casas had spread to other schools. Students from Engineering had seized the rectory. They did so, probably unaware of the risks that they took. Motivated by an idealism upon which more cynical political sharks played, the students suddenly found themselves at the center of a real dogfight. Public sentiment against the seizure of the buses clearly blamed the students for abusing "university autonomy."

Meanwhile, where was Ornelas? Like all Mexican governors, he was in Mexico City at the time, present there for the *Informe Presidencial*. In the early hours of September 4, Ornelas returned from Mexico City. He closeted himself with his advisors to review the situation. Ten students gained entry to the government palace and were able to talk to Ornelas. An announcement came from the Governor's Office that a solution would be found for the university. Ornelas' press secretary went so far as to say that the seizure of the buses was a "passionate action without appropriate thought. If the students would quit listening to those who push them toward violence, they would easily discover that they are the ones principally affected."

Ornelas knew that he had a serious problem that needed to be dealt with firmly. On the evening of September 4, the police moved in and began to disperse the students, mainly with tear gas. Students retaliated by throwing rocks. Surprisingly, there were few injuries.

In Mexico City, Ornelas' nemesis, Fidel Velázquez, pompously pontificated. He declared unequivocally that the chaos in Chihuahua required federal intervention. Coupled with this declaration, a demand went up from Ornelas' opponents that a state and federal audit should be conducted of the entire finances of the university.

Ornelas found himself in a precarious predicament. He needed to act quickly and struck upon his one-time student and collaborator, *El Pato*. In an interview with De las Casas, Ornelas excoriated the rector for his "repressive and intransigent" actions. While he promised more money for the university, Ornelas reprimanded De las Casas for his initial firing of the deans of Animal Science and Chemistry.

El Pato also was on the defensive. On September 5 he declared his refusal to resign and blamed venal politics on the mess at UACH. In a press conference, one reporter sympathetic to the strikers accused De las Casas of wearing fine silk shirts and imported suits bought with money suspiciously obtained. Impulsively, De las Casas began to strip off his shirt to show the reporter that it was not in fact made of silk. When a photographer attempted to get a picture, *El Pato* asked that he be allowed to put his shirt back on, for he did not want to appear "in poor rags."

The opposition continued to hammer away at the rector. Organized as the Frente Democrático Universitario (Democratic University Front), this group accused De las Casas of a continuous assumption of power reserved to other units of the university. He did this, they said, "to further his own interests rather than those of the University community."

Even with the disruption of the bus seizure, students still remained in control of the rectory. On September 5 the Frente Democrática Universitario issued a statement of violations perpetrated by the rector. They included:

1. Illegally convening the University council for the selection of a new rector.
2. Illegally presiding over the session in which he was elected.
3. Illegally dismissing the heads of Chemistry and Animal Sciences.
4. Violation of personnel statutes that govern UACH.
5. Illegally naming new deans of Chemistry and Animal Sciences.
6. Rescinding the contracts of tenured faculty.
7. Failure to present a budget or submit reports to the board of trustees or the University community in general.
8. Revising the academic calendar without the approval of the University council.
9. Impairing the free functioning of the University council.

The early days of September were fraught with political danger for De las Casas as well as Ornelas. All of the demands made by the Frente Democrático had some basis in the organic charter of the university. The economic impact of the seizure of the buses for a twenty-four-hour period rose into millions of *pesos*.

In opposition, the PAN tried to take advantage of the students' upheaval. They hoped to capitalize on the student unrest to further their own political causes. But when *panistas* offered their support, they were soundly rejected by student leaders. This clearly indicated that the fight at UACH was a family affair within the PRI. No outsiders were welcome.

De las Casas still refused to resign. He claimed to have been reelected legally. In addition, though the buses now were under police control, public transportation remained slow to resume normality. The pressure continued to build on De las Casas.

In the early hours of September 11, *El Pato* announced his decision to resign following a four-hour meeting with Ornelas. Ornelas had specifically come from Mexico City to meet with the beleaguered rector. The conflict at UACH assumed national proportions. Political observers had for the last few years focused on Chihuahua as a center of political discontent. In Hermosillo, capital of the neighboring state of Sonora, the local newspaper trumpeted the news: "*El Pato* resigns!" Four days later, the students returned the rectory to administration control.

De las Casas was forced to resign. He had visited the *secretaría de gobernación* in Mexico City and was told to leave his post. Apparently, some intimations were made that Ornelas was next. It became obvious that *El Pato* did not inform Ornelas of his fate. The resignation of the rector also saw the fall of other high university officials. When Rubén Acosta, the Law School dean, was named as interim rector, opposition began to form against the appointment.

The return of the university to normal functioning did not include the School of Philosophy and Letters. Rafael Cereceres, head of the Frente Democrático Universitario and a member of the Philosophy and Letters faculty, declared that a condition for reopening the school was the resignation of Luis Nava Moreno as dean and Hildeberto Villegas as the technical secretary. Until they left the school administration, the school would remain closed.

By September 22 classes and administration normalized and calm prevailed. The schools, however, began to organize politically

for the election of a new rector. On a broader political front, the
ouster of Ornelas was now orchestrated.

Pressure increased on Ornelas. The national **PRI** now wanted
him out, as did Velázquez and local opponents in Chihuahua.
Thus, on September 19, Ornelas went before the state legislature to
ask for *licencia,* a leave of absence. It had become apparent to most
observers in Chihuahua that Ornelas took this action under orders
from Mexico City, not because he genuinely wanted to leave his office. *Panista* legislators refused to vote for the leave. Some members
of the private sector even urged Ornelas to continue in office, even
if it meant defiance of Mexico City. But Ornelas, a good party
man, succumbed to his own and party discipline in spite of the fact
that he knew he was a political sacrifice.

Ornelas resigned because of pressure from Mexico City. *Chihuahuenses* resented the intrusion from the center of the country.
While Ornelas may have had his local critics, he was still a local
boy with whom they could work and who would work with them.
On the day that Ornelas resigned, the legislature named State
Treasurer Saúl González Herrera as interim governor. As an aside,
in 1988 González Herrera had become the successful **PRI** candidate to the national senate. A political payoff had been made.

Change in state government at first left the *panista* administra-
tions at the local levels in some consternation. A few days after the
change, **PAN** leaders in Ciudad Juárez declared that they saw no
problem between themselves and the new administration. Francisco Barrio Terrazas, however, joined other **PAN** leaders in con-
demning the way in which Ornelas was forced out of office.

Left-wing parties also voiced their discontent at the ouster of
Ornelas. The **PPS** declared that the deficiencies in Mexico City
were not Ornelas' fault. The **PDM** stated that the people of Chihuahua had elected Ornelas for a six-year term, and that it was un-
fair for the political gurus in Mexico City to intervene in state affairs in order to serve their own political ends. The **PPS**, however,
did say that **PAN** support of Ornelas clearly demonstrated how the
major party had moved to the right.

With González Herrera ensconced in the governor's palace, all
aspects of *ornelismo* were ousted. *El Pato* became the first step, then
a brother who was an accountant for the state preparatory school
system. The new rector, Rodolfo Torres Medina, was González
Herrera's *compadre.* Obviously, the heavy pall of *personalismo* per-

meated the political maneuverings of late summer and early fall 1985.

Two months after Ornelas received his leave of absence, the state legislature did in fact remove him from the governorship and confirmed González Herrera as the interim appointee. In related action, a series of electoral reforms began to cause consternation among the *panistas,* for these appeared to be attempts to restrict their freedom of action (see Chapter 6). By December, PAN screamed foul.

No question exists about the importance of Chihuahua on the national scene. The growth of the PAN as a viable opposition group gave the official party sufficient pause to reassess, at the very least, their methods of operation. At the same time, the PRI took strong measures to stem the spread of *panismo* and its growing support when it appointed Manuel Gurría Ordóñez as an official watchdog for the state of Chihuahua. In 1986 he would see to it that the electoral laws passed by the state assured a PRI victory.

PAN also began to make its preparations for the upcoming gubernatorial elections. Presumptive candidates began to insinuate their interest in the nomination as party standard bearer. A significant amount of backroom juggling occurred throughout the PAN state organization in the late fall of 1985. One candidate, Francisco Barrio Terrazas of Ciudad Juárez, did not wait. He brazenly announced his candidacy for the nomination. This move forced the hand of Luis H. Alvarez, the distinguished looking mayor of Chihuahua City. Alvarez's announcement meant that the party convention would be a dogfight between young party activists and the more established *panistas.*

More traditional established parties of both the right and the left played by certain rules, often not of their liking, but understandable within the system. In the early 1970s, however, a new group came to represent large blocs of disenfranchised and poor citizens who wanted lands for the purpose of building homes in and around major cities in Chihuahua.

The Comité de Defensa Popular (Committee for the People's Defense, or CDP) became a major element in the political equation of Chihuahua. Born in early 1972, the CDP began its rise through a series of three bank robberies of branch banks of the Bancomer system in Chihuahua. A group of urban guerrillas assaulted the banks in order to raise funds for their organizing activities and to play at terrorist games. Housed in the university Law School under the leadership of Rubén Aguilar Jiménez, a forty-three-year-old graduate of the school, the CDP grew into a major pressure group making demands of state and local governments for lands and the delivery of public services to their followers. In 1974, when Manuel Bernardo Aguirre became governor, he hoped to undercut the CDP by handing lands out directly to the squatters. The squatters, known as *paracaídistas* (parachutists, because they landed wherever they felt like it), received lands legalized under the Programa de Desarrollo Urbano (Program of Urban Development). The government acquired the lands on which the squatters had already established themselves and handed the title directly over to the occupants. In this way, it was hoped the CDP would lose a lot of its punch.

CDP leadership also wanted to exercise major influence at the university. They definitely despised Oscar Ornelas when he was rector and pressured to get rid of him. In the early 1980s, many CDP adherents inhabited the various schools of the university and had taken on the ideological trappings of the left, including some of its own paranoia.

One student of mine was an ardent CDP man. All he wanted to do in class was to argue about United States policy. Finally, we agreed that such discussion was inappropriate for a course in historical research methodology, but he persisted nonetheless. Bright, energetic, and articulate, this student still shared the left-wing paranoia. He absolutely insisted that the drought that plagued Chihuahua in 1984 resulted directly from cloud seeding operations by the United States to control hurricanes in the Caribbean. He had no evidence for this contention but persisted in its articulation.

As the CDP grew in influence, it brought pressure to bear on the *panista* governments of Ciudad Juárez and Chihuahua City. As opposed to PRI-controlled *municipios*, those under PAN management — Chihuahua City, Ciudad Juárez, Casas Grandes — responded forcefully. Mass rallies without permits were dispersed. Civil disturbance of any kind received short shrift from PAN. The polarization led to an open declaration of war between the two. PAN's position hardened: There would be no negotiations with the disrupters of public order. This PAN attitude presaged more problems for the 1986 election.

In 1985 the corruption of the Mexican political system reached a high point in the state of Chihuahua and generally in the north. Toleration of opposition by the PRI's national leadership became more than a fossilized institution could bear, for it was obvious that the dreaded PAN could conceivably wrest control of state and municipal governments from the PRI. Northern Mexico and especially Chihuahua emerged as the focal point for PRI activity against the PAN.

To combat the conservative party, the PRI and some of its captive left-wing groups asserted a series of shibboleths that touched nationalistic chords in the Mexican. Principal among these were charges of the intervention of the United States, its ambassador, John Gavin, and the CIA. Like lemmings, many Mexicans believed these contentions and wavered away from the PAN.

To assure its victory in Chihuahua, firm PRI control needed reestablishment. But first it was necessary to get rid of the governor. Oscar Ornelas may have been a party hack, but he was a *chihuahuense* party hack elected by the people of Chihuahua. Ornelas also proved to be an honest man; he genuinely wanted to respect the electoral will. For an honest man to be a politician, he must either be ingenuous or a little stupid. Ornelas was not stupid. In all probability, he believed in the promises of Miguel de la Madrid to have open and clean elections. Yet cynical forces wanted Ornelas deposed. Party officials who were starting to carbonize like long-dead dinosaurs demanded that this honest man be removed from office. To remove him, the national party manipulated state factions opposed to Ornelas. Their first target became the university.

By nature, university students are volatile and probably a little naive. They are blinded by their idealism, a dangerous trait that can be exploited by political manipulators. The students engaged in a closure of UACH that left permanent scars on its various faculties and on the perceptions about it by the people of Chihuahua.

Even the radical CDP became a factor in the 1980s. They pressured the conservative municipal governments and met with firm responses, thus creating political polarities that would have lasting effects.

But overall, the overthrow of Oscar Ornelas meant that once again Mexico City was dipping its oar into local affairs, something that has always infuriated the localistic *chihuahuenses*. One observer wrote:

The great distance that separates Gran Tenochtitlán [Mexico City] from the *chihuahuenses* has accustomed them to be independent from decision from the center. The same economic progress and exemplary development that the north of the country has achieved has made them self-sufficient. They do not render tribute to the center of the country.

CHAPTER 6

The Boogyman is Coming: PAN, PRI, and the 1986 Election

His eyes glinted with the fire of reborn fanaticism. Righteously, he addressed his audience, convinced that he carried the true word about the salvation of his state and his nation. Like an Old Testament prophet, there was utterly no arguing with the man. He was absolutely right, and the system that sought to continue its imposition upon the state remained unarguably wrong. He intended to right the injustices brought on by years of one-party control. Francisco Barrio Terrazas, the mayor of Ciudad Juárez, prepared to launch his race as the Acción Nacional candidate for the governorship of Chihuahua.

Never before had state elections in Mexico drawn so much national interest. In the past, they had brought a foregone conclusion: PRI candidates would inevitably win, so why bother to vote? But now, the experiences of 1983 in Chihuahua drew national and international attention. Would the PAN actually succeed in dislodging the ever-powerful PRI? Should Acción Nacional succeed, the social and political consequences for Mexico would be far-reaching and would take years to disentangle. Just what was happening in Chihuahua? Was the system undergoing a type of meltdown? Was the body politic actually changing? On a national level, far more was at stake than a governorship and local and state offices.

The national PRI could not afford a major loss. Chihuahua, always a bone in the throat of Mexico City, could cause the very problems that the national party wanted to avoid. As a consequence, 1986 proved to be a repeat of 1985. The federal government reneged on its promise of fair and clean elections. The usual ballot box stuffing occurred; expulsion of opposition pollwatchers and tampering with voter rolls joined the list of fraudulent practices. While to many it seemed to be politics *a lo mexicano,* the protest, engendered by the continued desire of the PRI to retain its hegemony in the state, shook the powers-that-be in Mexico City and again made them cognizant of Chihuahua as the singular most powerful entity in the Mexican federation. Civil demonstrations took place, hunger strikes became part of the PAN protest, bridges were seized that connected Mexico to the United States, and even some leftists joined the PAN in demanding either nullification of the elections or a clean recount.

And, finally, there lay the United States, directly across the border from Mexico. Chihuahua occupies a unique geopolitical position in Mexico. Not only is it the largest state in the federation, but it borders extensively on the most powerful nation in the world. "For good or ill," wrote Contreras Orozco, "the luck and political destiny of Chihuahua is of interest to the northern neighbors. They consider this state the doorway to Mexico."

PAN geared up for the elections in 1986. They had plenty of ammunition, for in late 1985 new electoral codes passed the state legislature that severely restricted opposition campaigning and the eligibility of opposition voters. The early months of 1986 saw PAN select a nominee and launch a series of acts of civil disobedience that threatened to upset the body politic of the state.

Acción Nacional, while seemingly unified, also suffered some internal divisions. A group of Young Turks, headed by Barrio Terrazas, seized control of the party machinery. Dubbed *neopanistas,* they controlled the January nominating convention. As a result, Francisco Barrio Terrazas bested Luis H. Alvarez, the mayor of Chihuahua City. Alvarez, legatee of the traditional *panistas,* was tall, gray-haired, distinguished looking, and utterly faithful to his principles. He had, as a young man, run for president in 1958 as the PAN candidate against Adolfo Ruíz Cortines. But now the youngsters had gained control of the PAN. Alvarez, ever the gentleman, accepted his defeat for the nomination and worked hard for a PAN victory in July.

Barrio, however, seemed full of his own importance. He declared the possibility of national aspirations. When he resigned as mayor of Juárez in order to devote full time to campaigning, he also announced that he would not engage in any debate with the PRI candidate, Fernando Baeza Meléndez. Barrio stated that such a debate would give Baeza "a standing that he does not have and that I earned on my own in recent years."

Tactically, PAN chose to protest electoral fraud early in the campaign. It became, in fact, a cornerstone of the campaign even before any election had been held and probably backfired. In late January, marches began against restrictive changes in the electoral codes. Barrio had gone on a twenty-one-day hunger strike until he collected 190,000 signatures from *juarenses* protesting the changes. To a significant number of *chihuahuenses* it seemed that Acción Nacional cried "Wolf!" a bit early in the campaign.

Meanwhile, PRI also began its selection process. In its usual backroom manner, party leaders selected Fernando Baeza Meléndez, whose family credentials would have made him equally acceptable to PAN. In part, this was a move by the state PRI to distance itself a bit from the national party, to show that it too could field truly *chihuahuense* candidates. Baeza had distinguished himself in state and national politics. He served as assistant attorney general of the country when the late Oscar Flores Sánchez, one of Mexico's most powerful political figures, acted as attorney general during the administration of López Portillo. Two *chihuahuenses* served in national office together and commanded respect. Baeza was the ideal candidate for the PRI.

Each major party in Chihuahua now had its candidates. Both Barrio and Baeza were popular. They had an appeal that exuded the openness upon which *chihuahuenses* prided themselves. Both men had proven extremely successful in their different activities. Barrio, an accountant in Juárez, helped to build the *maquiladora* program. Baeza had been successful within the PRI. Another factor that ultimately became an issue was the Church. Both men espoused being *muy católicos*, very Catholic. Like Manuel Avila Camacho, the official presidential candidate in 1940, they declared themselves *creyentes* (believers). The role of the Church would eventually become an issue in the 1986 election.

The Mexico City paper, *Proceso,* gave some thought to the two candidates. It speculated that PRI leaders must be wondering what would happen if PAN launched candidates in all municipal elections. Of Barrio and Baeza, it stated that both were honest and intelligent. Baeza looked like a university professor "and expressed himself as such. Barrio, on the other hand, known for his hunger strikes, is closer to the model of Ghandi or that of Ayatollah Khomeini."

And from out of the immediate past another voice emerged. Oscar Ornelas, forced from office in September 1985, broke silence. After eight months, he stated PAN had used his name badly. He declared that this would be his only statement. He affirmed his support for Governor González Herrera and the electoral reform, and stated that he was not forced out of office. All along, PAN had claimed that Ornelas' departure from the political life of Chihuahua resulted from his honesty in respecting the vote. Acción Nacional even averred that Ornelas' statement was forced out of him by a weakened PRI that wanted to demonstrate party unity.

Little by little, hints of national PRI displeasure with Chihuahua appeared. There was no doubt that the national party wanted Chihuahua firmly back in the fold. One such indication was a sudden shortfall of money for the university. Since a substantial part of the university budget comes from the national secretariat of public education, the allotment for May had not arrived by the first of the month. As a consequence, professors faced the possibility of no paychecks on May 15, and the cancellation of university travel and research costs loomed imminent. State officials took the hint and began to throw even more energy into the election of Baeza and all PRI candidates.

Both parties thus began their campaigns in an atmosphere of acrimony. They both began an early *promoción del voto* (get out the vote) drive and also disclaimed that they promoted violence. Barrio even claimed that on July 6 PAN and the state of Chihuahua would "remove the yoke of imposition that comes from the Federal District." Mighty words, but Barrio did not realize the depth of PRI commitment to bring Chihuahua back to the official party.

Another major part of the PRI campaign strategy was simply not to mention PAN. While *panistas* hammered away at electoral irregularities committed by the official party, Baeza merely proposed positive programs and refused to mention his opponent or the opposition party. By stressing *promoción del voto,* Baeza and PRI demonstrated the ostensible nonpartisan nature of their campaign.

Barrio, however, continually emphasized the abuses that plagued Mexico's political system. Even in an emotional statement of his beliefs, he could not resist the political cut and slash. He declared:

> I BELIEVE in a Mexico free of demagoguery and corruption.
> I BELIEVE in a prosperous, strong, united, and happy Mexico.
> I BELIEVE in an ordered and generous Fatherland and in a better and dignified life for all citizens.
>
> •   •   •   •
>
> I know that all this will require more than a day or even a few years because we drag with us the remnants and bad habits of centuries.
>
> •   •   •   •
>
> But I also know that these ends can exist and that there exists a means to achieve them:
> True democracy.
> To achieve this I shall deplete all of the resources and all of the deeds within my reach without falling into violence, whatever may happen to me: IT IS NOW TIME . . . .

PAN continued to pound away at PRI's fraudulent electoral practices. *Panistas* constantly emphasized a protection and respect of the vote. "Before voting," wrote Contreras Orozco, "they already talked about fraud." Added to his constant negativism came the program of civil disobedience. One thousand *peso* notes were stamped with "Respect for the Vote." Water bills went unpaid. License plates were covered in violation of Mexican law that state that auto licenses were to be unencumbered and wholly visible. Marking currency also violated Mexican law, though the practice was tolerated until March 1988.

Baeza, however, kept up his positive approach. When addressing a group of industrialists in Juárez, he stressed the need to clean up the city, to make it more presentable as a first impression of Mexico. On the same day, he visited a poor neighborhood and talked with people about transportation problems to and from the

Two recent Mexican bills, one for 1,000 pesos and the other for 5,000. On the face of the 1,000 PAN stamped the legend ``Respect for the Vote'' while on the 5,000 pesos note the PAN emblazoned ``The End to Dictatorship. Chihuahua, 1988.''

maquiladoras. There was no question that Baeza wanted his message carried as widely as possible. He successfully juxtaposed the esthetic concerns of the upper classes without coming into conflict with the survival concerns of the lower-class elements of Juárez.

But violence could not be avoided. In a demonstration in Chihuahua City, 30–40,000 workers pressed for increased salaries as they demonstrated in front of the State Police headquarters. A small riot broke out, and thirteen workers and six policemen received minor injuries. From Mexico City, Fidel Velázquez declared ominously: "We want goals . . . but also beans." In Spanish, the statement rhymed: *"Queremos goles . . . pero también frijoles."*

By early May, *panista* hints that more than peaceful protest might occur began to surface. Barrio Terrazas declared that in Chihuahua "a new revolution will be made to rescue democracy and give the popular will its value." Barrio continued that PAN had also sent a letter to the Human Rights Commission of the Organization of American States in which it decried the political repression that was occurring in Mexico. He concluded by stating that the strategy of civil disobedience had as its goal "respect for our condition as citizens and respect for the fundamental rights granted by the Constitution."

PAN launched more protests in mid-May. *Panistas* set up roadblocks all over the state as a means of showing their displeasure over PRI practices. Overall, the action was peaceful and police intervention did not occur. For an hour, roads to Parral, San Guillermo, Camargo, Jiménez, Saucillo, Juárez, and Delicias were blocked. In some respects, the PRI strategy of not mentioning PAN and its actions clearly showed up in the roadblocks. As long as they remained peaceful, there would be no police intervention.

But the PRI did have to make some sort of response to the program of civil disobedience. The national government instructed all banks to accept marked bills but to pull them out of circulation. Clearly, marking the bills was an effective strategy but could only be carried out by those who had a few thousand *pesos* to spare.

Dirty pool and disruption of PAN activity still remained an active part of the PRI game plan. In May, during a rally in Juárez, Barrio declared that he would not pay water or electric bills and that he had a blacklist of electoral frauds. During this speech a helicopter appeared overhead and flew back and forth across the area, hovering occasionally. The racket raised by the chopper made it extremely difficult to hear Barrio.

Electoral dirty tricks continued to abound. Toward the end of the campaign, a forged document bearing Baeza's name "confessed" to his intimate relations with drug smugglers. In response, on election day a handout bearing the PAN colors and logo asked voters to boycott the election as the ultimate act of civil disobedience.

The United States showed a high degree of interest in the state elections in Chihuahua — a first, in view of the usual lack of interest shown about Mexico north of the Río Bravo.

Immediately prior to the elections, the Gallup Organization conducted a poll that showed Fernando Baeza ahead by fifty-seven percent. PAN candidates, however, were expected to garner at least thirty-eight percent of the vote.

A false calm prevailed in the last phase of the campaign. Baeza had declared that he believed there would be clean elections and that there would be no need for spending extra money to assure their fairness. The state judicial police declared that it had 1,500 men ready, though it believed that they would not be necessary. Election day remained strangely calm, though reports of voting irregularities began to surface.

While a superficial peace covered the state, as election time drew closer, some of the uglier aspects of political polarization were felt. On July 1, Alvarez began a hunger strike to protest electoral fraud. In spite of the peacefulness and the integrity of most candidates on all sides, the spectre of violence continued to haunt Chihuahua. While there had been few direct confrontations, signs of polarization appeared. The simple sounding of an auto horn often led to the exchange of ugly words and vicious verbal recriminations.

Jaime Bermúdez, the distinguished Juárez industrialist and PRI candidate for mayor of Ciudad Juárez, declared that the economic crisis had given PAN its greatest impetus. Bermúdez, playing both sides of the political fence, had supported Barrio in 1983 when the latter sought to remain independent. But now the powerful industrialist wanted to sound every bit the independent *chihuahuense*. He made slashing attacks on the central government, declaring that:

The government has to pay us. I am going to México [D. F.] to collect what we are owed. I will demand what is owed with specific numbers. I am not going to ask for anything. Rather I will recover what the Seguro Social system has taken out of Juárez and with that we will do some marvelous things.

The local race in Juárez clearly seemed a contest between PRI and PAN. Bermúdez, the godfather of the *maquiladora* program, faced a formidable opponent in Gustavo Elizondo. Both men were considered honest and showed a high degree of integrity. In Bermúdez' case, this was in direct counterpoint to the political corruption that so often characterized the PRI.

In this atmosphere 200 foreign journalists presented their credentials to the state electoral commission. The foreign press correctly assessed the importance of Chihuahua in the political life of Mexico. American journalists and policymakers determined that in large measure Mexico's economic chaos grew from political disorder. Contreras Orozco said that "the financial disarray that daily complicates the external debt is the progeny of a disorderly and uncontrolled political system."

But in spite of the large presence of the foreign press, electoral irregularities did appear before the election. In an INFONAVIT housing development in Chihuahua City, there was only one polling place for 11,000 people. It was calculated that these citizens would have to vote at a speed of five milliseconds per vote between 8:00 A.M. and 6:00 P.M., nonstop. Moreover, an additional two million ballots were printed without explanation. The Mexican army also made its presence felt by patrolling the streets in cities such as Juárez, Chihuahua, Cuahtémoc, and Nuevo Casas Grandes, where problems were expected.

And then came election day, July 6. As expected, a massive turnout occurred. In 1983, thirty-one percent of the eligible voters cast ballots; in 1986, that figure jumped to fifty-one percent, about a sixty-seven percent increase. But the PRI overplayed its hand. The elections had been orderly. There was no violence. News of irregularities would creep into the picture later on, but Manuel Gurria Ordóñez, the representative of the PRI national electoral commission, announced at 7:00 P.M., barely an hour after the polls closed, that the official party had scored a statewide triumph. Very few counts had even been completed by then. The real problem with the Gurria announcement came in that he would exit from Chihuahua and leave a mess for the *chihuahuenses* to clean up, simply because the *secretaría de gobernación* panicked. Typically, the state found itself stuck with problems created by federal intervention.

The Gurria announcement touched off cries of fraud from PAN. Soon PAN began to enumerate apparent irregularities. They pointed out that PAN pollwatchers had been excluded from about one-half of the polling places. In addition, out of twenty-two major towns in Chihuahua, sixteen did not know how many polling places they had. One town only had 1,000 voters, while another had 25,000. These early reports led Baeza to conclude somewhat reluctantly that there might be some fraud, especially since PAN did not win a single *municipio*.

Thus, while PAN protested and Baeza acknowledged the possibility of error, political groups on the left decided to remove themselves from the fray until the battle lines had been defined. Early on, however, opponents to PAN, including PRI and parties on the left, had criticized the civil disobedience campaign. They noted that such action disrupted the functioning of an orderly society and was ultimately irresponsible.

Quickly, both Baeza and Barrio declared that there would be no violence. Barrio announced that the campaign of civil disobedience would continue, and PAN opponents quickly declared such action as subverting the public order. The CDP, an outspoken opponent of PAN, demonstrated in favor of the principle of civil disobedience. Declared CDP leaders: "We are disobedient with regard to the injustices of which we are victims." Additionally, they accused PAN of "copying us in our disobedience."

Barrio stridently decried the fraud that had been perpetrated. "Never," he protested, "will I say that I lost. Never!" He ominously promised to prove the widespread existence of fraud at a later date. Baeza joined Barrio in decrying fraud without ever admitting that it existed in the July election. He declared that no one benefited from such irregularities and declared himself the first to desire the prevalence of truth.

But Baeza also took advantage of the opportunity to state that "*chihuahuenses* want change. They have demonstrated that they want to believe, and we as candidates should respond to that conviction . . . . We have an obligation to have the *chihuahuenses* believe in us."

Two days after the election, PAN launched another part of its strategy. Party leaders began to talk about asking for a nullification of the election because the results of that contest had been clearly rigged by PRI. In Juárez, the Centro Empresarial (Enterprise Center) declared fraudulent elections.

Also two days after the election, the preliminary results of the hotly contested races appeared. *El Diario de Juárez* reported that Baeza had garnered 298,000 votes as opposed to Barrio, who trailed by 172,000. Additionally, the PRI won forty out of sixty-seven *municipios* outright. This announcement, however, did not meet with immediate approval from the opposition. The Movimiento Democrático Electoral (Democratic Electoral Movement) announced that it would convene a people's tribunal to analyze the election results. Immediate accusations of ballot box stuffing, people voting more than once, and the removal of opposition pollwatchers surfaced. Moreover, PRI was accused of slowing down the count in order to hold the people at bay. It was hoped that they would become disgusted and forget about the whole thing.

With eighty-four percent of the vote tallied by July 8, PAN claimed a sweeping victory. It also made the claim that had it not been for electoral irregularities, the party would have won even more handsomely. Of course, the PRI differed greatly from the PAN contention. Acción Nacional continued to hammer away at PRI about its unscrupulous electoral fraud.

Inexorably, National Action began to build its case against the official party. One action was to document instances of PAN pollwatchers being excluded from performing their function by election officials at the different polling places. The pollwatcher constituted the key to fraud in a Mexican election. If the individual was kept away from the polling place, government officials could do as they pleased. And this they did do. Without pollwatchers around, officials merely "voted" those who had not appeared to cast a ballot. Since voter lists are not signed at the precinct level, it proved relatively simple to cast a vote for an absentee.

Whether ingenuous or crafty, Fernando Baeza Meléndez, the putative governor-elect, declared that he wanted no votes that had been obtained fraudulently. He stated, however, that under no circumstance would his party concede a single honest vote. This was the democratic way.

But any statement by the official candidate failed to mollify *panista* leaders. Guillermo Prieto Luján, the regional president of National Action, declared that PAN would accept only a nullification of the election. He announced that "PAN has enough force to establish a power parallel to PRI's." What became a call to arms spread throughout the state of Chihuahua.

Panistas did not wait long before they made their feelings known. On July 8 a very mixed group of protesters — students, well-to-do matrons, known businessmen — participated in a blockade of the twenty-five most important intersections in Chihuahua City. There was no doubt that PAN feelings ran deeply about this particular election. On the morning of July 14, women activists staged demonstrations. Acción Nacional placed ballot boxes at the Plaza de Armas in Chihuahua City to show that there were more PAN voters than those subscribing to PRI, and certainly more than those counted by the electoral commission. In Parral, the protest went beyond demonstrations. They burned a PRI van and blocked access to the local electoral commission office when the results were submitted for consideration.

But the government also felt that it must do something to maintain order. Knowing full well that Juárez would be a hot spot, the Mexican army moved in and seized control of the police headquarters. Instantly, PAN began to scream "Martial law!" Cries of military repression forced a response from the Mexican army. The commander of the infantry battalion in Juárez declared that "it is untrue that Juárez is under a state of siege, nor are the police under the Army's orders. Further, it is untrue that the army could intervene if the order and tranquility of the city is disturbed because that is the responsibility of the Municipal Police." To assure a tranquil election remained the only function of the army.

A week had transpired since the election, but still, the results remained inconclusive. The longer the process dragged on, the more polemical the conflict became. Tension began to build, and leaders and candidates of PRI and PAN felt the pressure. As a matter of fact, the Mexican political system groaned under the strain. In all probability, the biggest risk in the days after the election appeared in the strong possibility of violent, fratricidal conflict among *chihuahuenses*. Complicating this were overt, unquestionable instances of fraud by the PRI and the obvious political immaturity of PAN, which refused to accept the idea that they might have lost legitimately.

Finally, in the long, grueling process of electoral results, the first official count appeared. On the surface, PRI scored a 2:1 vic-

Student protestors burning a plush duck, el Pato, in the courtyard of the Government Palace, Chihuahua City, August 1985.

Photo by the author.

Student protestors gathered outside the Government Palace, Chihuahua City, August 1985.

Photo by the author.

tory over PAN. Fernando Baeza won 401,167 votes, while Barrio gained only 231,109. To be sure, protests started. In Chihuahua City, twenty-four businesses shut down in an attempt to bring local commerce to a halt. In Juárez, an ugly tenor came to dominate the protest.

PAN leaders had every right to protest, as did all of northern Mexico. PAN could ascribe its phenomenal growth in the north to the relative prosperity in the area. Between 1980 and 1985, for example, Chihuahua sustained a growth rate of 8.5 percent — almost three times the national average. PAN simply wanted more local autonomy in order to let the big money operate more freely and to keep the federal government out of local economic affairs. As a consequence, this very factor served as a principal motivator for PAN protest. Since many of their followers constituted the economic backbone of Chihuahua, they wanted to share in political decision-making that directly affected them.

In this light, Pablo Emilio Madero, relative of Francisco Madero, the apostle of the Revolution, appeared in Chihuahua. Madero was the national president of PAN. He requested that Governor Saúl González Herrera nullify the elections since so much controversy revolved around them. He did not, however, satisfy all of his political coreligionists. He directly told them that no doubt existed about elements of fraud in the election, but there was no definitive proof that twenty percent of the voting places (the number required by law for nullification) had been involved. Madero also criticized the blockade of bridges, the hunger strikes, and the disruption of traffic through the blockage of streets and highways. He went so far as to ask Luis H. Alvarez to give up his hunger strike. He remained especially critical of PAN in Chihuahua because they rejected the seats allocated to them in the Chamber of Deputies.

President Miguel de la Madrid went public. He called for an investigation of the election and asked protesters to cease their activity. He was seconded in this by different labor organizations, which joined in the call for a peaceful solution to allow the judicial system to work. The Electrician's Union went so far as to say that PAN attempts to obtain the governorship could lead to "conflicts that would disrupt the peace." PAN stalwarts, however, refused to heed the call. On July 18, 5,000 *panistas* blocked the Pan American Highway outside of Juárez. In Cuahtémoc, protests also erupted, and intimations of Church involvement began to appear.

Ciudad Juárez proved to be the most volatile spot in Chihuahua. *Juarenses* genuinely believed that they had rejected PRI completely. They demanded that *gobernación* nullify the elections. They even staged a plebiscite to demonstrate that PAN did, in fact, have the votes. Transparent ballot boxes and ballots with indelible ink were used. The results of this unofficial tally: PAN — 83,309; PRI — 1,344.

Protests in Juárez continued to erupt. On July 25 the Córdova international bridge was seized. Francisco Barrio Terrazas exhorted his followers to remain firm in their convictions and justified the depth of their protests. He called for a rally on August 7 to maintain solidarity with those leaders on a hunger strike. He further claimed that a great deal of support existed for the blockade. In this he proved correct, for the protesters received ready supplies of food and refreshments throughout the five-day blockade.

The blockade had its economic effect in Juárez. From the first seizure in mid-July and then the lengthy blockade, business in Juárez fell by ninety percent. Usually, anywhere from 100 to 1,000 protesters manned the blockade stations. But a backlash did occur, for the business community of Juárez began to split.

There was no question that an effective boycott of business, the blockade of bridges, and sit-ins at government offices had an impact. Businessmen pointed out that they were in trouble and began to refuse to support the fight against the government. Such activities, it was claimed, could lead to anarchy. This clearly indicated that PAN had strayed from its ideals of order and progress. Moreover, such an unsettled state might convince foreign investors to pull out of Juárez, where the bulk of the *maquiladora* industry was located. To cap it off, tourists had quit visiting Juárez.

All of the brouhaha raised by PAN demonstrated that it could call out the forces if necessary. On July 29 they voluntarily ceased the blockade of the Córdova bridge that served as a major artery between El Paso and Ciudad Juárez. Traffic again began to flow normally. But PAN was far from finished, for Francisco Barrio Terrazas announced that on July 30 more protests would take place. He called a meeting that would terminate in a torchlight march to mourn the death of democracy. Rather weakly, PRI responded that it had won cleanly.

Political protest was all fine if the cash register was not affected. Juárez businesses more and more rejected the blockades and

shutdowns of businesses as a form of protest. The CDP — proverbial political gadfly — accused the government of excessive toler-
ance toward PAN hooligans because so much of the big money in
Mexico supported PAN. Aside from the usual blather from CDP,
the reality remained that industrial activity in both Mexico and the
United States suffered a forty percent drop and that some U.S.
firms had suspended credit to Mexican companies.

Throughout the spring and summer of 1985, the United States
took a keen interest in Chihuahua. Heavy United States investment
in the state clearly justified the interest. But this interest took on an
ideological overtone that more clearly placed the Reagan administration, wittingly or not, on the side of the PAN. In May, Senator
Jesse Helms, darling of the fundamentalist right, began to make
noises about the possibility of U.S. intervention in Chihuahua to
assure a clean election. The U.S. consul general in Juárez declared
that official U.S. policy respected Mexico's internal affairs and pro-
cedures. Mexico, however, still filed a formal protest with the Department of State. Edwin Meese, U.S. attorney general, declared
that Helms did not represent the administration's view about Mexico.

Throughout the summer, though, Helms refused to shut up.
He blasted Mexican efforts to clean up the drug trade. He accused
Mexico of foul political practices and unsavory international con-
nections. By July, he openly called for United States intervention.
What he did, according to one Texas politician, was to create a
sense of hysteria similar to the one that led to the invasion of Veracruz in 1914. Helms demanded that some American troops be re-
called from Europe and reassigned along the U.S.–Mexico border
because, in his judgment, no doubt existed about fraud in the July
6 election. Armed with a righteousness so typical of the fundamentalist right, Helms collared some of his Republican colleagues in
the senate to take up the cudgel against political corruption in
Mexico.

In August, five U.S. senators — all of them Republicans —
proposed that the senate request that President Miguel de la Madrid nullify the Chihuahua elections. All of the senators came from
border states or from heavily Hispanic ares. Denis Deconcini, the
lone Democrat, of Arizona said that the move was not aimed at offending "the fine citizens of Mexico" or in favor of any party.
Rather, he condemned "the Chihuahua elections where thousands

of voters witnessed widespread fraud." Mexicans viewed this as overt meddling into Mexican internal affairs. More than anything, Helms and his cohorts probably neutralized the good relations built up by Reagan and De la Madrid over a four-year period and retarded the growth of effective and durable relations between Mexico and the United States.

Panistas were encouraged by the senate statements. Some National Action leaders made noises about seeking political asylum in the United States. Chihuahua's attorney general, Enrique Aguilar Pérez, indicated that they would not be eligible for asylum, for such a grant came only because of political persecution. PAN was not being persecuted. It was merely held accountable for the damage caused by protest excesses. The government could not be blamed if it attempted to maintain order. Quite simply, those who broke the law would bear the responsibility for the act.

But *panista* leaders remained undeterred. In August, six of them plus the mayor of Parral asked for political asylum in the United States because of warnings that included death threats. The United States, already burned by Helms and his buddies, denied asylum. Prieto Luján declared that he thought the request for asylum unwarranted, though he indicated that PAN members had a right to protect themselves. He also declared himself unsurprised by the request considering the political situation in Chihuahua.

Still, the political process continued to function. On August 4, PAN went before the judge of the First Judicial District with a request for nullification of the election. This request had failed before the state congress, which transforms into the electoral college during an election year. Four days later, the electoral college declared Baeza the winner. PAN unity began to crack. *Panista* deputy Rubén Salgado Durán broke ranks and signed the verification of the election.

The move came as a great blow to PAN. Had Salgado Durán sold out to PRI? Should he be subjected to party discipline and expelled from the PAN? Salgado Durán declared that Barrio's *neopanismo* was causing serious injury to the party and that he was under no obligation to follow the dictates of Prieto Luján. As a consequence, Salgado Durán found himself expelled from PAN. *Neopanismo* struck yet another blow at the party traditionalists.

By August 10, Miguel de la Madrid tried to put the Chihuahua situation within a broad perspective. He saw it as nothing more than a propaganda war on all sides, and, since these were state and local elections, declared himself incompetent to sit in judgment. While this was an obvious ploy to avoid action, De la Madrid did state clearly that:

> Elections are won by votes and not with demonstrations, hunger strikes, or moral pressures. I know that PAN had an important percentage of the vote, but they did not, according to the information I have, win a majority of the votes.

He also assured Mexico that because of her internal stability, there existed little chance of violence in Chihuahua. But in that prediction, De la Madrid proved wrong.

Parral again showed some violent tendencies. Reflecting the PAN activism throughout the state, *panistas* blockaded eight banks in Parral as well as some government offices. In order to get the attention of the population, a sharp-sounding mining horn announced the PAN activity. Almost spontaneously, similar actions began in Coahuila and Tamaulipas, states to the east of Chihuahua where in late 1985 similar political problems existed.

By now, Francisco Barrio began to change his tune. In a speech at the University of Texas–El Paso in September, he outlined the history of official party dominance of Mexican politics. He also declared that his movement was essentially nonviolent but ominously noted that the potential for violence always existed when a government refused to concede basic political rights. PAN victories in other states would be difficult to achieve because the government feared a loss of power.

In late September, Barrio carried his message farther into the United States when he and other PAN spokesmen went to New York, where De la Madrid was scheduled to visit. Barrio and a group of thirty-five people participated in a demonstration in front of De la Madrid's hotel. They called for "justice in Chihuahua, Durango, and Oaxaca." So insistent were the protesters that Mayor Ed Koch moved the welcoming ceremony for Mexico's president inside the hotel. Most of the protesters came from Chicago, where a strong Mexican community exists. One PAN spokesman warned that these protests could spread to other cities.

But PRI winners in Chihuahua recognized the power of the opposition. Jaime Bermúdez, the successful mayoral candidate in Juárez, came under heavy political fire from his own party because of the multipartisan nature of some of his appointments. The PRI head in Juárez criticized Bermúdez for not consulting the party leadership about some of his appointees. One appointment that met with particular rancor was that of Luis Calderón Trueba, the son of a prominent *panista* family, as municipal secretary. Obviously, Bermúdez was turning away from the party hacks and looked for competence more than affiliation.

PAN continued its protests into October. The acting mayor of Juárez declared that PAN would be held liable for all damages incurred by its activities. PAN responded that allegations of excesses would receive appropriate investigation and also assured local authorities that there would be increased security at all future party functions.

Meanwhile, in Chihuahua City, Barrio held a rally on the steps of the Palacio de Gobierno. Insults between PAN and PRI almost turned to physical violence. Newly inaugurated Governor Fernando Baeza declared that the events in Parral, Juárez, and Chihuahua clearly showed how strongly freedom of expression was guaranteed and further stated:

> Sometimes it is better to tolerate the consequences of excesses of this freedom than to restrict. There will not be violent repression. Democratic processes will be maintained, but in cases of excess in which the laws are broken, legal action will be taken.

Despite Baeza's good intentions, Barrio continued to press. Almost messianically, Barrio and Gustavo Elizondo Aguilar, the PAN candidate for mayor of Juárez and newly elected state leader, went to Washington, DC, to carry their protests to the Organization of American States (OAS).

Barrio and Elizondo wanted to lay their alleged proofs of electoral fraud before the OAS and the Inter-American Human Rights Commission. While they did not appear hopeful that much could be done, at least for the time being, they did emphasize that if the Mexican government did not change its attitudes, they might have to go to the Commission on Human Rights in Costa Rica. Both Barrio and Elizondo stressed that their action was wholly that of PAN and not of any other political party in Mexico.

The PAN presentation brought a quick response from the OAS, so much so that Barrio and Elizondo were caught somewhat unawares. The OAS asked for documentation about fraudulent electoral practices. Rodolfo Elizondo Torres, the *panista* mayor of

Durango and ex-gubernatorial candidate, declared that OAS action did not constitute external intervention in Mexican affairs. What PAN did, he argued, was to take a protest of electoral fraud to a more neutral body. What he hoped to accomplish was to throw into question the entire electoral system of Mexico. This case became the first instance of electoral fraud brought before the OAS.

The 1986 election in Chihuahua also threw into stark relief the role of the Church in Mexican political life. For more than a century, severe restrictions on clerical political activity had dotted Mexican law. The Constitution of 1917 clearly made the Church a juridical nonentity. In the 1920s, a civil war was fought in which the Church remained outside the system. By the 1980s, however, all of that began to change.

In 1983 and 1985, the Church became increasingly vocal in its attempt to attain some political rights. Always couching their arguments in moral tones, Church leaders began to press for their rights as Mexican citizens and as moral leaders of the community. PRI and leftist opposition groups came to criticize the alleged alignment of the Church with the PAN. By 1986, the different episacies of Chihuahua took strong and concerted action.

No longer could the Church remain silent on the problem of electoral fraud. On July 9, 1986, clerics complained from the pulpits that ballot boxes had been stuffed and that other electoral irregularities had marred the political scene. Carefully, they refused to align themselves with any one political party and declared the Church position against violence. But Churchmen did emphasize that the people should not allow the imposition of candidates. In addition, the clergy supported civil disobedience when no other recourse remained open.

Four days later (July 13), a meeting of bishops from Chihuahua at Ojinaga brought on another attack on governmental imposition of candidates. In a pastoral letter prepared by the bishops, the Church referred to itself as a Good Samaritan who helped save the people from fraud. They also let it be known that on Sunday, July 20, all churches would close for the day in response to the grave social injustices committed in the elections. The spectre of the Cristero Revolt loomed before the official party.

But the Church merely acted in the tradition of a socially active corporate body. Following the dicta of councils and popes since

John XXIII, the Church in Chihuahua began to flex some muscles. In 1983 a pastoral letter entitled "Vote Responsibly" exhorted the citizens to exercise their right. Obviously, the large turnout in that election could in part be attributed to the Church's moral suasion. In 1986 the pastoral letter "Christian Political Coherence" reemphasized the importance of exercising the right of suffrage. In neither case did the Church leaders argue for PAN, though the majority of *panistas* openly identified with the Church. Implicitly, however, the Church became identified with PAN because of its criticisms of Mexico's political system. But PRI found itself in a quandary because its gubernatorial candidate declared himself a believer. As a consequence, the traditionally anticlerical official party ceased all references to the Church.

The Church kept up the pressure. The pastoral letter openly stated that if lay Catholics acted in a truly Christian manner, such corruption as existed would disappear. The extension of Christian principles to all facets of Mexican life would automatically cleanse the body politic of the evils that beset it.

Archbishop of Chihuahua Adalberto Almeida y Merino became the most vocal of the Chihuahua bishops. On July 9, at the popular tribunal held in the Plaza de Armas in front of the Cathedral in Chihuahua City, the archbishop said that citizens must defend their right to vote even if it meant taking steps beyond the law. Electoral fraud negated the right to vote because it made suffrage meaningless.

The PRI's only comment was to complain loudly that they had been prejudged. The threat to close all churches on July 20 was removed, but the bishops of Chihuahua kept up a steady stream against the official party. In a new pastoral letter issued in August and entitled "Moral Justice over the Electoral Process," the bishops called for a nullification of the Chihuahua elections. While they recognized that they had little legal standing with their letter, Almeida y Merino and his brother bishops did want to assert some moral authority. They also asked for the Vatican Council to assist in the fight against injustice, oppression, intolerance, and the dictatorship of a single-party system. Such episcopal activism would have consequences for both the Church and opposition parties in the future.

While PAN had an ally in the Church, it also had an implacable enemy in the CDP. All attempts at business boycotts were undercut by CDP activity. Their ambulatory merchants went into the streets and sold their goods in front of the closed businesses. In Chihuahua City, Calle Libertad (the main commercial district) saw CDP vendors peddling smuggled goods. These *fayuqueros* (purveyors of smuggled merchandise) had an absolute bonanza and reaped large profits from their sales.

PAN attitude toward the CDP had hardened the latter's attitude toward the former. Clearly, CDP might have helped National Action. But because PAN refused to tolerate *defensa popular* and its civil disruptions, the lines were drawn. PAN could expect nothing but sabotage from CDP.

PRI probably overplayed its hand in the 1986 election in Chihuahua. Many state party leaders felt that with Baeza as a candidate there was no need for the central government to become actively involved. Instead, *"se les fué la mano"* (its hand slipped). The *secretaría de gobernación* overreacted. People voted for Baeza because he was a presentable candidate. He appealed to a sufficiently broad spectrum of the electorate. That made the usual political hanky-panky of the past unnecessary.

No doubt exists about the panic in Mexico City over Chihuahua. PRI won all sixty-seven municipal elections as well as the governorship. Yet, strangely enough, Mexico's political system did undergo change, for in 1986 the country came as close to true electoral pluralism as it ever had in the twentieth century.

What vitiated much of this new experience was the troglodytic attitudes of some of the PRI fossils in Mexico City who quaked at the thought of a *panista* or any opposition victory. The official political party existed for itself. A new majority party would sweep out job-holders in order to make room for its own party faithful.

At the same time, PAN acted like a somewhat spoiled and indulged child. The idea that they might lose simply escaped them. They had had a viable and attractive candidate in Francisco Barrio Terrazas. But then, so did PRI with Fernando Baeza Meléndez. This was a factor that eluded the *panistas*. Baeza was no mere party hack. He was as much a *chihuahuense* as the *panistas*, but he maintained his independence within the official party rather than outside of it. PAN had no monopoly on *chihuahuense* independence.

In its campaign, PAN proved a bit paranoid. Even before the election was held, they based a large part of their appeal upon official electoral fraud. While there was provable irregularity in 1985, a positive picture of PAN dissipated in 1986. Almost immediately, Barrio Terrazas and the *panistas* began to attack electoral corruption months before the election was even held. They hammered away at this theme. The positive aspects of the *panista* program became deluged in a wave of accusations about the upcoming fraudulent elections. While PRI certainly panicked, so too did the PAN.

PAN also committed another tragic error. It opened the door to criticism about its close ties with the United States and its open sympathy with some of the Republican Party's most vocal conservative spokesmen. With friends like Jesse Helms, there was little need for enemies. Helms' call for intervention provided the opposition to PAN with a perfect opening. They could point at PAN as mere instruments of Reagan administration policy. The PRI noted that a lot of anti-Mexican propaganda filled the U.S. press because of the Chihuahua election. Even the most virulently independent *chihuahuense* could respond to the allegation and leap to the defense of Mexico.

Finally, there is no doubt that corruption existed in the campaign. The instances of irregularities clearly indicate that the official party was absolutely determined to rescue Chihuahua from itself. *Chihuahuenses* rightfully felt angered by such an attitude from the central government. Barroom gossip — boozy but informative, if one can remember it — clearly expressed the general sentiment. Chihuahua had been taking care of itself for over two centuries without any help from Mexico City. They did not need it now. Such an undercurrent made the presidential election of 1988 an interesting and exciting contest.

The back page of a 1988 PAN leaflet. It shows a picture of the PAN presidential candidate Manuel J. Clouthier ``Maquio." The text reads ``Together we can accomplish the plan for change. Together we can assure that democracy and justice will prevail in Mexico. Together we can build a Mexico to which we anxiously aspire. MAQUIO. THE LEADER FOR CHANGE. PARTY OF NATIONAL ACTION."

CHAPTER 7

Mexico Elects a President, We Think!

December 1, 1988. Mexico City. There he stood — diminutive, bald, an almost Chaplinesque mustache under his nose, and ears like satellite dishes protruding from the sides of his head. He had a bookish look to him, almost a stereotype of a shy, retiring academic rather than an active member of an all-powerful political party. Carlos Salinas de Gortari prepared to accept the presidential sash from his predecessor, Miguel de la Madrid Hurtado, and become yet another president in the long succession of official candidates to fill Mexico's presidential chair.

Yet there remained a critical difference. Salinas' election, disputed from the outset, still left the uneasy feeling in the guts of most Mexicans that the PRI had again rigged an election and thwarted the popular will. Opposition members of the Chamber of Deputies walked out of the inauguration, protesting the alleged fraud. In so doing, they left Salinas and the PRI with the smallest majority in twentieth-century Mexican history. PRI hegemony seemed to be breaking down, and all of Salinas' promised reforms might not be able to keep the party in power the next time around.

Salinas de Gortari already had a nickname. Even before the

inauguration, *chihuahuenses* called him the mushroom, *El Hongo* —
short, bald, in the dark, and possessed of hallucinogenic promises.
The growing cynicism about Mexico's political future continued to
permeate Chihuahua, and in the long, grueling preparation for the
presidential struggle, *chihuahuenses* provided a mixture of optimism
and cynical realism about the future of democratic institutions in
Mexico.

Salinas' selection as the official candidate followed the time-
honored traditions of the PRI. Prospective candidates had their
names floated among party faithful and the public in general. By
the time the president of Mexico decided on his successor, the number of candidates had narrowed to two or three. The selection, usually made in the summer before the election, still remained a secret
except to a very few PRI sachems. Salinas de Gortari had occupied
the old cabinet post formerly held by De la Madrid, secretary of
planning and budget. Another candidate, Manuel Bartlett Díaz,
served as secretary of *gobernación,* a man who was instrumental in
the ultimate removal of Oscar Ornelas from the governorship of
Chihuahua.

Party war-horses much preferred Bartlett Díaz. He was a
party hard-liner who was less prone to the reformist rhetoric of the
bookish Salinas. The latter, a Harvard-trained Ph.D., was the consummate technocrat — highly trained as a theoretician but who
had never held an elective office.

A degree of tension began to build in the summer of 1987. Who
was the *tapado,* the covered one? By October of that year the announcement was made. Carlos Salinas de Gortari would carry the
PRI banner in the electoral lists in July 1988. A major difference in
the *destapamiento* (the uncovering) took place. Fidel Velázquez, the
labor czar of Mexico, did not make the announcement as in the
past. Mexicans took this as a signal that the old man's power was
waning, that he was being shunted aside by other, more powerful
elements within the PRI.

While political maneuvering took place within the PRI, the
opposition also began to gather force. A major threat to the ranks of
the PRI came from the governor of Michoacán, Cuahtémoc Cárdenas, son of the late President Lázaro Cárdenas. By 1986, Cárdenas began to voice his criticisms about the lack of reform and
commitment to revolutionary ideals by the official party. By late
1987, he formally broke with the party and formed the Frente De-

mocrático Nacional (National Democratic Front, or FDN). Soon dissident left-wing elements coalesced around Cárdenas and posed a definite threat to the PRI hegemony, especially in central and southern Mexico.

PAN leaders also began to make bellicose noises. As early as January 1987, the national PAN declared that it had no objection to a woman as its candidate in 1988. PAN leadership emphasized that many capable women filled its ranks, and that it would select its candidate on the ability of that individual to draw votes and the capacity and experience of the candidate. Unlike the PRI, it would not rely on the secretive and undemocratic *tapado* system.

One month later, Francisco Barrio Terrazas gave a lecture at New Mexico State University in which he flatly stated that the 1988 race would be controlled totally by the PRI. He said: "We are completely certain that the 1988 elections will be controlled 100 percent by the PRI, and we are also sure that this will no doubt push the population toward a revolution." Barrio's statement, coming in early 1987, already showed the promise of PAN bellicosity and the threat of social disruption should the PRI win the election.

By this time, Barrio had taken himself out of the presidential race. Although he had made earlier intimations about national aspirations, he announced himself preparing for the presidential contest of 1994. He endorsed two potential candidates: Fernando Canales Clarión, former candidate for the governorship of Durango, and Manuel Jesús Clouthier, PAN candidate for the governorship of Sinaloa. Both represented northern Mexico and drew upon the strong northern linkages that connected the PAN in the north.

In mid-February, the national PAN elected Luis H. Alvarez as its president. Alvarez moved quickly to take some of the fire out of Barrio's firebrand speechmaking. The white-haired, slightly aristocratic Alvarez decried violence and pledged PAN to follow a course of nonviolence and to combat government corruption. He declared: "I don't believe in violence because violence has shown us that fear builds governments that are irrational, unjust, criminal, and dishonest. It is efforts of human conscience that produce historic events that benefit humankind."

During the early months of 1987, the PRI struck at a strong, informal base of PAN support. A revised electoral code imposed strict, heavy fines on priests and nuns who overtly became political activists. The bishop of Juárez openly criticized the new code. As a consequence, the government suspended the sending of goods from San Diego, California, to the Diocese of Ciudad Juárez for the support of the needy. The government averred that Church officials used these goods for PAN propaganda. Archbishop of Chihuahua Almeida y Merino protested vociferously. He stated that the goods were distributed on the basis of need, and he added that in all probability PRI worthies also received their fair share of the goods. In large measure, the move by the government against the Church was interpreted in Chihuahua as reprisal for the Church's criticism of the electoral fiasco of 1986.

In March 1987 the newspaper *El Norte,* of Chihuahua City, awarded Archbishop Almeida y Merino the Prize of Excellence because of his social services for the people of Chihuahua and for his public consciousness. Archbishop Almeida had founded "democracy workshops" as a means of protesting electoral fraud. The general director of the newspaper, Juan Antonio Rodríguez, declared that for many years the archbishop had been "an enthusiastic social fighter."

One year later, candidate Salinas de Gortari met with the archbishop of Chihuahua and the three other bishops of the archdiocese. He hoped to reach an accord with these influential prelates, for he sensed that subtle though active Church opposition would jeopardize the PRI position in Chihuahua and the north in general.

While the PRI and Church officials fenced with each other, PAN set about nominating a candidate. In open convention, they selected Manuel Clouthier, nicknamed Maquio, of Sinaloa. Clouthier, born of a French father, was educated at the Instituto Tecnólogico de Monterrey, one of the country's most prestigious private schools. He also attended school in the United States. In both the U.S. and at Monterrey he played American football, a game quite popular in northern Mexico. He was a 250-pound defensive tackle. Bearded and burly, Clouthier remained essentially a patrician farmer. He launched early into his criticism of the government.

In early spring 1988, Clouthier decried the constant meddling of the government in economic matters and advanced the traditional PAN position *vis à vis* a free market. He viewed the *ejido* system as a sham that stole incentive from the peasants and made them less productive. He believed that the *ejidatarios* should receive title to their lands in order to give them the impetus to produce. Always a bit earthy, Clouthier drew a fecund analogy about land reform. He saw the earth as a woman. "You must love it," he said, "caress it, make it fertile. I want my wife for myself. I don't want her on loan from the government."

PAN also struck at the central government's almost constant intervention in local affairs. To Clouthier and his followers the local unit of government constituted the basic sociopolitical organization of Mexico. This governmental form chronically suffered the tampering of Mexico City to the detriment of local interests. Clouthier and his staff hammered away at the PRI, hoping to make a dent in the almost invincible nature of a party owned and controlled by the government.

Throughout the early spring of 1988, the hard-hitting PAN campaign brought shouts of derision from the *chilangos* in Mexico City. The sobriquet of *bárbaro del norte* (northern barbarian) was applied to the *panistas* in Chihuahua and throughout the north. They revelled in it. Clouthier proudly declared his barbarity. Bumper stickers issued by PAN in Chihuahua said, *"Soy bárbaro del norte"* (I am a northern barbarian). Emblazoned on the sticker along with the PAN logo was a revolutionary-looking character somewhat reminiscent of Pascual Orozco.

In many ways, Clouthier seemed a rebel chieftain, a role he played with real gusto. He lambasted the government for its chronic interference and its violations of personal freedom. To many *chihuahuenses*, Clouthier seemed a reincarnation of Pancho Villa. Though not from Chihuahua, he still had that streak of northern pride and independence that separated the north from its more malleable brothers to the south.

One campaign leaflet issued by PAN drew parallels between Pancho Villa, Francisco Madero, and the *panista* tradition in northern Mexico. The party sought to capitalize on some of the revolutionary imagery that emanated from northern Mexico. In so doing, they hoped to dispel the notion that they were "conservative" but rather in line with the revolutionary traditions of Villa and Madero. In fact, they accused the PRI of being conservative because the official party refused to admit change.

Throughout the campaign, PAN hammered away at its free-market themes and at the possibility of continued civil disobedience in the event of political fraud. PAN wanted to demonstrate that it did have the vote-getting capacity to surpass its sixteen percent showing in 1982. Yet it would not compromise and make common cause with other opposition parties who were philosophically opposed to PAN principles.

Various leftist parties began to make noises about a coalition to protest electoral fraud and to defend the vote. Not surprisingly, however, PAN refused to join with the left because of the differences that separated them.

In Chihuahua the CDP, the proverbial PAN nemesis, began to think of itself as a political party rather than a mere advocacy group. It drew up petitions to be included as a political group on the ballot in the upcoming election. This dispute would drag on throughout the spring of 1988. While ultimately successful, the CDP succeeded more as a gadfly than as a powerful political force.

In mid-April the CDP demanded 500 lots for housing its constituents from the municipal government in Chihuahua City. CDP leaders announced that neither PRI nor PAN would be allowed to campaign in areas under CDP control. This prompted an immediate response from PAN leaders in Chihuahua. They met with Governor Fernando Baeza Meléndez about the CDP threats. Baeza assured the PAN that they had free access to all areas of the state for campaign purposes. With this assurance, PAN announced that it intended to go to all parts of Chihuahua. The major issue would be the crisis that afflicted Mexico.

Salinas de Gortari demonstrated a keen political sense when he traveled to Chihuahua in late March. In Ciudad Juárez, he began to underscore his own northern roots. Salinas pointed out that his family came from Nuevo León, one of the hotbeds of *panismo*, and that he understood how northerners felt. Fifty thousand party faithful greeted his statements in Juárez. He did a fine job of stealing the show. For two or three days, Chihuahuan newspapers did not mention Manuel Clouthier, but their pages were filled with stories about Carlos Salinas de Gortari.

Chihuahua remained the active seat of *panismo* during the 1988 election. At the state level, the wife of Luis Alvarez, Blanca M. de Alvarez, stood as a senatorial candidate for the PAN. She promised to serve as a loyal Chihuahuan in the national senate and to represent the state's interests. In addition, Sra. de Alvarez promised to fight for a limitation of presidential power. She was opposed by

Panel 1

In Parral a group of priistas *who were once* panistas *got into a rock throwing spree with another group of* panistas *who were once* priistas. *"What is the difference?"*

Panel 2

"The panistas *throw the rock and then hide their hand."*

Panel 3

"The priistas *do it in reverse."*

Panel 1

The export of cattle [to the U.S.] was suspended except for those used for sport. "Sport cattle???" "It's the ones they use in rodeos."

Panel 2

Armando Concha, another disaster from Parral, had a genial idea. "He crossed all of his cattle." "How? Armando doesn't have rodeo stock."

Panel 3

"Well, he put T-shirts, shorts, and tennis shoes on all of his calves. Who was going to say they weren't sports cattle?"

Saúl González Herrera, who had served as interim governor when Ornelas was deposed in 1985. The political payoff was apparent.

Meanwhile, Manuel Clouthier gave the PRI a dose of its own epithets. In 1986 the PRI and some of the leftist parties had accused the PAN of being creatures of the CIA, Ambassador John Gavin, and the Republican Party. In the spring of 1988, George Bush, then a candidate for the Republican nomination, met with Carlos Salinas de Gortari. Clouthier bluntly accused Bush of being a PRI supporter and implicitly pointed to Salinas as a toady to the United States. He emphasized his complete lack of interest in the primary races occurring in the U.S. at the time, indicating that he had quite enough to do in his own presidential campaign without worrying about what his neighbors were doing.

With less than two months left in the campaign, the PRI accelerated its activities. Instructions were issued to party workers who were to distribute literature that explained all the reasons that voters should cast their vote for the official party.

PAN responded in kind. They began to organize neighborhood watches in order to assure the fairness of the election. Stressing the importance of local organization, they distributed literature to party workers, instructing them on how to organize local groups for the purpose of political action and electoral surveillance. The literature was effective, concise, and aimed at all levels of society.

In addition, Manuel Clouthier planned to go to Chihuahua in mid-May to organize civil resistance against electoral fraud. Clearly, PAN planned to follow the same pattern it had in 1986: anticipate fraud and prepare to fight against it even before the election occurred.

In Ciudad Juárez some tensions began to build. Already PAN was calling for a nullification of the election results in Juárez because of the refusal of the electoral commission to verify voter signatures. Election officials, however, stated that "great advances had been made in the demoncratization of the country." PAN refused to be satisfied.

In Chihuahua, Clouthier thundered that "in spite of everything, Mexico has changed. It is no longer the same nor will it ever be again." The country, he stated, "needed a leader in which it could believe and confide."

By early June, President Miguel de la Madrid increased his

activity in support of the official candidate. He planned to stop in Chihuahua and visit various cities, including Juárez and Chihuahua City. When he arrived in Chihuahua City on June 3, *El Heraldo*, the city's leading newspaper, carried a complete section of advertisements welcoming the president to the state capital. Different businesses and organizations fulsomely welcomed their national leader. Among those that welcomed De la Madrid was the Unión Regional Ganadera de Chihuahua, the cattlemen's association. While the cattlemen opened their doors to the president "with the hospitality characteristic of this northern entity," they also pointedly declared that they survived on exports and needed more freedom in the sale of cattle to the United States. They also noted that the difficult Chihuahua terrain increased the difficulties of cattle raising in that area.

De la Madrid clearly wanted to restore PRI favor in Chihuahua. In an act of federal generosity, he returned two buildings to the municipal presidency that had been sold because the city needed money. Eventually, they had been taken over by two banks and flanked the municipal headquarters. With the nationalization of the banks in 1982, the buildings now were federal property. De la Madrid hoped to gain some local favor for the PRI through the restoration of these buildings to local authorities.

At the same time, De la Madrid took some potshots at United States critics of Mexico's electoral process. He emphasized Mexican independence and Mexico's political maturity. She did not need lessons on how to pick her political leaders. Mexicans were free to do as they wished in that regard.

But the PAN did not stand still for De la Madrid. The next day, *panistas* began to protest the existence of electoral fraud in Delicias, a mere hour south of Chihuahua City. They remonstrated with De la Madrid, accusing local authorities of suppressing PAN campaign efforts in that area. Finally, *panistas* asked if Miguel de la Madrid Hurtado came "as president or as a *priísta*."

The tension increased throughout June. PAN began to gear up for a campaign of civil disobedience. The leadership told *chihuahuenses* that "you, the citizens, are ready for the change, the liberty, and the democracy to which we aspire."

But it was not all rhetoric. The tension turned to occasional violence. One PRI congressional candidate in Chihuahua was attacked by CDP sympathizers. Gunshots punctuated the political rally. While the candidate himself was unhurt, one of his supporters took two bullets when he moved to save his leader.

The election of 1988 drew close scrutiny in the United States. Polls by the Gallup Organization and other pollsters showed that Salinas led both Clouthier and Cárdenas. In late June, it seemed as if Salinas would garner about fifty-six percent of the vote, while Cárdenas would run off with twenty-three percent and Clouthier with nineteen. The remaining two percent would be split among the other three presidential candidates.

Salinas again made a pitch to the north. In late June, he was again in Chihuahua. He confidently stated that the PRI would win because it was the middle road and avoided excesses. He accused the PAN of wanting to wipe out years of social progress achieved under revolutionary leadership. Salinas also began to increase his pitch to the businessmen and industrialists of Chihuahua, and he successfully weaned some away from PAN. He again emphasized his northern roots. In this he succeeded, for Eloy Vallina, one of the most powerful, wealthy, and influential men in Chihuahua, had openly declared his allegiance to Carlos Salinas de Gortari earlier in the spring. In so doing, he brought a significant segment of the business community to the side of the PRI.

As soon as Salinas left Chihuahua, Clouthier returned. He declared that *"México se tuvo que chihuahuizar"* (Mexico had to become like Chihuahua). There was no doubt in his mind that this would be clearly reflected in the PAN victories on July 6. As a nation, the country was ready to remove the yoke of officialdom, and Chihuahua had led the way.

Northern Mexico and Chihuahua specifically became a two-way battleground. The PRI and PAN fought it out doggedly. The FDN of Cuahutémoc Cárdenas, while it enjoyed some support, did not fall within the northern traditions. Cárdenas wanted a more active government involvement in the economy, a clear contradiction to the fierce independence of the north.

Four days before the election, the opposition parties began to call for nullification of the elections should there be any provable fraud. While outwardly unified, the opposition, including the PAN, still continued to bicker among themselves. Joining the clamor was the Church. Without taking political sides, Church authorities in Chihuahua called for a free expression of the electoral will.

The PRI, as well as the Partido Mexicano Socialista (Mexican Socialist Party, or PMS), was unfortunate to condemn the archbishop for his political statements. The PMS continued and lambasted clerical intervention, calling such action by a prelate unacceptable. The statement drew a response from Catholic laity and resulted in a march by the laity in Chihuahua City. They marched from the Villa statue on Avenida Universidad to the Cathedral, where they heard Mass and prayed for clean elections. Local Mexican Baptists joined other critics of the Catholic clergy by decrying the violation of electoral laws by the priests.

Conditions began to reflect the tension of the moment. PAN declared that it would quit campaigning in order to avoid violence born of tension and frustration. PRI presented itself as the only viable program, while the other groups all tended to lean toward Cárdenas. PAN declared that in Chihuahua it would cover about ninety-five percent of the polling places.

Local authorities in Chihuahua refused to allow conditions to worsen. They announced that twenty-four hours before and after the election, bars and liquor stores would be closed. Thus, from midnight of July 5 until midnight, July 7, Chihuahua would be dry. Electoral violence, often resulting in exchanges of gunfire and knifings, would not mar this election.

Political prognosticators saw the real possibility of the opposition picking up some senate seats, especially in Chihuahua, Baja California Norte, Guanajuato, Yucatán, and Michoacán. This in itself would shock the PRI, for it had never lost a senate race while it had relinquished seats in the Chamber of Deputies.

There was no question that the state of Chihuahua generally, with Ciudad Juárez and Chihuahua City specifically, posed real trouble spots for the PRI. The official party needed to concentrate on that area, for more than a hundred electoral districts were at risk. The loss of these could severely threaten the hegemony of the official party in Chihuahua.

By election day, July 6, the opposition parties began to stake out territory in order to build their cases about electoral fraud. PAN hoped to do more than that. Clouthier's job was to assure that the PAN improved its showing, hoping to garner twenty to twenty-five percent of the vote as opposed to sixteen percent in 1982. The election ultimately revolved around the electoral process itself.

While all opposition groups blamed the PRI for the crisis,

clean elections would have put competent leaders in office rather than corrupt party hacks who fleeced the national treasury and drove Mexico into bankruptcy. In many respects, PRI opponents sought a scapegoat in the official party, for they wanted to heap the blame on the force of inertia rather than on a society that tolerated poor leadership and allowed officialdom to enrich itself while the general populace suffered economic deterioration.

Then came election day, July 6, 1988. Throughout the country conditions seemed peaceful, though there had been a large turnout of voters. In Chihuahua, the PRI boasted its victory barely before the polls closed. As in 1986, they gave the appearance of a foregone conclusion. The head of the PRI electoral commission declared Salinas de Gortari "roundly victorious."

Almost immediately, suspicions began to surface. PAN had only carried Ciudad Juárez, while the PRI claimed the rest of the state. PAN protested while the PRI crowed. Fernando Baeza reported that throughout Chihuahua calm prevailed. Quick to react, PAN soon made rather pointed allegations. *Acción Nacional* leaders in Chihuahua and throughout the nation claimed that their poll-watchers had been physically removed from polling places and occasionally beaten physically, especially in Chihuahua and Veracruz. But the secretary of *gobernación*, Manuel Bartlett Díaz, declared the 1988 election a visible show of the great strides made in Mexico's electoral processes.

The atmosphere continued to emit suspicious and occasionally noxious airs. The electoral commission at all levels refused to release preliminary results. In Chihuahua and Mexico City they excused this as a mere computer malfunction. At the same time, PRI claimed a mighty victory for Carlos Salinas de Gortari. Clouthier countered with the assertion that PAN had clear advantages in the north and parts of central Mexico. He pointed to Ciudad Juárez and Guadalajara as concrete examples.

Four days after the election, it became clear that PRI had lost Mexico City to Cárdenas and the FDN. Nearly 21 million people inhabit the Valley of Mexico, always considered a PRI fiefdom. This time severe cuts were made in PRI hegemony by Cárdenas' narrow victory over Salinas in an area where twenty-five percent of the Mexican population lives. The increasing rumors of irregularities prompted outbursts of civil protest.

The Chihuahua PAN announced that on July 10 and 11 they would close the Pan American Highway as well as seize the three international bridges that led into Ciudad Juárez. Blockades were set up running from Juárez through Chihuahua City to Meoqui, Delicias, Camargo, Jiménez, and Parral. The only way south in the state was on the new highway that ran from west of Chihuahua City to Parral and then on south to Durango. Leading the blockade of the bridges was Francisco Barrio Terrazas, still looking messianic, fiercely determined to break the back of the official party. Clouthier, no less determined but more judicious in statement and action, declared that PAN would launch a campaign of "peaceful civil resistance" to protest "the most vulgar vote fraud in Mexican history."

On July 11, rain and pressures from semi-truck drivers forced those blockading the highway and the bridges to abandon their vigil three hours early. The PRI and the Partido Popular Socialista (Popular Socialist Party, or PPS) condemned the blockade. They claimed that any protest that affected third parties was clearly antisocial.

Thus, while PAN engaged in civil protest, the government of Chihuahua prepared for the delivery of the first electoral tallies. Baeza again declared a dry period to last from July 10 through the 11th. In addition, the army was put on alert.

On July 11, the official tally gave the state of Chihuahua to Salinas. The federal electoral commission confirmed that Salinas de Gortari had won nationwide. Clouthier declared: "Mexico has had two elections in two days. The election of July 6, in which the PRI was decisively defeated and the opposition emerged as the majority, and the one whose results have just been given."

Nationally, Salinas carried 52.8 percent of the vote while Cárdenas was awarded 29.1. PAN came in a poor third, with 16.6. Three days later, hoping to mollify PRI opponents, some revisions were announced: Salinas de Gortari — 50.4; Cárdenas — 31.1; Clouthier — 17.1. More importantly, PRI suffered a major setback in the Chamber of Deputies. Of 500 seats, the opposition controlled 240. The problem for the opposition became how to find some consensus among disparate points of view.

But *panistas* in Chihuahua remained dissatisfied. On July 11, the day of the first announcement, thirteen of them seized the office of the secretary of government and held it for four hours. They demanded to see Governor Baeza to lay before him their protests about electoral fraud. Finally, the police broke up the demonstration. Baeza, however, did meet with the PAN leadership in which he heard a repeat of the allegations that had marred his gubernatorial victory in 1986. Pollwatchers were kept from their duties; names were left off of voting lists; ballot boxes were stuffed. Baeza made his usual promises about investigating any clear violations.

The national candidates knew that they needed to make their appeals fully public. Both Cárdenas, working in central Mexico, and Clouthier, operating from his base in the north, began to appeal for public support for a nullification of the elections. Oddly enough, they did not join forces. They only agreed to have daily protests in one form or another.

In part, the PAN position was stated clearly by Luis H. Alvarez, PAN's national chairman. "Never," he declared, "would PAN ally itself with the left. PAN," he continued, "will never compromise its principles . . . . There is no point of convergence with other parties."

Throughout August, political tension continued to build. Dissident elements in PRI began to question whether or not they should support Salinas in the Congress when it became the electoral college. Some of the more cynically corrupt, usually those who supported the oil workers' union, demanded "support payments" for their affirmative votes. If the little bald man wanted the job, he would have to pay for it.

The CTM, headed by Doroteo Zapata in Chihuahua, wanted some retribution for the humiliation it had suffered in 1986. Probably acting under orders from Fidel Velázquez, Zapata promised to fight for a PRI victory in the VII Congressional District of Chihuahua. While the electoral commission gave the victory to PAN, Zapata said it was merely a technical decision. The real fight would be in the Congress.

PAN began a massive petition drive to demand a nullification of the electoral results in Chihuahua. It hoped to collect 200,000 signatures and force that action. In so doing, it wanted to demonstrate to the federal government that *Acción Nacional* in Chihuahua did, in fact, have clout and would use it. Additionally, this prepared the groundwork for further protests.

But there were irregularities on a national scale. In Iguala, Guerrero, two sacks filled with ballots marked for the PRI were found dumped in the countryside. For once, PRI and opposition parties joined and demanded an investigation of the flagrant act.

As August progressed, the political tension failed to abate. Mexico prepared for Miguel de la Madrid's final *informe presidencial*. On September 1 he addressed the nation and congress for a final time. He declared that changes that better the life of a nation cannot be achieved with "illusory promises." He also emphatically stated that, while a majority might exercise power, the rights of the minorities needed to be guarded and respected. Derisive hoots greeted his words as opposition members of Congress walked out.

One week later, the federal electoral college declared Carlos Salinas de Gortari the victor in the July 6 election. They did, however, reduce his margin. They awarded him 50.2 percent of the vote, the smallest margin ever won by an official candidate. The fragile victory left Salinas with only a ten-seat majority in the Chamber of Deputies that could dissipate given the dissension within PRI ranks.

The fall of 1988 proved no better. While tensions seemed to relax, the atmosphere in Chihuahua specifically and Mexico in general still reflected the acrimony generated by the election. State officials in Chihuahua began to distance themselves from the national party once again.

In late November, Governor Bacza said in a speech in Ciudad Juárez that every time he entered the Governor's Salon in the Government Palace he felt small. There were portraits of the greats: Abraham González, Francisco Villa. How could he possibly accomplish what they had done? He asked *chihuahuenses* not to expect too much of him. But he did issue a warning to Salinas de Gortari. He called government centralism "asphyxiating." He also noted that Chihuahua, a state rich in resources and honest, hard-working citizens, had never had a president of Mexico. Clearly, this was a warning to Salinas not to tamper with Chihuahua.

The presidential election of 1988 produced tensions in Chihuahua and in Mexico that continue to plague it. The hold of the PRI showed definite signs of slippage, while PAN campaigned on a platform of putative electoral fraud. It seemed that neither group learned the lessons of 1986.

Fearful of losing hegemony and concomitant prestige, the PRI continued to rig electoral results. It needed a majority, and if a rigged election was the only way to achieve this result, then so be it. It could not admit that as a party PRI might be beatable.

PAN, however, continued to act politically immature. While its campaign literature advanced positive programs, its pronouncements concentrated on electoral fraud in an election which had not yet been held. PAN's position, *vis à vis* an alliance with the left, clearly reflected its political inexperience. It refused to make pragmatic decisions but rather stuck to ideological ones. In one instance, however, it did succumb to practicality. Prior to the election, PAN refused to accept any government money for campaign expenses. Finally, in the fall of 1988, it took the cash. Economic necessity forced it to compromise.

For Chihuahua, the presidential election again acted as a prelude to the upcoming local and state elections in 1989. How those would go was anybody's guess. Much of it depended upon Salinas de Gortari. Would he, unlike Miguel de la Madrid, live up to his promises about clean elections? Would he reform the PRI as promised? To what degree would new blood replace the dinosaurs who control much of the PRI?

Chihuahua has always been a bone in the throat of the federal government, and it continues to assert its independent nature. The state's growth, progress, and peculiar ethos present problems for the central government that require a sensitivity not yet demonstrated by the *chilangos* of Mexico City.

PART III

The complexities of social organization in Chihuahua still require an enormous amount of study. Impressions based on long periods of time spent in Chihuahua in addition to the sketchy information that can be gleaned from newspapers and official publications form the basis of the following section.

Socio-economic aspirations impel a people to make political decisions. In addition, how a people perceive themselves also accounts for the political decisions that they make. As a consequence, this section of the book reflects one writer's impressions of how the people of Chihuahua view themselves in relation to each other, to the nation as a whole, to the United States, and to the world in general.

Brahma bulls, EXPOGAN 1985.
Photo by the author.

Black Angus bulls, EXPOGAN 1985.
Photo by the author.

CHAPTER 8

Cowboys, Society, and Culture: *Al Estilo Chihuahua*

Cattle bawled. Men shouted greetings to each other as they sought seats in the crowded area that overlooked the small arena. In the center stood a large podium. Men in cowboy hats placed themselves behind the podium, and one grasped a microphone. Soon there began a rhythmic chant familiar to all denizens of livestock sales. But something strange was going on here. It wasn't English they were speaking; it was Spanish. One of the many cattle auctions of EXPOGAN (the *Exposición Ganadera,* or Cattle Exhibition) in Chihuahua had begun.

In many respects, the cattle industry in Chihuahua specifically and northern Mexico generally provides a microcosm to examine provincial-central government relations in Mexico. Centralism, an integral part of Mexico's political tradition, had clashed constantly with a fierce sense of local autonomy that antedates national independence. Centripedal tendencies in the twentieth-century coupled with the reformism of the Revolution of 1910 intensified attempts by central authority to impose a particular vision on the entire nation. Thus, tension between Chihuahua cattlemen and planners in Mexico City has thrown state and federal government into almost constant conflict.

But the disagreement involves more than mere politics. It encompasses lifestyle and a perception of self that deep in the heart of every *chihuahuenses* pulsates as his reason for being. He knows his worth; he is confident that he and Chihuahua in general will survive the vicissitudes of economic crisis, political chicanery, and the vagaries of life in the hard land that he calls home. The Chihuahuan, whether he is a cattleman or not, has absorbed that particular ethos and perceives himself as the rugged individualist of the desert plains who has braved the elements and survived.

In many respects, walking around Chihuahua City today is like taking a step backward in time. It is reminiscent of Fort Worth when the stockyards still functioned. Pick-up trucks jam traffic. In the back windows of these rigs are gun racks from which hang lariats. Stores abound where cowboy boots can be purchased, and western wear is almost *de rigueur* for the well-dressed *chihuahuense*. In fact, it is almost impossible to tell the real cowmen from the drug store variety. Cow culture in Chihuahua is ubiquitous and permeates everywhere. Food (beef is the preferred nutrient), language, and attitudes all stem from the common tradition that binds the southwestern United States and the Mexican border region. One bumper sticker that has been popular in Chihuahua shows a caricature cowboy in a large straw hat with dark glasses and a simple look on his face. The legend says quite pointedly:

> *Con lente obscuro,*
> *bota y sombrero,*
> *cualquier pendejo es ganadero.*
>
> (With dark glasses,
> hat, and boots,
> any idiot can be a cattleman.)

Cattle forms the basis for all economic activity in Chihuahua. *Maquiladoras*, mining, forest products, commercial enterprises, diversified agriculture, and other activities all take a back seat to the sheer volume of dollars generated by the cattle industry. As a consequence, the constant tinkering with export quotas and taxes by the federal government introduces a chronic irritant into the relations between Mexico's largest state and the denizens of Mexico City.

Even politically, the PRI in Chihuahua pays more than pass-
ing homage to the role of cattle in the state's economy. Chihuahuan
governors in the twentieth century have done regular battle with
Mexico City to assure the smooth continuation of the cattle industry. The Cattlemen's Association in the state constitutes one of the
most powerful pressure groups in both state and national politics.
When they bark, state and national authorities listen and begin the
dialogue.

But this is not to say that the cattlemen always get their way.
On the contrary, they are constantly engaged in a battle to preserve
their enterprise. After all, Mexico City must attempt to attend to
the needs of the megalopolis (21 million strong and malignantly
growing), and pressures are brought to bear on the provinces.

The need to expand continually besets the cattleman in Chihuahua. Breed improvement and state-of-the-art technology become constants in the *chihuahuense* attempt to gain more from the
hard and violent land on which he lives. In one sense, he must ex-
tract more from this land if he is to keep up with the exigencies of
federal authorities, for the demands for more taxes and more support for federal programs by the cattle industry imposed by central
authority mandate increased production. Since cattle, like other
forms of agriculture, must produce in volume in order to be profitable, the Chihuahua cattleman has begun to institutionalize means
by which he can advertise his product and at the same time make
information available about the newest innovations in animal nu-
trition, breed development, and agricultural technology. To do so,
Cattlemen's Exhibitions became an almost annual event of the
1980s.

The *Exposición Ganadera* of 1983 became the first such cattle
fair in over thirty years. But it was not a dinky little affair where a
few ranchers showed off their stock. International competition underscored the wide interest that United States and Canadian cattlemen had in Chihuahua. Large breeders from the U.S. and Canada
exhibited cattle in Chihuahua in that year, and a Canadian outfit
ran off with the majority of the prizes.

While the U.S. private sector was intensely interested in EX-
POGAN '83, the U.S. government did not even know it existed.
While in Mexico City in the early days of October 1983, I met a
young man attached to the office of the U.S. agricultural attaché.
We exchanged impressions about Mexico, and then circulated at a

cocktail party held for Fulbright Scholars. When I returned to Chihuahua City a few days later, it dawned on me that our official representatives in Mexico City knew nothing about Chihuahua and about the cattle business that constitutes Chihuahua's major economic activity. Therefore, I called this individual. The American Embassy in Mexico City, so it seemed, was totally unaware of EXPOGAN, and there was no official U.S. presence in Chihuahua in that major cattle fair. Two years later, I noticed that the U.S. government did, in fact, have a booth at EXPOGAN '85, as it did in 1988. It seemed that the American view coincided rather neatly with the *chilango* position: if it is not happening in Mexico City, it merits no attention. The shift that occurred in a two-year period was gratifying.

At all three cattle exhibitions I attended, a large foreign contingent was there from Canada and the United States. Chihuahuan cattlemen actually find it less expensive to buy their breeding stock from the United States and Canada than from local breeders. As their purebred stock increases, the prices will drop; but until then, breeders in the U.S. and Canada will have an excellent market in Chihuahua.

While dominated by major breeds of cattle (Angus, Red Angus, Beefmaster, Zebu, Hereford, etc.), EXPOGAN also featured dairy cattle, hogs, goats, and some sheep. A large number of horses competed as well. There was a preponderance of Quarter Horses, though Arabians, Appaloosas, and Paints also made their mark. Thoroughbreds, coming principally from the army equestrian team, were also evident. In 1988 a few rabbits were even on display. The exhibition sponsored by the Cattlemen's Association is beginning to expand and become the major agricultural fair in northern Mexico.

In the quest to improve the product that they send to the United States, Chihuahua cattlemen constantly travel to the United States and Canada. In 1984, for example, the presence of cattlemen from northern Mexico at the Livestock Show in Denver was so apparent that the *New York Times* reported the phenomenon. Two very successful cattlemen traveled to Kansas in 1988 to purchase Salers bulls and cows in November 1988. Travel and expenditure of often large sums of money are required to keep the Chihuahua cattle industry competitive.

But Mexico City constantly places obstacles in the way of Chihuahuan cattlemen. What seems to be a capricious "playing around" with export quotas perpetually irritates cattlemen who must then send delegations to Mexico City to force a reinstitution of permits from both the Secretariats of Agriculture and of Commerce and Industrial Development (SECOFI). In mid-1985, for example, SECOFI authorized the export of slightly more than 50,000 calves to the United States. This meant a revenue of about $3 million. But SECOFI imposed some restrictions. First, domestic meat supplies could not be cut. Secondly, the foreign exchange accumulated from the sale of exported cattle had to be deposited in the Banco Nacional de México (Bank of Mexico). In light of Mexico's foreign exchange problem, cattlemen saw their dollar profits dwindling as their deposits were converted to a depreciating *peso* (worth about 350 to the dollar in mid-1985; sliding to nearly 2,300 to the dollar in 1988; and, in 1991, valued at about 3,000:1).

The ever-declining *peso* wreaked havoc on cattlemen. In 1985 a program for fattening cattle in Texas while held in bond was canceled. These cattle were destined for the domestic market, but the lack of foreign credit and the scarce supply of dollars made it cost-prohibitive to ship cattle to Texas for fattening. Chihuahuan cattlemen had to pay about 350 *pesos* per kilogram of weight gain, but cattle only sold for 330 on the domestic market. Unfortunately, Chihuahua as yet did not have a strong feedlot industry. Three years later, there was some evidence that feedlots were becoming a part of cattle production in Chihuahua in spite of federal government inaction and apathy. As ranchers diversify and raise their own alfalfa and feed supplements, a local feedlot industry will emerge.

The Unión Regional Ganadera de Chihuahua in 1986 found itself joined in conflict with the Secretariat of Agriculture and Hydraulic Resources (SARH). In its wisdom SARH canceled permits for the export of 41,000 head of feeder cattle as opposed to weanling calves. This cattle had an approximate value of $15 million. The state of Chihuahua lost a substantial chunk of revenue because of the SARH ruling that cattle only bearing one brand could be exported. This forced the president of URGCH to accuse Mexico City of being wholly illogical. Since when, he asked, was it illegal to buy and sell internally? Again a delegation went to Mexico City and forced modifications.

The panic approach induced by Mexico's ever-widening financial crisis provoked yet another surge by SARH to control the Chihuahua cattle industry. No longer would the Unión Regional Ganadera handle the distribution of export permits. Instead, in a malignant web of centralism, SARH dictated that it would allocate these permits. For exported calves, a federal levy of 500 *pesos* per head would be imposed. Ostensibly, this was to assure a supply of meat for the Federal District during a time of crisis.

In October the secretary of agriculture visited Chihuahua and authorized an export quota of 305,000 head for 1987. In addition, he called for the promotion of dressed and deboned meat as well as beef by-products such as leather for export. Beef on the hoof was all very good, but additional exports would bring more dollars into Mexico.

Chihuahua received approximately one-third of the national export quota for 1987. SARH authorized an export of slightly more than 1 million head. But inflation and the declining value of the *peso* proved to be the largest impediment to profitable enterprise. The head of the National Cattlemen's Confederation declared that most ranchers worked "out of vocation" because of the difficulty of disposing of their herds. Yet they made no real profits. In late 1986, and beyond, Mexican cattle herds stood at about 30 million head, with the largest beef herds located in Chihuahua.

The effect of Mexican cattle exports on the United States in the 1980s brought cries of alarm from Texas Senator Lloyd Bentsen. He calculated that in 1987, Mexico could import 1.9 million head to the United States. This clearly threatened U.S. producers, he averred. Of course, he failed to note that it was principally U.S. producers who had bought this feeder cattle from Mexico because of the inability of U.S. cattlemen to meet the demands for beef in the United States.

By 1988, the perpetual battle between Chihuahua cattlemen and the central government failed to abate. In June, cattlemen refused to export stock because they were required to sell twenty percent of their stock to Mexico City at fixed prices. Chihuahua cattlemen argued that such capriciousness had a detrimental effect on the entire industry. Some butcher shops in Chihuahua closed, while others sold horse meat because it was so much cheaper. Slaughterhouses either closed or worked at a minimal capacity.

Butchers demonstrated in front of the SECOFI office in Chihuahua City and demanded a regularization of meat supplies. Governor Baeza, feeling somewhat out of his element, temporized.

Cattle producers from *ejidos* also voiced their complaints. They, too, accused SECOFI of inhibiting the cattle trade for both export and domestic consumption. Since SECOFI discouraged feedlots, the cost of producing cattle merely escalated and resulted in a scarcity of beef for local consumption.

Beef shortages in Chihuahua brought an increase in cattle rustling throughout the state. Whole trucks filled with cattle were hijacked, in addition to individual small operators stealing one or two head at a time. The problem throughout 1988 became so pervasive that local and state police authorities did not know where to begin.

Two months later, cattlemen continued to hammer away at the central government. The constant theme of capriciousness filled the complaints. Last-minute announcement of export quotas constantly left cattlemen wondering what they could produce for export and what for the domestic market. This resulted in cattle being kept off the market and in a continuing and aggravating meat shortage.

The imposed export tax exacerbated relations between cattlemen and Mexico City throughout 1988. In some magical way, SARII and SECOFI agreed that export calves weighing under 300 pounds would be taxed at a rate of twenty-nine percent of the value; animals over that weight fell to a twenty percent tax. By late November 1988, Governor Fernando Baeza Meléndez of Chihuahua finally saw the critical damage being done to Chihuahua's cattle industry. When he struck out against "asphyxiating centralism," he spoke for the cattlemen. He also viewed the export tax as repressive and voiced the hope that the new administration would lift the burden from the cattlemen. Into the 1990s, an export tax remained on cattle.

Baeza spoke from strength. Chihuahua cattle do not suffer from a trade deficit, and the industry outdistances all production in the state in all economic enterprises, including the resurgence of the mining of nonferrous metals. Cattle formed the springboard for the economic prosperity of Chihuahua. In many respects, the situation became somewhat reminiscent of the 1890s, for cattle provided the key to economic development in the entire state. What was missing was an intrusive federal authority.

Chihuahua's cattle industry kicked off a dizzying growth of economic activity in the state. Between 1970 and 1980, the state geared up for major economic growth in the 1980s. In large measure, *chihuahuenses* viewed economic growth as a sure sign of social progress, for jobs were created and unemployment was held in check. But the 1980s proved to be a time of economic disaster for the nation as a whole. Only northern Mexico and especially Chihuahua was able to maintain a growth rate far in excess of that experienced by the nation.

Nationally, prices almost multiplied ten times between 1981 and 1985. While Chihuahua also experienced the same price increases, the state continued to experience an unprecedented growth that became the national envy. Between 1980 and 1985, Chihuahua's economy grew at a rate of about 8.5 percent. The nation generally only expanded at a 2.3 percent rate.

A principal cause of this growth in Chihuahua could be attributed to the expansion of the *maquiladora* program. In Chihuahua there existed eighteen industrial parks as of 1987. Nearly 6,200 acres of land (2,500 hectares) scattered between Ciudad Juárez, Chihuahua City, Delicias, Cuahtémoc, Parral, Nuevo Casas Grandes, and Camargo provided the industrial base for the burgeoning *maquila* industry.

The effect of the *maquiladoras* on the state has been extremely important. In terms of jobs, for example, in 1980, the *maquilas* employed a little more than 43,000 people, predominantly women. In May 1987 that figure jumped to nearly 126,000 with more men coming into the work force in the industry. This growth of industrial jobs gave Chihuahua a preponderant lead (forty-six percent) in the escalation of the *maquiladora* program nationally.

The *maquilas* have produced a social revolution in Chihuahua. Women who once stayed home or worked as domestics found employment in the *maquiladoras*. At first most of the jobs went to women, who were considered better suited for the monotony of assembly lines. Though men have joined the *maquila* work force, the problems brought about by female employment shattered the Mexican *macho* image.

In many families the woman became the principal wage earner. Increases in violent crime and alcoholism among unemployed men attested to the disruption caused to the traditional family structures by the *maquilas*. Additionally, the scarcity of domestic help brought on by *maquiladora* employment of women deprived middle-sector women of housekeepers, cooks, and babysitters. Now that they could afford the help at cheap prices, that help was no longer available. The few available domestics demanded high salaries and fringe benefits.

The onset of Mexico's financial crisis in the early 1980s provided an incentive for *maquila* growth. Since 1982, over 200 *maquiladoras* have grown up around Ciudad Juárez. The desperate need for dollars prompted Mexico to allow for the rapid expansion of the *maquiladoras* since the bulk of these enterprises are foreign-owned.

One major company to invest in Chihuahua was Ford Motor Company. Just north of Chihuahua City, Ford opened a motor assembly plant that produced motors for all Ford cars built in Mexico. In 1986, Ford enterprises expanded, and they began to move into the production of automobile clocks and other car accessories. Thus they created more jobs and continued to stimulate the local economy.

The need to make Mexican exports more competitive prompted some programs in Chihuahua that returned a portion of taxes to approximately 180 businesses. In this way, they could purchase raw materials, fuels, and packing substances at a cheaper rate and thus make export products more profitable.

The Chihuahua–Texas linkage existed in more than the cattle industry. In May 1985, Chihuahua City Municipal President Luis Alvarez visited San Antonio, Texas, in order to negotiate direct flights between Chihuahua and San Antonio. Alvarez noted that Texas businessmen in Odessa as well as San Antonio viewed Chihuahua as a likely place for investment. San Antonio Mayor Henry Cisneros and Alvarez agreed to approach their respective governments about direct flights. By early March 1986, only technical details about crews and the needs of specific classes of planes needed to be arranged.

During the time that Alvarez and Cisneros talked with their governments, the director of economic development for Chihuahua also attempted to increase the number of high-tech jobs for Chihuahua. To do this, he needed to provide stimuli for investment and thus create a sophisticated business base for the state.

Obviously successful, the governors of Chihuahua and Texas signed agreements for trade and the exchange of information between the two states. They aimed to promote technological centers, agribusiness information, and technical information through the universities and technological centers of each state. At the same time they aimed to reduce the vast amount of paperwork required for each transaction.

Chihuahua's good fortune in the 1980s seemed almost like a Midas Touch. To add to the almost fairy-tale quality of Chihuahuan progress, oil added to the economic picture. Studies by United States, French, and British firms showed oil strata all over the state. Some petrologists theorized that this was an extension of the Gulf of Mexico finds in the early 1970s. In Janos, in the northwest, oil and natural gas wells began production, and by 1990 it was estimated that around thirty-five wells would be producing in Chihuahua.

But the downside of these finds was price. In 1985, oil prices surpassed $20 per barrel. By 1986, these had plummeted to between $10 and $15 per barrel. Consequently, the rich oil reserves that lay beneath Chihuahua might be too cost-prohibitive to exploit.

One eminently exploitable resource for Chihuahua, however, could be found in tourism. With the exception of Ciudad Juárez, the rest of the state was virtually ignored by tourists. Since the 1986 programs began, many of them centered at the Autonomous University of Ciudad Juárez, to stimulate tourism throughout the state. Hotels were remodeled. Documentaries and written materials rolled out of the typewriters of public relations specialists. Chihuahua's beautiful mountain country including Copper Canyon received major publicity. More and more tourists were being attracted to Chihuahua. The area does not have the immediate attraction of a Cuernavaca or a Lake Chapala (near Guadalajara), and the tourists do not linger for long. But they no longer just drive through to the border either.

The phenomenal economic growth of Chihuahua has failed to trickle down to the entire population. The *ejidos* continue to be a problem. The bulk of agricultural production, including cattle, is in the private sector. *Ejidos* still remain a principal problem to a central government committed to a communitarian land system that has been a failure in Chihuahua and apparently in the nation.

As a consequence, where struggling crops once grew, vigorous marijuana plants sprout. In Chihuahua's countryside, those who failed to make it as small farmers often engaged in drug growth and trafficking. By 1986, the nation's attorney general estimated that Chihuahua had become one of Mexico's leading drug centers. Between January and October 1986, 173 drug trafficking trials took place in Chihuahua. Additionally, there was a massive destruction of marijuana operations as well as the destruction of opium poppies used for heroin production.

Chihuahua's drug traffickers are scattered throughout the state. In the mountains, the Tarahumara Indians engage in the growth of marijuana. Around Delicias and Nuevo Casas Grandes, drugs constitute a part of the local economy. In the last few years the number of drug-related arrests in these areas have been graphically depicted in the state's newspapers.

In one instance in 1985, a major marijuana operation in northwestern Chihuahua brought in workers from central Mexico and literally enslaved them on the land. Increased vigilance brought the situation to light, but it required pressure from the United States to convince Mexico to become more vigilant.

In large part, the increase in Mexican vigilance came as a result of the kidnapping and execution of an agent of the United States Drug Enforcement Agency near Guadalajara. Intensified pressures on Mexico forced the country to step up its drug enforcement program. By August 1986, Mexico augmented its drug control forces by thirty planes and 100 agents in the states of Sinaloa, Sonora, Chihuahua, Durango, and Nayarit. The principal thrust of this program was to find and destroy commercial plantings of marijuana.

But the exploitation of less fortunate peoples by drug traffickers was cruelly underscored when, in early 1987, four Tarahumara Indians were found dead. It was generally believed that they died because they had displeased drug traffickers for whom they raised opium poppies. In the Sierra, more and more rumors are heard about the slave-like treatment meted out to Indians by drug dealers.

By the mid-1980s, Chihuahua not only became a production center for marijuana but also served as a trampoline for cocaine into the United States. The long, empty border between much of Chihuahua and the United States provided a haven for smugglers who export marijuana and cocaine plus Mexican-grown and produced heroin into the United States.

Cooperation between United States and Mexican authorities, resulting from increased pressure by the United States, accelerated vigilance at the border. At international bridges, principally between Juárez and El Paso, cars and trucks are regularly stopped on the bridges. Drug-sniffing dogs are brought out, and lanes of traffic are examined. In March 1988, for example, 130 kilograms of cocaine were found by these dogs on the Córdova bridge.

With Chihuahua a principal center for drug trafficking, the health implications of drug use needed to be emphasized. In 1986, about 200,000 students in Parral, Juárez, and Chihuahua City received information about the dangers of drug use. But this still did not keep drug trafficking from becoming an integral part of the Chihuahuan economy.

By mid-1988, the illicit drug trade became even more apparent in Chihuahua. The Mexican army regularly patrolled highways and searched vehicles. For those cars going into the mountains, the army looked for liquor and arms that could be traded to the Indians for marijuana. Daily reports in Chihuahuan newspapers told of more drug arrests.

One Chihuahua newspaper, while acknowledging the health dangers of drugs, also saw the drug problem as an excuse for United States intervention in Mexican internal affairs. This paper even extended the logic to include all Latin American countries where the United States needed a pretext for some sort of intervention.

Drugs have formed the negative side of Chihuahua's economic growth. On the positive side, the industrial and agricultural growth of the state has made it the premier producer in Mexico. As a consequence, the socio-political implications of this growth have accounted for Chihuahua's designation as a political maverick.

The political and economic power of Chihuahua lies in its energetic and heterogeneous population. Conditioned to survive in a harsh environment, the *chihuahuenses* developed an individualistic mentality over the centuries that made them mavericks in a country whose principal population centers revolved around communitarian indigenous cultures. Orientals, Spaniards, Mormoms, Mennonites, and other groups have contributed to the heterodox nature of Chihuahua. While not always understood and occasionally scorned by the bulk of the citizens, these groups have provided a source of stimulation for the progress of the area which often prompted *chihuahuenses* to keep pace.

Part of the ethnic component of Chihuahua that has never been resolved is the Tarahumara Indian from the Sierra. The Tarahumara walk to the cities to beg. Life in the mountains remains difficult, and squeezing an existence out of the Sierra is often unsuccessful. Tarahumaras beg on street corners, *cantinas,* and wherever people congregate, including outside of the supermarkets. They constitute a problem that will not go away and that needs incorporation into the mainstream of Chihuahua's life.

Chihuahuan prosperity in the 1980s, and into the 1990s, in light of the economic crisis and futile efforts by the government to stem the decline of the *peso,* only set in stark relief the contrasts between that state and the rest of the nation. Unemployment and underemployment in Mexico approaches twenty-five percent in some areas. In Mexico City unofficial estimates place this at nearly forty percent. Population pressures in Mexico City dictate that people look elsewhere for livelihoods. Chihuahua has suddenly become a magnet for those disillusioned with Mexico City and the ability of the federal government to resolve their individual problems.

The state of Chihuahua has undergone steady population growth. In 1900, the entire state had slightly more than 325,000 people. By 1980, this had grown to more than 2 million, and in 1988 unofficial estimates put its population at about 3 million. This growth has been principally in urban areas — Ciudad Juárez, Chihuahua City, Nuevo Casas Grandes, Delicias, to name a few. Like the rest of the nation, Chihuahua is becoming increasingly urbanized, and a majority of its citizens live in urban areas.

The rapid growth of Chihuahua City in the 1980s put pressure on *ejidataros* immediately outside of the urban areas. As the city expanded, lands usually used for agriculture were expropriated by municipal authorities in order to put residential housing on them. Reserve lands that belonged to the *municipio* fell prey to the urban pressures that beset Chihuahua City. Thus, the *ejidos* surrounding the capital city felt threatened, and they organized to avert the loss of their lands. While only moderately successful, the communal *ejidos* remain a part of Chihuahua.

Chihuahua's economic prosperity has attracted people from all over Mexico. *El Heraldo de Chihuahua* speculated that the state has become "the honeycomb that attracts citizens from other states who are looking for jobs." This, of course, means that the loathed *chilango* showed up in profusion in Chihuahua, a phenomenon not to the liking of most *chihuahuenses*.

The increase in people from central and southern Mexico in Chihuahua aggravated the tensions between Mexico City and Chihuahua. *Chihuahuenses* pride themselves on their openness and general friendliness and their willingness to accept each other's foibles with a certain amount of grace and humor. But the arrival of these people from the south, the "midgets from the south," utterly aggravated the local Chihuahuan. One description of the southern midgets was that they were "of closed personality, short, Indian, ugly, and stupid." While not very flattering, this description remained wholly consistent with the utter contempt with which the Chihuahuans view Mexico City, its environs, and its inhabitants.

Chilangos gave impetus to the increased growth of the CDP. It began initially as a strictly Chihuahuan group in the 1970s, but the arrival of homeless Mexicans from central and southern Mexico provided a fertile area for CDP exploitation.

CDP leaders organized their followers, Chihuahuan and outsider alike, into a political pressure group that took advantage of the divisions in the traditional Mexican left. CDP members have become the principal dealers in contraband goods, or *fayuca*. This group's success in Chihuahua City, for example, has resulted in their ownership of real estate where they peddle their goods. The CDP even named one section it controlled in Chihuahua City "Mercado Francisco Villa," in an attempt to equate their anarchism with the great revolutionary leader. It is here, in the middle of downtown Chihuahua, that the CDP sells its *fayuca* and foodstuffs. Ironically, for an outfit that claims to be quasi-Marxist, it has enjoyed remarkable success in what is essentially a free market system. While contradictory, it is also thoroughly *chihuahuense*.

Whether urban or rural, the bulk of the population of Chihuahua prides itself on its successes. A growing and powerful middle sector found economic prosperity. When it began to lose that prosperity because of the economic crisis, it defected to the PAN in the hope that a change in the political power structure might improve economic conditions.

While the revolutionaries of 1910–1920 might have been brutal toward their enemies, principally the big landholders such as Luis Terrazas and company, these people did in fact survive. Currently, through a complex web of intermarriages, the Terrazases,

Lujanes, Creels, and others again appear among the respected names of Chihuahuan society. The survival factor engendered by centuries of fighting one's own battles facilitated the reappearance of these families. They are in all of the professions — medicine, law, teaching, engineering, banking — and politically they run the gamut, from PAN to PRI. Very few are identified with the left. While no longer dominant, they still constitute a part of the power structure of *chihuahuense* society and politics.

But not all *chihuahuenses* have been satisfied. Mexico's National Population Council estimated that one out of seven Mexicans living in the United States comes from Chihuahua. Geographic proximity in part accounts for this. But the harsh environment that keeps all but the most ambitious and hard-working on the land also contributes to a population flight to the United States.

Usually these immigrants cross as illegal aliens. They usually do agricultural work, though many have worked at other occupations, some of them a bit sleazy. Male prostitutes from Chihuahua have worked their trade in the United States for limited periods of time. Many illegals have returned voluntarily; some have suffered the indignity of a bust by the Immigration and Naturalization Service. But Chihuahua has an enthusiasm for the United States.

The majority of the *chihuahuenses* are fascinated by the U.S. If they can afford it, they go to El Paso to buy everything that they can get into the country. When restrictions were relaxed early in 1988, it became easier to bring more consumer goods into Chihuahua from El Paso. A kind of frenetic consumerism began to grip the middle sector of Chihuahua. They still hope to hang on to their prosperity through a demonstrable acquisition of consumer goods. Parenthetically, they also hoard dollars, and some even have bank accounts in El Paso in case the situation in Mexico fails to improve.

The large Chihuahua middle sector that experienced unprecedented prosperity in the 1970s and early 1980s began to feel the squeeze of economic crisis. Technicians and other public employees at the Instituto Tecnológico de Chihuahua had not had pay raises for five years (as of 1986), and more and more they began to protest this lack. Since they were not professors, they were not covered by the contract between the teachers' union and the administration. But the failure to grant raises in a period of inflation failed to respond to the need to keep up with price increases.

In 1988 the Mexican government attempted to stave off inflation and a declining *peso* with the Pacto de Solidaridad Económica (Economic Solidarity Pact) in which prices and wages were frozen. In some respects, the agreement proved successful, for inflation did in fact abate to about forty percent, an unpredented low in the last six years. But by mid-year *El Pacto,* as it was called, began to crack. Demands for increased prices for milk and eggs by producers, for example, showed that production costs remained high. In some parts of Chihuahua, milk shortages appeared occasionally. While the state has a thriving dairy industry, the cost of milk production was high. As of November 1988, there appeared pressure to raise the price of bread and tortillas. Thus, even middle and upper sector *chihuahuenses* began to feel the squeeze, and more dissatisfaction with the monstrous and anonymous government in Mexico City surfaced.

In many respects basic costs are more expensive in Chihuahua. There is less government subsidy of basic products — milk, bread, tortillas — and prices are concomitantly higher than in the rest of the country. While housing costs are relatively inexpensive, food costs make up for some of the difference.

Also, as a primary producer of foodstuffs, Chihuahuans often suffer from shortages or inferior quality food. The bulk of their best product goes to Mexico City, and this is mightily resented. Fruit, much of it brought from other states, is of inferior quality; again, the best goes to Mexico City. This does nothing more than aggravate the resentment of *chihuahuenses* toward the *chilango* and this insensitivity to the needs of Chihuahua.

The people of Chihuahua have become more and more insular as they have seen their prosperity erode. The *chihuahuense* sees his state as the only bastion of freedom in Mexico. The southerners are foreigners who refuse to recognize the obvious superiority of the north. Parral, for example, calls itself the capital of the world. Chihuahuans smuggly deprecate those who are not fortunate enough to share in the *chihuahuense* ethos. But they have become disenchanted with a political system that ignores Chihuahua. Increasingly cynical about the political system, they still gave overwhelming support to the PAN in 1983. They still supported the PAN in 1986, though they encountered a political buzz-saw in the PRI's decision to have its way in Chihuahua. The political immaturity of the PAN was offset by the political cynicism and heavy handedness of the PRI and the centralist tendencies of Mexico City. Not surprisingly, disaffected segments of the society as well as the PRI have evoked the image of Pancho Villa as a rallying point.

Symbols and imagery constitute a large part of how Mexicans perceive themselves. Ironically, Villa has come to symbolize for *chihuahuenses* of all political stripes the iconoclastic nature of that which is autochthonously from Chihuahua. Whether from the conservative PAN to the centrist PRI to more radical elements like CDP and PSUM, they all call upon the image of Villa as a rallying point. In this, *chihuahuense* society has shown how quirky its makeup is and has demonstrated the very maverick nature of its relation with the rest of Mexico.

A PAN bumper sticker declaring ``Victory! It is now time!''

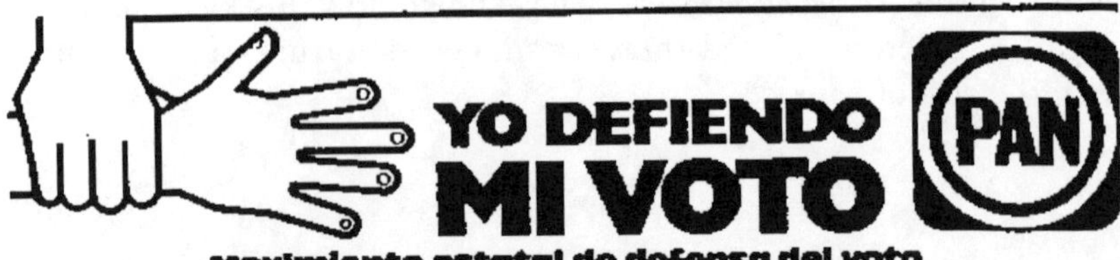

A PAN bumper sticker stating: ``I defend my vote. State movement for defense of the vote.''

A PAN bumper sticker that states: ``Democracy .... the solution.''

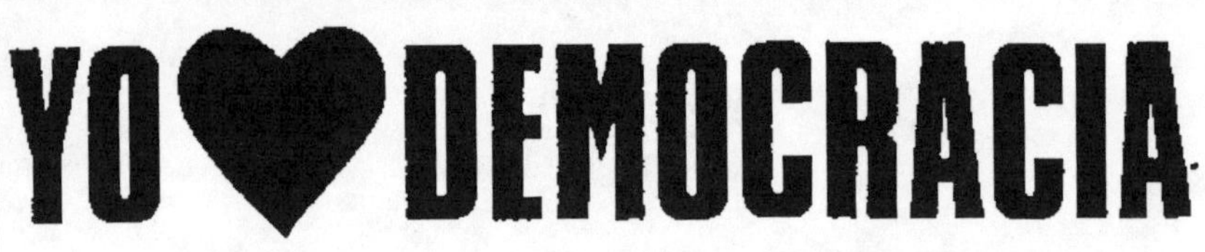

A more generic bumper sticker that says: ``I Love Democracy.''

Bumper sticker that says: ``With dark glasses, boots, and hat, any idiot can be a cattleman.''

CHAPTER 9

Villa Lives!

A controversy erupted in the spring of 1984 between Chihuahua and Durango. Someone had made a death mask of Francisco Villa when his body lay in the Hidalgo Hotel in Parral immediately after his assassination in July 1923. The death mask eventually ended up in a historical collection in a Texas school. Once it was discovered by an art teacher at the school, he made a cast from the mask which still contained mustache hairs and flecks of blood.

Mexican newspapers got wind of the find and demanded that the mask be returned to Mexico as part of its national patrimony. While the school seemed perfectly willing to relinquish the mask, to whom should it go? Durango claimed it as part of its state heritage. Pancho Villa had been born in Durango; he was a native son. Chihuahua, however, claimed that Villa's greatest impact on Mexico came when he was an adopted *chihuahuense*, a major revolutionary leader, and the most potent force of the Revolution in the north.

Throughout the spring and summer, the controversy between the two states continued. Finally, in September 1984, Chihuahua ended up as the recipient of the mask, which now resides in the Regional Musuem of Chihuahua in Chihuahua City.

167

Villa lives, or at least the idea of Villa lives. Villa has been claimed by all sides politically. PAN, in its attempt to appear modern, uses Villa as a symbol of northern resistance. The PRI, since Villa's resuscitation as a genuine revolutionary hero in 1967, has a claim on him. On November 20, 1988, marking the seventy-eighth anniversary of the Revolution, the Zócalo (main plaza) was decorated with lights. The day has become a major Mexican holiday. Images of principal revolutionary leaders — Madero, Carranza, Zapata, and Villa — were created by thousands of lights. Villa's recognition as a hero made a concession to the north. In a period when northern Mexico is critical to the government, more and more symbolic acknowledgment of Chihuahua occurs. The far left, especially the PSUM and the CDP, use Villa as a symbol of the fight against oppression and the restoration of the rights of the underdogs. His image also shines on leftist propaganda.

And what would Villa think? He would probably laugh heartily, for he was all of those things, depending on how one perceived Francisco Villa. Villa represented the very contradictory nature of the *chihuahuense,* and for that reason he is claimed by all sides. They find in him something that personifies particular aspirations. But in the way of the committed, all factions conveniently leave out those aspects of Villa's character and ideas that fail to coincide with a particular point of view.

Chihuahua has come full circle historically. Her colonial beginnings were sporadic and not very well organized until the eighteenth century. Even then, the province of Chihuahua had to fend off its Indian enemies with little, if any, assistance from the central authority in Mexico City. In the nineteenth century, at least until the 1870s, *chihuahuenses* under the leadership of different governors withstood Apache raids and foreign invasions without appreciable support from the central government.

The vicissitudes of politics in Mexico City left Chihuahua isolated and very much on her own. As a consequence, there developed an independent spirit that is even more idiosyncratic than in the rest of the north, an area that prides itself on its independence and ability to do things in its own manner. This independence created havoc in terms of relations with Mexico City, for the centralizing tendencies of the federal government, even in the nineteenth century, proved nothing but a harbinger of the tensions that currently characterize state-federal government relations in the twentieth century.

Chihuahua had a major advantage when the Terrazas family controlled the area. The family had reached an accommodation with Porfirio Díaz, the man who ruled Mexico for more than thirty years. Personal antagonism between Díaz and Don Luis forced a recognition on both sides of each other's power and influence. Terrazas exercised his will in Chihuahua, and Díaz worked out whatever arrangements he could with the rest of the nation.

The Revolution underscored the tensions that existed between Chihuahua and the central government. At critical junctures in the twentieth-century history of Chihuahua, that state resisted federal impositions and dicta. Certainly, Villa's activities as civil governor of Chihuahua speak for themselves. His relations with Carranza continually deteriorated because of Carranza's refusal to recognize the autonomous nature of the *chihuahuenses*. In the 1920s, during the Cristero Revolt, the governor of Chihuahua reached an accommodation with the local bishop, and while the forms of protest were observed, state and Church did cooperate in the resolution of common problems.

The 1980s posed a different set of problems for Chihuahua. The establishment of the PRI as the official party, beginning in 1929 with the PNR, left little room for local political maneuvering. No longer could independent candidates be placed in nomination for local and state offices without running afoul of the PRI. Rarely did opposition groups attain office in Chihuahua until the 1980s. Previous to 1983, Chihuahua had a high rate of abstentionism in local, state, and federal elections because of the general feeling that voting was a wasted effort.

But the local and state elections of 1983 changed all that. The Partido de Acción Nacional swept the state and threw the official party into a panic. Never had *el PRI* suffered such ignominious defeat. For two years, the PRI licked its wounds, and blamed the governor for the losses of 1983. Oscar Ornelas was, unfortunately, an honest man who demanded that PAN victories in the state be recognized. His honesty ultimately cost him his job. National PRI officials demanded that Ornelas be dumped in his final year as governor.

To do this they found factions within the PRI that opposed Ornelas. Opposition was organized, and the Autonomous University of Chihuahua became the vehicle by which Ornelas would fall.

Politically cynical PRI hardliners insisted that Chihuahua toe the political mark. To accomplish this, they needed to create a disruptive situation that could be blamed on the governor. They had this in the university, always a potentially volatile ambience.

PRI oppressiveness came to bear upon *chihuahuense* businessmen, many of whom were *panista* sympathizers. They were pointedly warned to be careful about becoming politically active. The example of Manuel J. Clouthier of Sinaloa has been mentioned. Clouthier, who would run for governor of Sinaloa in 1986 and then for president in 1988 under the PAN banner, had his business afflicted by a labor strike and vandalism when he made his political ambitions known. Rather than intimidating Chihuahuan businessmen, such action galvanized much of their support for Barrio Terrazas in the 1986 gubernatorial race.

From that point forward, the PRI worked its will in Chihuahua. In 1986 it manipulated the gubernatorial election when there was no need for such legerdemain. PAN did not carry a single municipal election in 1986, and it lost the gubernatorial race by a margin of 2:1.

There was no doubt that Fernando Baeza would win. He was a candidate who appealed to *chihuahuenses*. His opponent, Francisco Barrio Terrazas, was too much the fanatical zealot who diminished the support for PAN. Barrio's control of the PAN at the state level placed Acción Nacional in the hands of Young Turks, who approached their political task like a religious mission.

While the PRI in Chihuahua used heavy-handed methods to capture the governorship in 1986, PAN underscored its political immaturity through its campaign. Its allegations of fraud before the fact sent a message that PAN had no real program when in fact they did have a positive approach to the solution of local, state, and national problems. The fraud *leitmotif* carried over into the presidential election of 1988. Again, positive programs were ignored by PAN as it hammered away at possible fraud. That they were correct in the end is irrelevant. PAN needed to present a positive alternative rather than a negative one.

The 1986 election also brought into sharp focus the role of the Church in Mexican politics. Activist prelates in Chihuahua voiced their hopes that clean elections would be a characteristic of Chihuahuan politics. Archbishop Almeida y Merino strongly opposed any attempts to nullify the votes through electoral sleight of hand by the PRI. Church opposition to electoral fraud continued through 1986 and into the presidential election of 1988. At no time did the Church endorse any particular candidate or party in 1986. Both gubernatorial candidates had declared themselves good Catholics. It was not a contest between a believer and a secular anti-Christ. Instead, the Church prayed for clean elections in order to have a true expression of the popular will.

Opposition to Church involvement made itself felt. Under the Mexican Constitution of 1917, the Church was effectively excluded from all political participation. Clerics and religious groups were disenfranchised. The archbishop and his brother bishops in Chihuahua challenged this notion and demanded the individual right of expression. Almeida y Merino caused so much fuss in Mexico that in 1988 Salinas de Gortari met with him and the other prelates in order to smooth over Church–State relations. The Vatican also took a hand. Because of the fear that Almeida y Merino might cause some problems for the Church in Mexico in general, Pope John Paul II appointed an auxiliary bishop for the Archdiocese of Chihuahua. This appointee became a Vatican watchdog meant to keep Almeida y Merino in check.

The national PRI successfully alienated Chihuahua through its high-handed actions. As a result, even PRI officials in Chihuahua began to distance themselves from the national party. Governor Fernando Baeza Meléndez strongly attacked the centralism of the government. So, too, did Jaime Bermúdez, the PRI mayor of Ciudad Juárez. They began, in fact, to sound more like *panistas* in their demands for the recognition of states' rights.

In this political milieu, Chihuahua could count itself as the most prosperous area of Mexico. It had high economic growth. Mining, industry, and agriculture all boomed. Cattle served as the springboard for other economic enterprises. But all of this success had to be accomplished in spite of federal interference and not because of federal support. In large measure, the monstrosity that has become Mexico City dictated federal policy. With twenty-five percent of the Mexican population living in the Federal District, the national government finds itself with a terrible problem: how to feed and provide social services to this burgeoning population. The answer, of course, has been to take it out of the hides of the provinces. In the case of Chihuahua, the juggling of cattle export permits caused constant consternation among cattlemen in the state, and they were chronically joined in battle with the Secretariat of Agriculture and the Secretariat of Commerce; this, in spite of the fact that cattle brought millions of dollars into the state and nation.

It is this almost chronic interference that has intensified the tension between Chihuahua and Mexico City. *Chihuahuenses* expressed the idea that they did not mind paying taxes — one had to pay for government services — but that those taxes should go to Mexico City was more than an intelligent being could bear. Why support an area that is becoming rapidly unsupportable? Why should Chihuahua and other states bail out a city that treats them with such contempt?

For all of the political cynicism and heavy-handedness, the PRI in Chihuahua needed a visible symbol of economic betterment: roads — kilometers of roads. The major project was a new highway from Juárez to Jiménez in addition to a new highway from Parral to Chihuahua City. This last one cuts the trip between cities by almost two hours. The Juárez–Chihuahua City stretch extends about forty kilometers north of Chihuahua City. A new highway from Delicias to Chihuahua City marks southern progress. Governor Baeza launched a campaign, *"hacia el año 2000"* (toward the year 2000), as a major goal for Chihuahua. Remarkable progress was made between 1986 and 1988. But even Baeza acknowledged somewhat bitterly that continued road development depended on funds from Mexico City. By 1992, the network was essentially finished throughout the states.

The bulk of Chihuahuans feel comfortable with their situations. They have worked hard. They have a heterogeneous, contributing population that is industrious and honest. Yet they face daily programs imposed by the federal authority that have no relation to *chihuahuense* reality. While Chihuahuans acknowledge some of the problems that they face, they are conditioned to survive in the face of adversity. Some *chihuahuenses* have left the state for the United States, but the bulk of them want to remain at home to work and enjoy their earnings.

Nevertheless, the federal government wants to get more and more out of Chihuahua. Unreasonable export taxes on cattle, for example, underscore the feeling that the provinces merely exist for the benefit of Mexico City. Thus resentment continues to smolder in Chihuahua and often finds outlet in bizarre expressions. At times these are emitted while in a condition of drunkenness; at other times they constitute mere political palaver. But they are genuine sentiments.

Secession! It is an ugly word that brings back memories of the Civil War in the United States and its attendant fratricide. *Chihuahuenses* proudly announce to all who would listen that they do not need Mexico City. With the resources available to Chihuahua in agriculture, livestock, mining, forest products, and some basic industries, the state could exist rather nicely on its own. Many a time I have heard this sort of discussion. Usually, a healthy shot of liquor served as the inspiration, but it is a sentiment genuinely felt and profoundly expressed. To the *chihuahuense* the government in Mexico City refuses to recognize the richness of the largest state in the Mexican federation. To the accursed *chilango* the wealth of Chihuahua exists merely for exploitation and the advantage of central and southern Mexico.

Beef cattle from Chihuahua feed Mexico City, while Chihuahua receives very little in return, in terms of goods, services, and foodstuffs. Consequently, *chihuahuenses* continually declare their belief that the state would be better off without the parasitism of the center.

To the *chilango* the *chihuahuense* represents the barbarism of the north. Even people who leaned toward PRI hated the sort of condescension shown them by the *chilangos,* and these individuals displayed their barbarity with pride in the form of bumper stickers which said, *"Soy bárbaro del norte!"*

Such a manifestation of regional feeling has always escaped Mexico City. Mexico City views itself as the center of the universe, around which all of the little provincial satellites must whirl. Historically, this has always been the pattern and has touched off conflicts that go back for hundreds of years. Today the consequences of such an attitude when directed to a state like Chihuahua ultimately spells trouble for the central authority.

And then there is the United States. Relations between Chihuahua and the United States, while not always cordial and friendly, have been constant. Since 1806, when Zebulon Pike and his merry band made contact in Santa Fe and then were incarcerated in Chihuahua, there has developed a mutual dependency between Chihuahua and the southwestern United States. That the United States depends on Chihuahua today for a primary source of feeder cattle goes without saying. The statistics bear out that dependency. Chihuahuan cattlemen gear their production toward the sale of feeder stock to feedlots in the United States. American cattle producers, especially feedlot operators, depend on the production of quality feeder stock from northern Mexico.

But Chihuahua also does more than produce cattle. The *chihuahuenses* are primary consumers of United States goods. They go to El Paso, Houston, Dallas, Las Cruces, Los Angeles, and other areas contiguous or near Mexico and purchase all manner of items. When the financial crunch first hit Mexico in 1982, independent businesses in El Paso suffered traumatically. One estimate placed the number of business in bankruptcy or on the verge of sinking at sixty percent. Clearly, the loss of revenue from Mexico had a profound and painful effect on the El Paso economy. Since the 1982 crash of the *peso,* conditions in El Paso have improved, but Mexicans find it difficult to acquire sufficient dollars for shopping.

In the rush to acquire goods from the United States lies an odd paradox. *Chihuahuenses* are probably as nationalistic as any Mexican, but they define their nationality in different ways. They, too, possess an anti-*gringo* stripe that typifies many Mexicans. Yet they love American goods and some of the material manifestations of United States culture. If possible, *chihuahuenses* put their money in Texas banks. They purchase everything from microwave ovens to clothing to VCRs to major farm equipment, for they know that if they encounter trouble when returning to Mexico a well-placed *mordida* (bribe) will usually permit entry of the merchandise. Even with the *mordida,* it is still cheaper to get goods from Texas.

The United States finally awakened to the reality of Chihuahua. Interest in state and local elections in Mexico had never been high in the U.S., but in 1986 reporters crowded into Chihuahua to cover state contests. The interest also had an ugly side. Talk of intervention in one form or another was heard clearly in the United States Senate. Led by Jesse Helms, the reckless chatter about monitoring Chihuahua's elections aggravated more than a few *chihuahuenses.* Insultingly, Helms and his cohorts felt that United States pressure needed to be brought to bear upon the Mexican government to assure clean elections in Chihuahua. President Ronald Reagan, speaking through the State Department and the consul general in Ciudad Juárez, disavowed Helms' statements. But the fact that this sort of sentiment still existed in the United States indicated quite clearly that the jingoistic days of Teddy Roosevelt

and Woodrow Wilson continued as a part of American perceptions
of Mexico.

Historians get into trouble when they become prescriptive. We
should weigh evidence judiciously, make thoroughly reasoned
judgments about the past, and not try to be policy makers. However, policy is often based on the past, and who better than a historian to talk about the past?

Politically, Mexico's official party needs to set its own house in
order. It must reform and open itself to change, or else, like some of
its elder statesmen, it will ossify. The government needs to separate
itself from the PRI, for that close union between party and government resulted in the political crisis that Mexico faced in the 1980s.
Chihuahua is a case in point of this sort of crisis. When PRI officials declared that Mexico could survive a PAN governor in Chihuahua, they acknowledged the need to bring about a political pluralism that was genuine rather than the sort of tokenism in which
the PRI has engaged for decades.

At the same time, the PAN needs to advance the positive side
of its program. Constant protestations about electoral fraud before
an election is even held can do PAN candidates no good, for the cry
becomes monotonous. When montony sets in, so does apathy. With
apathy comes the sort of electoral abstentionism that occurred before 1983. The same prescription could be made for the other opposition parties as well, though in Chihuahua it remains essentially
a contest between PAN and PRI.

Economically, Mexico needs to recognize the intrinsic worth of
Chihuahua rather than look at that northern entity as a mere supplier of revenue, foodstuffs, and a complacent electorate. The *chilangos* have never really understood what makes a *chihuahuense* tick.
Party officials in Chihuahua, however, have made it clear that their
candidates — though *priísta* — will first and foremost represent
Chihuahua aspirations and goals. Rather than bleed Chihuahua
for revenue, they should allow the dollars brought in through the
sale of cattle, mining products, the *maquiladoras*, and other enterprises to circulate. This, in turn, would create additional jobs
through the expansion of existing and new enterprises. Instead, the
central government attempts to reduce *chihuahuense* entrepreneurs
almost to penury through taxes and export fees.

And the *ejido*? In Chihuahua, the communal land system has

been a nightmare. Plots are too small, and the land is too harsh. Yet the federal government through its Secretariat of Agrarian Reform tenaciously clings to a system that leaves its beneficiaries without substantial means of support. A few *ejidos* have worked fairly well, but without title to the land the incentive for making it productive reduces dramatically. In this, PAN presidential candidate Manuel J. Clouthier was quite right. Give the *ejidatarios* title, make them feel that they have a vested interest in the land, and thus provide incentive for making it productive.

A Chihuahuan reality is its prosperity and the attraction that prosperity has for other people in Mexico. Magnetically, Chihuahua draws people from central and southern Mexico, including *chilangos* who can no longer tolerate the stress of Mexico City. As a result, *chihuahuenses* need to temper their own antagonisms and demonstrate the open hospitality of which they are justly proud. It will be hard, but much will be done toward improving relations between Chihuahua and the rest of Mexico.

As for the United States, Chihuahua already has agreements with Texas and looks to the U.S. as a principal market for its products. This relationship needs to continue. The newly-signed North American Free Trade Agreement (August 1992) offers a plethora of advantages for Chihuahua. Moreover, United States investors need to expand their enterprises in Chihuahua to help maintain the level of prosperity that has characterized the state. All of this, of course, comes from the use of private sector monies. Mexico is trying to separate itself from economically unfeasible state-run enterprises. Already it has sold airlines to the private sector, and there is talk of selling telephone and utility companies as well. Some rumors have circulated about the sale of PEMEX, the nationalized petroleum industry. Should that happen, the howls of protest would be heard on Hudson's Bay. Therefore, government monies should keep out of economic expansion in Chihuahua. Let the private sector deal with this, for they are infinitely more adept at making money than are government bureaucrats.

Apropos of PEMEX, in January 1989 Salinas de Gortari brought the full force of government to bear on the leadership of the oil workers' union. For too long that union had held the nation in thrall. The corruption was of a magnitude that even made a generally corrupt system blush. Mexican army forces and judicial police nabbed the head of the PEMEX union and some of the other leadership on charges of arms smuggling. No doubt drug trafficking will eventually be added to the list of charges. Mexican army units assured the continued work at **PEMEX** installations. While it is still too early to assess the profundity of the clean-up of **PEMEX**, Salinas de Gortari let it be known that he was in charge of Mexico. Such a display of political *machismo* undoubtedly impressed some *chihuahuenses*, for Salinas also intimated that private sector participation in the oil industry would soon become a reality.

Chihuahua has provided an ideal microcosm to examine the relations between state and federal government in Mexico. The complexity of its social organization, the maverick quality of its politics, and its economic prosperity make Chihuahua almost paradoxical within the Mexican Republic. Where other areas have wallowed in poverty and ineptitude, *chihuahuenses* dug and scrapped their way to prosperity. They feel justly proud of this fact and challenge anyone to dispute the reality that is Chihuahua. And they constantly remind the nation: *Villa lives!*

``During the Torchlight Parade, Barrio Announced a Series of Surprise Moves.''

CHAPTER 10

Election 1989:

The Chihuahua Case

Bread and circuses met high-tech in the closing days of the municipal election in Chihuahua City. On June 28, 1989, the PRI staged a massive rally to close out the campaign for state and local posts. On Sunday, July 2, the election (or the PRI, Mexico's official party) would decide the outcome between the PAN (National Action Party), the PRI, and four minor parties.

On that Wednesday, various segments of the PRI joined to elect Rodolfo Torres Medina as *presidente municipal* or mayor of Chihuahua City. Hard, strident *rock azteca* (to steal a term from Carlos Fuentes) entertained the gathering mob. Speakers extolled the viability of the PRI and declared the inevitability of their victory.

Up and down Avenida Independencia, groups began to arrive before the 8:00 P.M. starting time. Some marched and bore PRI banners. Others came in buses, waving flags out of the windows. Some of those being transported were schoolchildren who could not vote but would look good on television and give the appearance of an enthusiastic gathering. Many wore T-shirts emblazoned with the PRI logo and declaring that they had made the best decision by backing Torres Medina, former rector of the state university, as the candidate for mayor of Ciudad Chihuahua. Hundreds of these T-shirts abounded as well as baseball caps, banners, organized groups, and the ever-present, incessantly loud music.

Beginning June 24, the different political parties began to close their campaigns. By law there could be no campaigning for three days before the election. First came the PAN. A diminished number of enthusiasts attended its campaign finale. On June 29, the five other parties, including the PRI, shut down their campaigns.

In Chihuahua, the main battle still remained PRI versus PAN. The four other parties, including the now directly politicized CDP (Popular Defense Committee), would not affect the outcome of the election one way or another. For seventy-eight days the two major parties hammered away at each other. PAN, in its usual paranoia about electoral fraud, already began to prepare the ground for its customary harvest of complaints about electoral irregularities. They had not waited to see if President Carlos Salinas de Gortari would in fact live up to his promises of clean and reformed elections. At the close of the PRI rally, Torres Medina declared that "everything has been done that could be done."

The rhetoric was great. The official party proudly announced that it had purged itself of impurity and that it could again become the repository of public confidence. But the rhetoric masked some of the ugliness that often accompanies these elections. During the PRI meeting of June 28, three *priístas* were assaulted and beaten by some of the CDP *aficionados* who, in another context, were described as using *tácticas gangsteriles* (gangster tactics).

Aside from that one minor incident, the next three days, June 29–July 1, proved boring. No campaigning could occur. No demonstrations filled the Plaza de Armas or the Plaza Hidalgo. The state electoral commission warned that it would be vigilant about violations of the campaign law as it applied to the dissemination of propaganda during the three-day hiatus before the election.

At the same time, Church officials in Chihuahua were quick to point out that the apostolic delegate to Mexico, Monsignor Gerónimo Prigione, did not single out the Chihuahuan archdiocese for his admonition to the Mexican Church. Prigione specifically exhorted the Church in Mexico from its participation in partisan politics. Influential Catholic laity quickly pointed out that the Church in Chihuahua headed by Archbishop Almeida y Merino had never been

Tendrá el PAN Mayoría en el Congreso

PRI Acepta Derrotas en los - Principales Ayuntamientos

Marco A. AGUIRRE RODRIGUEZ

Con la votación de 3,006 casillas contabilizada y faltando por computar sólo 30 de ellas, las elecciones para gobernador dieron 651.684 votos en total, de los cuales 340.056 correspondieron al Partido Acción Nacional (PAN), mientras que para el PRI fueron 298.941; lo que corresponde a 52.18% y 45.87% de la votación, respectivamente.

Datos proporcionados por el Partido Revolucionario Institucional reconocen a Jesús Macías, un total de 300.388, correspondientes a los del PRI más del Frente Cardenista, con el cual hizo coalición para este puesto.

Con esta misma base, el PRI reconoció su derrota en 10 distritos electorales y 8 ayuntamientos.

Sin embargo, el Partido Acción Nacional se adjudica triunfos en 11

El Triunfo de Barrio, Irreversible

Hoy Cumplimos 65 Años de Servicio a la Ciudadanía

Hoy, hace 65 años vio la luz primera este matutino.

Este día cumplimos casi tres cuartos de siglo de trabajo informativo ininterrumpido, con las metas invariables que han sido nuestra divisa por todo ese tiempo y constituyen un reto para todo el personal que en esta casa editorial trabaja, desde el más antiguo hasta el más nuevo en los menesteres del periodismo: comunicar de la mejor manera, lo más rápido y verazmente posible.

Hoy iniciamos nuestro sexagésimo sexto año de vida con las mismas ganas que lo hicieron quienes nos precedieron en la noble labor que nos ocupa como orientadores de la opinión entre la vasta familia

Macías Reconoció que Perdió la Gubernatura

Sandra I. JIMENEZ, Eva TRUJILLO R. y Marco A. AGUIRRE R.

La Comisión Estatal Electoral señaló que el Partido Acción Nacional llevaba hasta ayer una ventaja sobre el Revolucionario Institucional de casi un 16 por ciento en total, mientras que el candidato priísta Jesús Macías Delgado afirmó que había perdido ante el PAN la gubernatura del estado por ese margen de diferencia, y por su parte, el gobernador Fernando Baeza Meléndez anunció en rueda de prensa que el triunfo panista es irreversible, como producto de una democracia.

Con el 33.80 por ciento de casillas computarizadas, y en lo que respecta a la elección de gobernador, la Comisión Estatal Electoral (CEE) reflejó que el PAN aventaja al PRI con un 15.89 por ciento de diferencia en votos.

Durante la sesión de la CEE —efectuada ayer a las 10:50 horas— el órgano electoral informó

Salinas de Gortari Felicita a Barrio y Villaseñor

Carlos Fuentes: EU es el País más Corrupto y con más Drogadictos del Mundo

MADRID; España, (EFE y ANSA).- El escritor mexicano Carlos Fuentes opina que "Estados Unidos es el país donde más droga se consume, el que tiene la deuda más alta y el más corrupto del mundo". En una entrevista que publica en su último número el semanario español Tribuna, Carlos Fuentes sigue empeñado en extraer conclusiones positivas de la conquista de América, al tiempo que critica con dureza

Vea "CARLOS", Pág. 11-A

Contarán con Absoluto Respeto y Total Apoyo de la Federación, Asegura

MEXICO. (OEM).- Después de conocer ayer las tendencias que extraoficialmente apuntan al triunfo electoral de Francisco Barrio Terrazas en Chihuahua y, de Eduardo Villaseñor en Michoacán, el presidente Carlos Salinas de Gortari conversó telefónicamente con ellos y los felicitó por los resultados en los comicios de este domingo.

Vía telefónica les dijo que, a partir de la oficialización de sus triunfos por parte de las autoridades electorales correspondientes, contarán con el absoluto respeto y total apoyo de la federación para llevar adelante el desarrollo de sus respectivas entidades.

También, el jefe del Ejecutivo recibió ayer por la mañana una llamada telefónica del candidato del PRI a la gubernatura de Chihuahua, Jesús Macías, quien le notificó su aceptación de los resultados adversos en la jornada electoral de este domingo.

Macías comentó al jefe del Ejecutivo que durante la campaña electoral realizó su mejor esfuerzo

Vea "SALINAS", Pág. 11-A

Reconoce el PRI Naciona la Derrota de Macías

MORELIA, Mich., (OEM).- El dirigente nacional del Partido Revolucionario Institucional, Genaro Borrego Estrada, reconoció ayer la derrota del abanderado priísta en Chihuahua, Jesús Macías, y desfió al PRD a contar los votos en las actas de escrutinio en Michoacán en ceremonia pública.

El PRI estatal aseguró anoche que ni sumando todos los vot

Vea "RECONOCE", Pág. 5-A

Headlines from El Heraldo de Chihuahua *announcing the PAN victory at the polls in the July, 1992 elections.*

partisan. He and his brother bishops had merely called for honest votes and honest elections.

But in spite of all of the music, the political blather, the colorful banners, and the posters that appeared everywhere, the political atmosphere still seemed pessimistic. In Villa Aldama, twenty-two kilometers northeast of Chihuahua City, the political splits that had occurred divided the residents and a pessimism about the efficacy of the vote surfaced. *El Heraldo de Chihuahua* editorialized that "the real winner of the elections will be abstentionism," a direct result growing from the lack of faith in the validity of the electoral process.

On July 2, five states would hold state and municipal elections. In all of them, including Chihuahua, it seemed that the PRI would have to use all of its resources to defeat the opposition. In Baja California Norte, a powerful *panista* looked to seize the governorship. Ciudad Juárez in Chihuahua seemed ready to go over to the PAN again. In Michoacán, supporters of defeated presidential candidate Cuahtémoc Cárdenas threatened PRI hegemony. *El Heraldo* wondered if in the next few days the PRI would resort to past tactics: "steal elections, use alchemy, and mock the citizenry."

Meeting in Tijuana, Baja California Norte, on June 30, the PRD and the PARM, along with the PAN, met to make common cause for the defense of the vote. These three centrist to conservative parties called upon the government to assure peaceful and orderly elections. They asked the electorate to act calmly and maturely. At the same time, these groups vowed to have observers at most polling places to avoid any anomalies. The PAN also responded to allegations that it had made a deal with the government for the governorship of Baja California Norte. Since blatant dealmaking constitutes such an integral part of the Mexican political scene, speculation immediately saw back-door arrangements between the opposition and the government.

In Chihuahua, political prognosticators, including the Gallup Organization, saw the PRI winning all major *municipios* in the region, even Ciudad Juárez. In Chihuahua City Gallup projected a seventy-three percent to twenty-three percent victory for the PRI, while in Juárez it stood at PRI — fifty-seven percent, PAN — forty-one percent. In its projections, the other parties did not even have statistical significance for Gallup. Increasingly, *chihuahuenses* placed more faith in polls, especially since Gallup called the 1983 elections so exactly.

Governor Fernando Baeza readily acknowledged that the opposition had excellent opportunities for capturing some major mayoralties. He said: "If they didn't, they wouldn't be in the race. Everybody is in it to win, not to lose."

But not all of the preparations went smoothly. Missing electoral identifications — many of them belonging to anti-PRI voters — were found and had to be recovered at the state electoral commission office. PAN saw this as yet another attempt by the PRI to skew the election results in its favor.

By election day, PAN hoped to capture twenty of sixty-seven mayoralties in Chihuahua as well as make an impact in other states of Mexico. A PAN national deputy arrived in Chihuahua to observe the elections and to act as an advisor to local groups.

But the cry of fraud already had begun to resound in Chihuahua. Luis Alvarez, now national PAN president, said that last-minute changes of polling places in Chihuahua would leave the non-PRI faithful wondering where to vote. Other parties were not informed of the changes, and Alvarez opined that this was another PRI maneuver to steal the elections. Meanwhile, in Delicias, some outraged *panistas* seized the offices of the National Registrar of Voters because about 1,000 voters had been omitted from the list by secretaries who were PRI members. The intervention of local officials resolved the problem.

On the day before the election, PAN state president declared that a number of already apparent irregularities could impugn the electoral results. He pointed out the mountain city of Madera as an example. Moreover, he predicted — quite correctly, as it turned out — a seventy percent abstention rate from voting.

The advent of election day, July 2, came in a blistering heat. Temperatures into the 100 + degree range rendered air conditioners useless. In the heat, few people wanted to stand in line to vote for what they believed would be an inevitable outcome. Chihuahua was undergoing a vicious drought. More than a month had passed without measurable precipitation and with temperatures that were extreme. To exacerbate the heat, a forty-eight-hour dry law was in effect. Bars and liquor stores could not open until Monday.

In the fall of 1988, Governor Baeza tightened the strictures on the sale of liquor in the entire state of Chihuahua. The effect of his decree on election day was to make bootleggers a lot of money and to cause a run on the sale of soft drinks and ice. It was rumored that a bottle of Presidente Brandy that normally sold for around 12,000 *pesos* could be had from a bootlegger for about 30,000. Luckily, this observer's companions for that weekend had had the foresight to stock up on beer and other potables that efficaciously quench the thirst on a hot day.

But enough of alcoholic privation and back to the election.

By the late evening of July 2, some preliminary results clearly indicated that except for one district in Juárez the PRI had probably swept the state. But the PRI itself, while claiming victory, carefully noted that the results were quite early and could change.

By all indicators, the election proceeded tranquilly. With the exception of Parral, where two persons were injured, and Juárez, which abounded with verbal violence, the entire state underwent the process peacefully. In some districts there were reports of the expulsion of PAN pollwatchers, but this did not seem to stir the passions as such an event had in the past.

On a broader scale, PAN carried the governorship of Baja California Norte. Luis Alvarez was quick to note that the PAN would contest each and every attempt to steal municipal elections in Baja California and throughout Mexico. The PAN victory in Baja California Norte at least superficially showed that Salinas de Gortari meant what he said about clean elections.

Luis Donaldo Colosio, the PRI national president, acknowledged the PAN victory in a televised address on July 4. While going through a list of PRI achievements, he conceded victory to the PAN. Colosio was especially proud of PRI victories in Chihuahua. He noted that the citizenry of that state was extremely tough, highly politicized, and very competitive. Also, *chihuahuenses* were extremely demanding of their political representatives. He did not mention, however, the high degree of abstentionism which favored the PRI.

Alleged irregularities kept cropping up in the days immediately following the elections in Chihuahua. On July 4, a PAN rally saw *panista* candidates and leadership burn credentials and electoral lists in front of the Palacio de Gobierno to protest fraud. Some uncounted ballots had been found. But there were insufficient irregularities to engender widespread demands for a nullification of the election.

Meanwhile, the only chronic sour note in the entire process was the CDP. Their squatters seized properties belonging to elderly citizens, who protested to Baeza. The governor wisely asked the protesters to wait until after the election in order to resolve the problem. He wanted to avoid the appearance of moving against a political party that was also engaged in the electoral contest. By July 4, the "gangster tactics" used by the CDP continued to dispossess some older Chihuahuans. Over 200 of them protested again to Baeza. By July 7, the problem continued unresolved.

Were the elections clean? Had Salinas de Gortari, through the PRI, fulfilled his campaign pledges about clean elections? At first glance, it seems that the elections, with minor local exceptions, were some of the most honest that Chihuahua has had since 1983. Local irregularities could not be eradicated totally, but this is true in any place where elections are held. Certainly, it is hard to consider a victory with only thirty percent of the electorate participating a resounding mandate; but still, the PRI did win rather handsomely in Chihuahua. The PAN victory in Baja California also attested to Salinas' desire to reform the political process.

But the jury is still out. What about close elections? What if there is another major thrust by the PAN in Chihuahua? It seems clear that *chihuahuenses* have become disenchanted with the direction of the PAN. In this regard Governor Fernando Baeza has clearly stolen the march on the PAN, for he continues to stand first as a *chihuahuense* and then as a *priísta*. It seems that the PAN will have to mature some more politically before it can again posit a major challenge to the PRI in Chihuahua. A newly formed political watchdog outfit operating out of Chihuahua City and Juárez, the Asociación Cívica Democrática (Civic Democratic Association), declared that the electoral results in Chihuahua demonstrated that the people distrust the government and the political parties. Mexican *desconfianza* again had come to dominate the politics of Chihuahua.

Panel 1
The time had come when a well-known politician from Parral had to make a declaration of personal goods. He says: "As demanded by law."

Panel 2
Said declaration contained the following questions: "Source of goods."

Panel 3
The response came immediately: "Two mayoralties, one deputation, and three fires."

Panel 1
[Secretary] Colokuris from the Secretariat of Agriculture sent a technocrat to Eloy Morales' ranch: "I've come to study the effects of the drought."

Panel 2
He observed the cattle chewing their cuds and reported: "Aside from what is going to be spent on pasturage."

Panel 3
"We need to add the millions of pesos that need to be spent on chewing gum for the cattle."

Afterword:

Chihuahua Picks a New Governor

Heat, both thermal and political, permeated the atmosphere as the gubernatorial race in Chihuahua reached its conclusion in July 1992. Francisco Barrio Terrazas, the PAN candidate, declared: "To say that at this moment there can be clean elections in Mexico is to say a lot. Yet, there are indications that it will be a better process than in 1986. That is without a doubt."

The usual political mudslinging began in the spring, when the PAN began to make sly allegations about the smoky dens that selected PRI candidates while the PAN, ever virtuous, would use an open convention to select its candidate for the governorship of Chihuahua. Already the PAN had scored some impressive victories nationally. In 1989, the conservative opposition party carried Baja California Norte. A year later it achieved a disputed call in Guanajuato. But would Chihuahua, the crown jewel of the Mexican republic, the economic powerhouse of northern Mexico, fall to the opposition? Would the Atomic Ant, President Carlos Salinas de Gortari, allow or be allowed to let Chihuahua fall to the PAN Antichrists, the barbarians of the north?

Certainly, the PRI dinosaurs recoiled tremulously at the thought of the economic goodies that Chihuahua offered falling into the hands of the National Action Party. But these were the general perceptions of the brontosaurus brigade in Mexico City. In the north, it was generally conceded that Chihuahua could well fall to the PAN, provided Salinas and Governor Fernando Baeza Meléndez lived up to their declared intentions to allow the political process to go unhindered by partisanship.

Baeza's critics within and without the PAN granted that he

had legitimized his political efforts. Having won one of the most disputed elections in contemporary Mexican history, Baeza set about to build his support around those people who were not political *aficionados* but rather individuals who strove to earn a living. They did not embroil themselves in demonstrations and meetings but sought to put a few tortillas on the table along with other increasingly scarce and expensive foodstuffs. Even one of his most vocal critics at the time of his election, Olga Leticia Moreno, wrote recently that Baeza sought to "extinguish the fire of dissatisfaction" and rather wanted to bring about conciliation with all *chihuahuenses*, political affiliation notwithstanding.

One of Baeza's major tasks was to convince the Church that it contained believers of all political affiliations. At the same time, he needed to disarm the more rabidly anticlerical elements of the PRI and demonstrate that the Church did not posit a threat to the secular political life of the state. In the end, he convinced his fellow citizens that he was really a fine fellow and that he strove first and foremost for the welfare of Chihuahua.

In an interview with Olga Leticia Moreno, Baeza declared that the Church had to be recognized as a social reality within the political, social, economic, and social fabric of modern Chihuahua. The Church's role in Chihuahua could not, declared Baeza, be negated. This conciliatory attitude toward the Church by a PRI governor clearly marked the improvement of relations between secular and religious institutions since 1986.

When asked if he had been responsive to the wishes of the *chihuahuenses*, Baeza responded that what had been accomplished in Chihuahua resulted from the convergence of all segments of the society working together for the betterment of the state. For a decade certain goals had been established. Schools and medical facilities had expanded, electrification projects undertaken and completed. More and more *colonias* and *comunidades populares* now had running water and electricity. A multitude of works projects occurred. Yet, Baeza declared himself personally dissatisfied, for he could not bring about all of the ends that had been established.

What Baeza accomplished resulted from his launching what seemed a constant political campaign. Baeza undertook whirlwind tours of the state. He was there for the opening of new schools. He inaugurated highways in profusion. He fought with the central authority in Mexico City to obtain the necessary resources for continual development of Chihuahua. Baeza was among the first to chastize Salinas about the neglect that Chihuahua had suffered in the past. With Baeza it seemed as if the PRI would be resuscitated within the state of Chihuahua. It merely needed a candidate who could approximate the charisma and charm of Fernando Baeza.

But destiny declared that the PRI in Chihuahua suffer from a "throw the rascals out" reaction. The PAN at its convention in early February 1992 unanimously nominated Francisco Barrio Terrazas, its 1986 candidate, to make another run for the governorship. But this was a new Barrio and a new PAN.

Much subdued were the stridency and the whiny protests about fraud rather than the advancement of a positive program. Barrio was not threatening bridge closures and boycotts. Hunger strikes seemed like a neurotic Ghandian fantasy rather than an instrument of political success. Shortly after his nomination, Barrio would meet with President Salinas de Gortari to assure the president that, if elected, he would cooperate with Salinas in the advancement of positive programs. Barrio also promised to meet with Governor Fernando Baeza Meléndez to assure a smooth, clean election. He praised programs that came from PRI functionaries. Barrio, as quoted in *4° Poder*, acknowledged that Salinas had taken important steps for the betterment of the Mexican people.

One week later, the PRI selected Jesus Macías Delgado, the former *alcalde* of Ciudad Juárez and the hand-picked heir apparent to Baeza. Like Barrio, Macías had been mayor of Ciudad Juárez. Like Barrio, Macías was also an accountant. But there the similarities faded. Macías had been involved in different governmental posts. He seemed a consummate PRI bureaucrat, colorless, faithful, a real party worker, the antithesis of the mercurial Barrio. Political gossip, namely that which comes from bartenders and cab drivers and often seems the most informative, advanced the proposition that Baeza selected Macías as his candidate because Macías was an accountant. Apparently, Chihuahua had a multibillion-*peso* deficit, and so, said the gossips, Baeza needed someone to cook the books. The resolution of the problem, it seemed, lay in creative accounting skills.

Though Macías was Baeza's fair-haired boy, PRI officials, including the governor down to local organizations, expressed concern over the possibility of a PAN victory. By mid-February the governor was already calling upon the party faithful within the bureaucracy to get to work for the advancement of all PRI candidates. Ultimately, the effort proved insufficient.

Problems beset the PRI nationally. Other governorships were up for grabs. Zacatecas, Durango, Sinaloa, and Michoacán, along with Chihuahua, were all scheduled to change governors. Of the remaining four, Michoacán, the home ground of Cuahtémoc Cárdenas, seemed the most likely to go to an opposition party. The other states, all northern or northwestern, had some indications of strong PAN influence. Meeting in Morelia, Michoacán, the executive committee of the PAN charged that three agents of the Secretaría de Gobernación had posed as journalists and left a "bug" in the suite where the meeting took place. By late March, Gobernación declared that the men were guilty of invasion of privacy but of nothing more serious. PAN officials called into question Salinas' sincerity about clean elections in line with the putative electoral reforms that had been passed. PAN officials asserted that the issue did not end with the mere prosecution of the three clumsy agents. Rather, higher ups were obviously responsible and needed to be exposed.

The spring political season began in earnest with the nomination of Macías as the PRI candidate. Two other parties, the CDP and the PRD, also fielded candidates. But, as the conventional wisdom had it in Chihuahua, the leftist parties simply were not a factor. While the CDP and the *cardenista* PRD conducted an active campaign, the real fight lay between the PRI and its conservative opposition.

For about the next four months, declarations of undoubted victory could be heard from Macías and Barrio. Both claimed to have the will of the people behind them and sought to influence those elements that wavered. Moreover, both major parties sought to get out the vote, for abstentionism had been a major factor in the Mexican political system that gave control of the Mexican political system to the PRI. Barrio and Macías both knew this and attempted to sway a cynical body politic.

In mid-June, Barrio was quick to point out that the PAN had answered its critics. The state of Chihuahua was again aflame with enthusiasm. It was a people not doubled over by oppression. "The dream of democracy," he exhorted his followers, "remains alive."

Meanwhile, Governor Baeza attempted to answer the charges of potential fraud that appeared usually aimed at the PRI. Baeza firmly stated that the state government would act firmly against any notable anomaly within the electoral process. No attempt to frustrate the electoral will would be tolerated.

Then, at the end of June, the president came to town. He planned a tour of the state and invited representatives of all parties to accompany him. The PAN, remaining aloof, turned down the offer but its representatives held a private interview with Salinas de Gortari. Salinas told the *panistas* that the electoral results would be respected. Baeza echoed Salinas' pledge and backed up the president's promise of severe punishment for those who attempted to disturb the electoral will.

PAN and the other opposition parties, of course, made the usual protests about fraud and the care that needed to be taken to avert any fraudulent activity in the electoral process. A struggle occurred between the PAN and the electoral commission of outside observers. The commission did not object to observers, but they could not be foreigners — only Mexicans. The PAN laid out its strategy by assuring that there would be sufficient pollwatchers to catch any irregularities.

But political promises could not avert personal tragedy. A couple of weeks before the election, an automobile accident claimed the life of Barrio's sixteen-year-old daughter and seriously injured his other three daughters. The driver and his son were also killed. Barrio, his wife, and infant son were not with the group.

It seemed as if Barrio might pull out from the race. Deep mourning engulfed the state. Politics aside, a personal tragedy that cut deeply into the core of the family had afflicted a prominent member of the society. Expressions of sympathy appeared in the newspapers in the form of paid advertisements from different groups and enterprises, some of them political opponents of Barrio. There was a certain amount of tension. Finally, Barrio announced that he would resume but would campaign only a little. He promised to close his campaign efforts on July 4, eight days before the election. State PAN officials refused to speculate as to whether there would be a sympathy vote for Barrio.

Two days before the election, Cuauhtémoc Cárdenas in Michoacán thundered about electoral irregularities in his state. *Panistas* in Chihuahua, however, remained more muted in their criticisms. A working relationship existed between the PRI and the PAN in the north, and the stridency of 1986 was relegated to historical debate. There were still the usual noises, but these had lost the sense of panic of 1986.

Chihuahuenses, of course, were expected to endure another dry spell during the time of the election. Stout beer drinkers as a people, they waited for forty-eight hours as the whole town went dry. In fact, the period extended to sixty hours because the dry period started on July 11 at 1:00 A.M. and ended on July 12 at midnight. Effectively, the bars would not open for the single hour that remained because closing time was 1:00 A.M. To be sure, there was a run on the liquor stores. An election could not be tolerated much less enjoyed without some sort of libation.

Two days before the election, a poll showed Barrio and Macías running with about forty-eight percent each. The undecideds, it seemed, would carry the election. The poll, conducted by the Centro para el Estudio de la Opinión Pública, also indicated that Barrio could win because of last-minute momentum.

On July 12, 1992, voters went to the polls in Chihuahua. Only minor irregularities seemed to mar the process. PAN officials carefully monitored the process. By the end of the evening, it seemed clear that Barrio would triumph. Luis H. Alvarez, national PAN chairman and former *alcalde* of Ciudad Chihuahua, brought Barrio forth just before midnight to celebrate the victory. For the second time since 1929, an opposition party had wrested the governorship of a major state from the official party. Cynics, noting Barrio's confidence with only twenty percent of the vote counted, felt that he had struck a deal with the Salinas government. Barrio denied any kind of deal, though he acknowledged that he had promised to cooperate with Salinas should he emerge victorious.

Jubilation broke out in the streets of Chihuahua. *Panistas,* spurred on by their leader's supreme confidence, took to the streets in celebration. Even with only twenty percent of the vote in, the overwhelming rout of the PRI by Barrio made final victory almost inevitable.

By July 13, Macías had conceded the election, and Salinas proferred congratulations to Barrio and to the PRI candidate in Michoacán, Eduardo Villaseñor. Barrio and Macías met briefly. Macías offered his congratulations and best wishes. Barrio, by the same token, underscored the fact that Macías had been "manly;

[he possessed] a mature attitude and [was] politically serious. [He was] *muy pantalonudo.*" This translates roughly as "having lots of pants, being a man." (Sort of a genteel way of saying "lots of testosterone production.")

There was no doubt by the end of the week. Barrio was the undisputed choice. PAN not only won the governorship but also carried the state legislature and some of the major municipalities, including Ciudad Juárez, Parral, Casas Grandes and Nuevo Casas Grandes, and Cuahtémoc.

In the rural *municipio* of Bachínava, an anomalous situation occurred. The listed PRI candidate withdrew from the race a few days before election time. Lo and behold, on the day of the election another PRI candidate was declared the winner, and his name was not even on the ballot. Apparently communications between Chihuahua City and the rural areas were not very complete. What occurred in Bachínava was simply business as usual. Of course, the PRI would win!

But the PRI lost and lost significantly. For the losers, especially Baeza, a promising career in Mexico City might be cut short. He had failed to deliver the state to the PRI. Much of his destiny might be determined by the strength of the brontosaurus brigade in the party. They had been instrumental in ousting one Chihuahua governor in 1985. The political exile of another would certainly not be beyond their ken.

There exists no doubt that Barrio won in large measure because there was a perceived need for change. Four hundred thousand *chihuahuenses* were not faithful *panistas*. Rather, there was simply the feeling that change might bring about a betterment of conditions. There was also the factor that Barrio lost a child. Sympathy votes were undoubtedly cast. One PRI official noted that many of those voters reasoned that "the poor man lost a child, the least I can do is vote for him." Such an intangible cannot be measured, but it certainly played a critical role.

Now, one month after the election, I sit here in Chihuahua City cursing my lap top computer. Of course, all of the amenities I have found here in the past remain. Access to facilities, consultations with people who might know something, and plans of action that should not be deterred because of partisan nonsense. Yet, the problem remains as to how well the PAN will govern. *Priístas,* of course, fear an outbreak of *revanchist* activity on the part of Barrio. What I hear constantly is *"que no sea vengativo"* — that he not be vengeful. That approach would be counterproductive and would only cause a greater polarization of the body politic. Barrio has pledged cooperation to Salinas, but like most political pledges, it has its share of caveats. Yet I, too, hope *que no sea vengativo*. I would really hate to start all over again.

Bibliography

Chronically, bibliographies present a problem to the writer. They demonstrate to the reader that the author has done his homework, but they also can serve as padding to an otherwise short book. A book such as this requires a bibliography, but so much of the work is based on personal experiences, observations, and conversations that it becomes difficult to determine what came from the written word and what from oral exchanges.

Much of this work is based on what was observed and experienced. A large portion of the general information about Mexico, the Revolution, and Chihuahua in the twentieth century derives from years of study and can be probably considered in the public domain. And then there are those delightful conversations, many of them conducted in smoky, crowded bars where a drop of spirits loosened tongues, while others took place in more formal, though no less convivial, settings. All of my informants were friends or acquaintances or former colleagues who knew what I was doing and yet felt comfortable in telling me some things about Chihuahuan politics that they might not reveal to someone else. Some of them are even well-placed in the state PRI.

Apropos of the state PRI, that office did not seem too cooperative about giving information — even published information — to an itinerant writer from the United States. Therefore, thank heavens for my friends who were willing to talk. On the other hand, the state office of the Partido de Acción Nacional loaded me down with bumper stickers, leaflets, handbooks for party organizers, and much of the printed matter they used in the presidential campaign for 1988. They no longer had materials for the gubernatorial race of 1986, but those working in the office certainly had no qualms in talking about it.

The contemporaneous nature of this topic required that the bulk of printed information come from newspapers, not one of the best sources for the historian but the only show in town when one writes the history of the last decade anywhere in Mexico. For that reason I do not claim this book as pure history, whatever that may be. In many ways it is a personal memoir of the 1980s, a decade that saw a *chihuahuense* renaissance and a flowering of the *chihuahuense* sense of identity. This had always been there, but in recent years, Chihuahuans have come to view themselves as something special, apart from other Mexicans, who had been ignored by the nation as a whole until Chihuahua became the major center of economic growth in a country devastated by economic collapse.

This bibliography represents, therefore, the mere tip of the iceberg of information sources. I personally perused those listed; the conversations constitute five or more years of memories.

Primary Materials

Chihuahua. Gobierno del Estado. *El Mundo, México y Chihuahua*. Chihuahua: Gobierno del Estado, 1987.

Comisión de Investigaciones Históricas de la Revolución Mexicana. Isidro Fabela, ed. *Documentos Históricos de la Revolución Mexican*. México, D.F.: Editorial Jus, various publication dates. This multivolume set constitutes a prime source of information for the Mexican Revolution in general and for much of what occurred in Chihuahua between 1910 and 1930.

Delgado, René. *La Oposición: Debate por la Nación*. México, D.F.: Gribjalbo, 1988. This book is made up of a series of responses to questions put to all of the opposition candidates in the 1988 presidential election.

Guzmán, Martín Luis. *Memorias de Pancho Villa*. México, D.F.: Cia. General de Ediciones, 1963.

Instituto Nacional de Investigaciones Pecuarias. Secretaría de Agricultura ye Recursos Hidraúlicos. *Encuesta Ganadera en Chihuahua*. 1985.

Moreno, Olga Leticia. *¿Qué Pasó en Chihuahua?* México, D.F.: Ediciones Edamex, 1987. This is a series of interviews done by Moreno relating to the election of 1986. She interviewed Barrio Terrazas, Baeza, Jaime Bermúdez, and other prominent political figures in Chihuahua.

Partido de Acción Nacional. Various leaflets and booklets supplied by the state office of PAN which were used in the 1988 presidential election.

Treviño de González, María del Pilar. *¡Enahorabuena, Chihuahua!* Chihuahua: Partido de Acción Nacional, 1986. Señora Treviño de González

served as a *regidora* (councilwoman) in the municipal government in
Chihuahua City when it was under PAN control.

United Nations. Comisión Económica para América Latina. *La industria de
la carne de ganado bovino en México. Análisis y perspectivas.* México, D.F.:
Fondo de Cultura Económica, 1975.

United States Congress. *Congressional Record.*

Newspapers and Magazines

Ahora (official publication of PAN in Ciudad Juárez).
Excelsior (Mexico City).
El Fronterizo (Ciudad Juárez).
El Heraldo de Chihuahua.
El Heraldo de Mexico.
Mexico City News.
La Nación (official publication of the national office of PAN).
El Nacional (Mexico City).
The New York Times.
Newsweek.
El Norte (Chihuahua City).
Novedades (Chihuahua City).
Ovaciones (Mexico City).
Texas Monthly.
El Universal (Mexico City).
El Universal de Ciudad Juárez.
Uno Más Uno (Mexico City).

Books and Articles

Almada, Francisco R. *Gobernadores del Estado de Chihuahua.* Chihuahua:
Centro Librero La Prensa, 1980.
———. *Resumen de historia del Estado de Chihuahua.* México, D.F.: Libros
Mexicanos, 1955.
———. *La revolución en el estado de Chihuahua.* México, D.F.: Biblioteca del
Instituto Nacional de Estudios Históricos de la Revolución Mexi-
cana, 1964. 2 vols.

Alvardo, Arturo, ed. *Electoral Patterns and Perspectives in Mexico.* San Diego,
California: Center for U.S.–Mexican Studies, University of California, San Diego, 1987.

Atkin, Ronald. *Revolution! Mexico, 1910–1920.* New York: John Day Company, 1969.

Brandenburg, Frank. *The Making of Modern Mexico.* Englewood Cliffs, New
Jersey: Prentice-Hall, 1963.

Contreras Orozco, Javier Horacio. *Chihuahua: Trampa del Sistema.* México,
D.F.: Edamex, 1987.

Fuentes Mares, José. . . . *Y Mexico se refugió en el desierto: Luis Terrazas, historia y destino*. México, D.F.: Editorial Jus, 1954.

Jordán, Fernando. *Crónica de un país bárbaro*. Chihuahua: Centro Librero La Presna, 1981.

Levy, Daniel C. "The Mexican Government's Loosening Grip?" *Current History*, vol. 86 (March 1987): 113–116.

Lister, Florence C., and Richard H. Lister. *Chihuahua: Storehouse of Storms*. Albuquerque, New Mexico: University of New Mexico Press, 1966. While outdated in some respects, this book is the key work for understanding Chihuahua. Much of the work on the colonial period in this book derives from Lister and Lister. They made a significant contribution to the study of regional history in Mexico.

Machado, Manuel A., Jr. *Centaur of the North: Francisco Villa, the Mexican Revolution, and Northern Mexico*. Austin, Texas: Eakin Press, 1988.

————. *The North Mexican Cattle Industry, 1910–1975: Ideology, Conflict, and Change*. College Station, Texas: Texas A&M University Press, 1981.

Martínez, Oscar J. *Border Boom Town: Ciudad Juárez Since 1848*. Austin: University of Texas Press, 1978.

Mejía Prieto, Jorge. *México y el narcotráfico*. México, D.F.: Editorial Universo, 1988.

Moreno, Olga Leticia. *Succesión 92. Chihuahua, Durango, Sinola, Zacatecas*. Mexico, D.F.: Edamex, 1992.

Riding, Alan. *Distant Neighbors: A Portrait of the Mexicans*. New York: Alfred A. Knopf, 1985.

Teissier, Ernesto Julio. *¡Ya Nunca Más!* México, D.F.: Editorial Grijalbo, 1988.

Wasserman, Mark. *Capitalistas, caciques y revolución: La Familia Terrazas de Chihuahua, 1854–1911*. México, D.F.: Grijalbo, 1987. Translated by Beatriz Guiza. The work was originally published as *Capitalistas, Caciques and Revolution: The Native Elite and Foreign Enterprise in Chihuahua, Mexico, 1854–1911*. University of North Carolina Press, 1984.

————. "Strategies of Survival of the Porfirian Elite in Revolutionary Mexico: Chihuahua During the 1920s." *Hispanic American Historical Review*, vol. 67 (February 1987): 87–107.

Index